WRITING WELL

"This is a book about what writing is, about how you do it so it works, and how you do it so it lasts."

Writing Well is a workbook on technique, style, and manners for everyone who writes and wants to do it better. It's a practical guide to making your prose sing. Writing is talk tidied and transcribed. It's speech heightened by art, and most of the art can be learned. And that's what this book is about.

Writing Well is a guide to the poetic disciplines of creative writing and the functional disciplines of professional prose, and it's a reflection on the moral obligations and creative agonies of the writing life. Enriched by examples of fine prose from great writers, flush with exercises, informed by the author's expertise in both creative and functional prose, *Writing Well* is a stylish and readable guide to stylish and readable writing.

WRITING WELL

THE ESSENTIAL GUIDE

Mark Tredinnick

CAMBRIDGE
UNIVERSITY PRESS

CAMBRIDGE UNIVERSITY PRESS
Cambridge, New York, Melbourne, Madrid, Cape Town, Singapore,
São Paulo, Delhi

Cambridge University Press
The Edinburgh Building, Cambridge CB2 8RU, UK

Published in the United States of America by
Cambridge University Press, New York

www.cambridge.org
Information on this title: www.cambridge.org/9780521727686

First published 2006 by University of New South Wales Press Ltd as
The Little Red Writing Book
This edition published in 2008 by Cambridge University Press
Not for sale in Australia or New Zealand

Printed in the United States of America by Edwards Brothers Incorporated

A catalogue record for this publication is available from the British Library

ISBN   978-0-521-72768-6   paperback

For Maree,
  the meaning and the music

and for the children,
  whose world it is we're trying to tell

Do but take care to express your self in a plain, easy Manner, in well-chosen, significant and decent Terms, and to give an harmonious and pleasing Turn to your Periods: Study to explain your Thoughts, and set them in the truest Light, labouring, as much as possible, not to leave 'em dark nor intricate, but clear and intelligible: Let your diverting Stories be express'd in diverting Terms...

MIGUEL CERVANTES, "Preface," *Don Quixote*

CONTENTS

ACKNOWLEDGMENTS

I learned to write by listening and, later, by reading; I learned to write by writing; I learned to write by teaching others how to write. I didn't so much write this book as remember it; what you have here is everything I haven't forgotten of what's come to me from a life lived in sentences—most of them other people's.

So, thanks to all the poets and essayists, the historians and novelists, the biographers and memoirists whose works have been my truest teachers. Thanks to the people close to me—first of all my parents, from whom I heard the first sentences of my life, and most of all my wife Maree—who've let me sit for long stretches to write and read when there was the rest of life to be getting on with. And thanks to the students who've shown up to learn how to make better, truer, and more beautiful sentences and who've taught me more, I'm sure, than I ever taught them.

I've spent my life, as you see, getting ready to write this book, but I wrote most of it in two weeks in two cabins in Tasmania. I stayed at Lake St. Clair and Cradle Mountain as the guest of the Parks and Wildlife Service of Tasmania, and I thank them for having me and for caring so well for the country that inspired me. I'm grateful, too, to Wildcare Tasmania and *Island* magazine for sponsoring the residency that took me there (part of the Wildcare Tasmania Nature Writing Prize). I finished the book in a borrowed house in the Christmas heat of Brisbane; thanks to Elizabeth and Simon Porter. And then the rewriting began, and most of that happened in a loft two stories above my family, in a terrace house in Glebe, and then later in a cowshed in Burradoo; thanks to the children for surrounding my silence with language and helping me recall what all this writing is for.

Maree began encouraging me to write this book many years ago; so this book, in a way, is her fault. Blame me, though, for its imperfections. She has been my muse, my in-house editor, my companion, and my angel. She never stops listening. She has borne more than her share of the parenting so that this book, which she conceived and christened, could be born. I'll never stop being thankful to—and thankful for—her.

For over a decade I've taught creative and business writing at the University of Sydney's Centre for Continuing Education. This book and I owe much to them; thanks especially to Jennifer Dustman, Lisa Elias, Jo Fleming, Rebecca Johinke, Brett Myers, Liselle Pullen, Jan Sayer, and Danielle Williams. I've run other programs over the years at the ACT Writers Centre, the Fremantle Arts Centre, the New South Wales Writers' Centre, Varuna, and elsewhere. Thanks to those places, too, and the committed people who run them.

For her faith, grace, and nous, I thank my friend and colleague Lesley Evans Nelson. Among the many people I've worked with in business and government I particularly acknowledge Gordon Carey, Steve and Louise Meyrick, Liz Roberts, Jenny Steadman, and Kaaren Sutcliffe. Thanks also to Roland Hemmert, Philippa Johnson, Lucia Rossi, Kim Stafford, Frank Stewart, and Henryk Topolnicki—friends and listeners, whose work and lives inspire me.

Thanks to my agent Fran Bryson and her assistant Liz Kemp. In Emma Driver I had the perfect editor—adroit, intelligent, and generous. At University of New South Wales Press, my publisher Phillipa McGuinness understood this book at once, when it was just an idea, and she saw it through. Thanks to her, and everyone at the press. At Cambridge University Press, thanks to Andrew Brown for carrying these coals back to Newcastle; to Kate Brett for reading my antipodean words so carefully and shepherding them through so swiftly and graciously, even via Cornwall; to Gillian Dadd for picking it up from there; to Kay McKechnie for her smart and supple editing; to Angela Alrey for the fine index; and to Rosina Di Marzo, production editor, and Sue Watson, designer, for making out of all of this such an elegant volume.

Finally, I acknowledge and thank the copyright-holders (authors and publishers) of every work I quote from in this book. In particular:

Lines from "One Art" by Elizabeth Bishop, published by Farrar, Straus, and Giroux, reprinted by permission of the publisher.

Passages from *Out of Africa* by Karen Blixen, published by Gyldendal, reprinted by permission of the publisher and the Rungstedlund Foundation, literary representatives of the author's estate.

Passage from *Being Dead* by Jim Crace, published by Farrar, Straus, and Giroux, and Penguin, reprinted by permission of the publisher.

Passage from *The Hours* by Michael Cunningham, published by Farrar, Straus, and Giroux and HarperCollins, reprinted by permission of the publishers.

Passage from *The White Album* by Joan Didion, published by Farrar, Straus, and Giroux, and HarperCollins, reprinted by permission of the publishers and the Lois Wallace Literary Agency.

Passages from *An American Childhood* by Annie Dillard, published by HarperCollins, reprinted by permission of Russell & Volkening Inc. and the author.

Passage from *The Blue Jay's Dance* by Louise Erdrich, published by HarperCollins, reprinted by permission of the publisher.

Passage from *Middlesex* by Jeffrey Eugenides, published by Farrar, Straus, and Giroux, reprinted by permission of the publisher.

Passages from *The Lost Thoughts of Soldiers* by Delia Falconer, published by Soft Skull, reprinted by permission of the publisher.

Passages from *The Little Virtues* by Natalia Ginzburg, translated by Dick Davis, published by Seaver Books and Carcanet, reprinted by permission of the publishers.

Passages from *Plainsong* by Kent Haruf, published by Alfred A. Knopf, a division of Random House, and Picador, an imprint of Macmillan, reprinted by permission of the publishers.

Passages from *For Whom the Bell Tolls*, *The Sun Also Rises*, *To Have and Have Not*, and *The Essential Hemingway* by Ernest Hemingway, published by

Simon & Schuster and Jonathan Cape, reprinted by permission of the publishers.

Passage from "The Redfern Address" by Paul Keating, reprinted by permission of the author.

Passages from *A Grief Observed* by C. S. Lewis, published by Faber & Faber, reprinted by permission of the publisher and the C. S. Lewis Pte. Ltd.

Passage from *A River Runs Through It* by Norman Maclean, published by The University of Chicago Press and Picador, an imprint of Macmillan, reprinted by permission of the publishers.

Passages from *All the Pretty Horses*, *The Crossing*, and *No Country for Old Men*, by Cormac McCarthy, published by Alfred A. Knopf, a division of Random House, and Picador, an imprint of Macmillan, reprinted by permission of International Creative Management.

Passage from *Rising From the Plains* by John McPhee, published by Farrar, Straus, and Giroux, reprinted by permission of the publisher.

Passages from *The English Patient* by Michael Ondaatje, published by Alfred A. Knopf, reprinted by permission of the publisher and Trident Media Group.

Passages from "Politics and the English Language" and "Why I Write" by George Orwell, published by Harcourt Brace and Penguin, reprinted by permission of A. M. Heath, literary representatives of the author's estate, and Houghton Mifflin Harcourt Publishing.

Passages from *A Place of My Own* and *The Botany of Desire* by Michael Pollan, published by Random House and Bloomsbury, reprinted by permission of the author and publishers.

Passage from *Bad Land* by Jonathan Raban, published by Pantheon Books, a division of Random House, and Picador, an imprint of Macmillan, reprinted by permission of the publishers and Aitken Alexander Associates.

Passage from *Maps of the Imagination* by Peter Turchi, published by Trinity University Press, reprinted by permission of the publisher.

Passages from *More Matter* by John Updike, published by Alfred A. Knopf, a division of Random House, and Penguin, reprinted by permission of the publishers.

"This is just to say" from *Collected Poems: Volume One* by William Carlos Williams, published by New Directions and Faber & Faber, reprinted by permission of the publishers.

Passages from *Cloudstreet* by Tim Winton, reprinted by permission of Jenny Darling Associates and the author.

Passages from *Mrs Dalloway* and *The Waves* by Virginia Woolf, published by Houghton Mifflin Harcourt Publishing Company, reprinted by permission of the publisher and the Society of Authors, literary representatives of the author's estate.

STEPPING OUT
A prologue on diction, structure, magic, and democracy

A short walk in a southern wood

I sit down to write the book, and nothing happens.

It's summer out there. I'm working at an office desk in a ranger's hut close to a visitors' center by a glacial lake, and I'm a long way south of home. Being here's a gift, part of a prize I won for writing something else. And I want to spend my time here well; I want to spend it writing this book. If I don't, my publisher might kill me.

Though it's summer, it fell below freezing last night, and I was cold in my bed. But the morning is warm and still and clear. There are black peppermints standing up in it and black currawongs crying their guttural cry, and there's a light as clean and a sky as blue as any you're ever going know. I've come here to write a book; I walk out into the morning to find it.

And it's on the gravel track to Fergy's Paddock at the edge of the lake that my book comes to me. Between steps, it occurs to me (though not for the first time) that to write is to make sentences, and out of them to make a story or an argument, a business case or a poem. Whatever you want to write, it's sentences you'll need to master. Your task is to get to the end of each one and then the next until the end, but not just any old how. You have to get somewhere and take your reader with you; and you want to get there well—elegantly, economically, gracefully, reasonably. You don't want to trip, and you don't want your reader to stumble.

What the morning tells me is that a sentence is like a walk—like this one in particular. A good sentence is a gravel path through a forest. It's a track, not a road; it's a trail, not a footpath. You want it finished, but not anonymous. It needs personality, modulation, topography—a little rise and fall. And it needs to take a sensible, and reasonably straight, path to wherever it's meant to be going.

But a sentence is not just a trail; it's also the walk the writer, and after the writer, the reader, takes upon it. For sentences live. They move, and they breathe. They travel, making themselves up as they go. A sentence—making it and taking it—is the walking, not just the walk.

And this is how you'd want your sentence to feel; this is how you'd like your reader to feel, reading it—the way I do, taking the track, this morning. You'd want them to trust it, the way I trust this path. It's sound. I can hear it under my feet, but it doesn't distract me. Because I can be sure it's not going to lose me, I give myself over to everything it opens out upon.

You'd want your reader to hear the cries of birds—sweet crescent honeyeater, harsh yellow wattlebird, distant yellowtail. You'd want your reader to smell the eucalypts and the leatherwoods; to catch a vivid crimson glimpse of waratah; to feel this waft of cold air; to sense, without seeing it yet, the deep glacial lake beyond the tea-trees; to guess at the whole long natural history that makes and goes on making the place she walks through. You wouldn't want her bitten by these bull-ants or centipedes or by that tiger snake. You probably don't want mud. Or mosquitoes. But there are always mosquitoes. And mud. And you'd want your reader to know that all of this was here, even the bugs and the snakes, going about their ancient business.

For you'd want all these qualities of your sentence and its world— what it says and what it implies—to catch your reader's attention without distracting her from the path or its destination, without tripping her up or putting her off.

A sentence is a morning walked through, some place on earth. It is an act, and a piece, of creation.

So, if you have something to write, concentrate on your sentences, and take them one at a time. Put down the burden of the whole huge book, the suite of poems, the letter, the report or the essay. Don't carry that monster on your back. When walking, as the Buddhists say, just walk. When writing, just write. Specifically, just write that sentence. And then write this one. Walk it elegantly, and let it suggest, let it even express, everything you mean to say, in the way it tells its own short story—for every sentence is a short story. The way it takes the bends.

If you want to write, take a walk. Take it again, sitting down at your desk.

 Try this

Take a walk. Come back home and write what you encountered. Try to write so that your sentences feel the way the walking felt.

Diction and structure

Actually, there was something else I did this morning before walking out into my sentence. There's a big whiteboard in the meeting room, and I did some thinking on it. I made a mindmap of the pieces of this book I still had to write—which was most of it. Then I flipped the board over and drew a gesture drawing of the book and all its parts.

Then I walked out, and my beginning began.

Writing is a dance—sometimes not all that pretty—between the big picture and the small. So much of the writing happens when you're not really writing at all. Sentences seem to come looking for you if you map their territory first.

So it was this morning. Plans are for starting out with and very often abandoning. You discover more interesting territory in your writing than you imagined in your map. You plan in order to compose yourself so you'll recognize a decent sentence when it arrives—so you'll know if it belongs and where and why.

This book is like my morning. It's about diction and structure; it's about what you have to do to hear just the right words at just the right time to speak them in just the right rhythm to say what you wanted to say. My book is about making beautiful sense.

What this book is and whom it's for

This is a book about what writing is—how you do it so it works and lasts.

Chapter 1 "Lore" is about first principles. It explains why and how good writing sounds like the very best kind of talking—clear, careful, animated, and memorable. Good writing means something fast. It speaks. Sometimes it even sings.

Chapter 2 "Sentencing" describes how sentences work and why verbs matter so much within them. It's a study of sentence craft, a guide to skilful sentence making. Nothing matters more in writing than making sound, astute, and elegant sentences, and varying their length and character. This chapter shows you how.

Chapter 3 "Grace" is about style. It's about writing—above all else —*clearly*. It's about saying more with less; about making the complex simple; about resisting fashion and cliché; about avoiding false eloquence and abstraction; about being particular; about writing (mostly) in the active voice; about using just the right word or phrase; and about a few other points of writing etiquette. "Grace" is about how to be cool, without outsmarting yourself, on the page.

Chapter 4 "Poetics" is for creative writers. It covers some skills and ideas that novelists, memoirists, essayists, and poets—literary artists —are going to need to master. While it doesn't aim to be complete, it speaks about most of what matters to me as a writer, and everything I've found useful. It talks about why literature matters so much. It covers poetics and politics; it speaks about listening and the importance of finding a form and sustaining a writing practice; it traverses beginnings and places and fragments and moments and stories and plots and characters; it considers the power of rhythm and the uses of tropes; it talks fairly straight about telling it sideways (indirection) and making your exposition sing and varying your pace and managing your points of view and rationing your modifiers and undoing, finally, everything you've done to leave behind the thing you really meant.

Chapter 5 "Attitude" is about writing for your reader and remembering your manners. If you want to write well don't think too much about your particular reader. Neglect your reader benignly. Please yourself, this chapter argues, but make yourself hard to please.

Chapter 6 "Shapely thoughts" is about structure. It's about thinking (wildly but well), planning (thoroughly but not too tightly), and linking (sentences and paragraphs). It's about what would once have been called "rhetoric." And in it you'll learn (again, perhaps) the four kinds of paragraph you can build and the ten ways you might make your point. Know what you want to say before you say it, this chapter suggests, but let yourself discover what that really is in the act of composing orderly paragraphs.

I'm writing this book because I'm losing patience with pedestrian prose; with loose constructions; with techno-babble and psychobabble; with babble of all kinds; with the dreary, dumbed-down, polysyllabic diction of public and corporate life; with the desiccated abstractions and clichés and with the group-think of too many bureaucracies and professions and businesses. I'm not the first person to notice that we have entered deeply into an era of bad language—ill-conceived or carelessly, or even mischievously, expressed, or both. I fear we will live with the consequences of bad language for a long time if we don't do something about it now. Democracy—not just art—depends on the lucid expression of careful and independent thought. And that's another way of saying what this book is about. I'm writing this book because I'd like to encourage richer and smarter writing. Writing that's clearer and more pleasing and useful. I'm writing this book to do something about bad language and its consequences.

But mostly, I'm writing it out of love for the mystery, the hard labour and the beauty of good writing and the conversation it enables each of us to carry on—with each other and with the world we spend our lives trying to plumb. I write it in the knowledge that there are still a few of us left who know you can never know too much about how to write elegantly. I write it for the people who have been my students for twelve years now and for people like them, and I write it largely out of what they have taught me about what I thought I already knew about writing. I write it for the muses among us, as my friend Kim Stafford calls all the poets out there who have no idea they're poets—people who speak with the kind of personality and vividness and particularity a writer wants in his prose, even if he doesn't know he does.

Writing Well has been insisting upon itself for six or seven years now. About that time I heard its heartbeat within my teaching materials.

But six years ago, I had no books of my own in the world. It seemed precocious to write a writing book before writing a real one. Three, nearly four, books later, its time has come.

But this book began before all that. It began when I did. It is the upwelling of what I've learned over twenty years as a book editor, as a writer of essays and books and poems, as a teacher of creative and professional writing, as an instructor in composition and grammar, as a reader, and as scholar and critic. And from twenty-odd years before that, as a child becoming a man becoming a writer. It describes the ideas and techniques I've learned from far better writers than I am—disciplines I follow daily. There's nothing here I haven't seen help my students, in functional and in creative writing. And there's nothing here I didn't learn from other people.

These are one writer's thoughts about his craft. But this is more than a philosophy and a critique of writing. It's a book of both craft and technique. It's a writing primer; it's a manual of ideas; it's a box of tricks. I aim to be as practical as I can. I don't intend to say a single thing I haven't found useful myself. In fact, I've already started. For the most useful things I know are sound first principles.

This book is for everyone who wants to write.

It's for all of us who just want to get something said, so that something will get done—people for whom writing is a means to an end. But it's also a book for those for whom writing is an end in itself. This is a book of the disciplines (of diction and structure, of thought and sentence construction) that apply whatever one is writing. You may want to write, for instance,

- to get a job
- to win a tender
- to tell a woman that you love her and how and why—or to tell a man
- to make sure the children know the kind of life you lived and the kind of world you lived it in
- to change the world
- to change the government's mind
- to teach the children well

- to honour a place on earth
- to tell a story that wants you to tell it
- to find out what it is you have to say

or for some other reason. All of it is writing. And writing is a profession, or something like one. Like any other profession or any art (dancing, say, or football, politics, acting or accounting), you ought to know what you're doing. It goes better when you know enough craft to be yourself.

Writing that's any good sounds like someone talking well. Voice and personality matter more, you might think, to the writer-as-artist than they do to the writer-as-parent or as executive or policy wonk. But, in fact, voice matters whatever you write, because writing transcribes speech, and if your transcription lacks the qualities that make speech engaging your tale, however businesslike, will die in the telling.

This book will show you how to write tunefully. It may school you in many of the moves a writer needs to make, but it will have failed if it doesn't help you turn out writing that sounds like elegant speech. Like talk tidied up. That's the point of everything this book describes. For the trick to writing better is to make your writing less like you always thought writing had to be and more like yourself talking about something you know among people you trust. The tricks and techniques of wording and phrasing and sentencing and paragraphing are meant to help you, paradoxically, sound as natural on paper as you do, sometimes, when you talk.

Ten ways of saying the same thing well

William Strunk thought the best writing was vigorous (*The Elements of Style*). Here are ten tips for writing vigorous prose.

1 "The golden rule is to pick those words that convey to the reader the meaning of the writer and to use them and only them." (Ernest Gowers, *The Complete Plain Words*)

2 "Vigorous writing is concise. A sentence should contain no unnecessary words, a paragraph no unnecessary sentences, for the same reason that a drawing should have no unnecessary lines and a machine no unnecessary parts. This requires not that the writer make all of his sentences short, or that he avoid all detail and treat his subject only in outline, but that every word tell." (W. Strunk and E. B. White, *The Elements of Style*, 4th edition)

3 ". . . words are the only tools you've got. Learn to use them with originality and care. Value them for their strength and their precision. And remember: somebody out there is listening." (William Zinsser, *On Writing Well*)

4 "Short words are best, and the old words, when they are short, are the best of all." (Winston Churchill)

5 The best writing is
   - clear
   - trim
   - alive

6 Grammar matters, but style matters more.

7 "Writing is the most exact form of thinking." (Carol Gelderman, *All the Presidents' Words*)

8 Writing is a process, and most of it happens when you are not writing.

9 Good writing is aware of itself—but not self-conscious. It does not happen accidentally. It results from the care the author takes with word choice, sentence structure and organization.

10 "Writing is only reading turned inside out." (John Updike)

CHAPTER 1

LORE

On voice, music, care, and thrift

To write well, express yourself
like the common people,
but think like a wise man. ARISTOTLE

Everyone knows how to write a bad sentence

Barry Lopez is a fine writer. If you wanted a model of humane and intelligent prose, of beautifully uttered sentences, and paragraphs as nicely arranged as the communities of lichen and moss on the sandstone rocks I passed this morning on my walk, you could do worse than study *Arctic Dreams* or one of his collections of fables— *River Notes*, say. A critic I know, reviewing *Arctic Dreams*, wrote once that Lopez doesn't seem to know how to write a bad sentence. It was a nice thing to say. Gracious and apt. But untrue. Barry Lopez knows perfectly well how to write a bad sentence. Everyone does. Even you.

What makes Lopez a good writer is that he knows the difference between those of his sentences that work and those that don't; between those he gets nearly right and those he nails; between those that sing and swing and those that mumble and fail. Sentences fail for many reasons. You may not know enough about what a sentence is, for instance, to reach the end with poise. Or you may, like Lopez, know more than enough, but you give them too much weight to carry; you work them too hard. And they break.

I know that Barry Lopez knows how to write (and right) a bad sentence because he rewrites everything—from essays and stories to his longest books—four and five times. And because he works on a typewriter, he writes every sentence from start to finish through four or five drafts. Think about the discipline that calls for—the care and the labour it entails. It's through such effort that effortless sentences are born.

Writing is the art of making an utterance perfectly natural through the perfectly unnatural process of making every word and phrase again and again, cutting here and adding there, until it is just so. It is contrived spontaneity. What the writer wants is something just like speech only more compressed, more melodic, more economical, more balanced, more precise.

Good writers take almost too much care with their work. Which led Thomas Mann to say that "a writer is somebody for whom writing is more difficult than it is for other people" (*Essays of Three Decades*). To be a writer you don't have to be the smartest soul on earth; you don't have to know the biggest words. You just have to commit yourself to saying what it is you have to say as clearly as you can manage; you have to listen to it and remake it till it sounds like you at your best; you just have to make yourself hard to please, word after word. Until you make it seem easy.

Writing, I'd say, is half gift and half hard work. And you can compensate for a want of the first by a surplus of the second. Let's not teach our students to be writers, pioneering writing teacher Wallace Stegner once said; let's just teach them how to write. It's not a lofty station; it's a job.

Work hard to make your writing seem to have cost you no effort at all. Struggle gamely to make it seem that your words came as naturally to you as the sun to the sky in the morning. Just as though you opened your mouth and spoke.

"The end of all method," said Zeno, "is to seem to have no method at all."

Here are some of Mr. Lopez's careful sentences:

If I were to now visit another country, I would ask my local companion, before I saw any museum or library, any factory or fabled town, to walk me in the country of his or her youth, to tell me the names of things and how, traditionally, they have been fitted together in a community. I would ask for the stories, the voice of memory over the land. I would ask to taste the wild nuts and fruits, to see their fishing lures, their bouquets, their fences.

I would ask about the history of storms there, the age of the trees, the winter color of the hills. Only then would I ask to see the museums. I would want first the sense of a real place, to know that I was not inhabiting an idea. (BARRY LOPEZ, "The American Geographies," *About This Life*)

▶ Try this

Here are some failed sentences of my acquaintance. Hear how awkward and inelegant they sound; notice how they fall apart, how loosely they are worded, and how confused they leave you; count the clichés they fall for; think about how many more drafts they could have done with to make them sound easy and clear. See if you can improve them; see if you can even understand them.

1 Certainly the combination of the sub-tropical rainforest and rich hues of sandstone that frame the paddocks of grazing dairy herds, lazy mountain streams and skies filled with flocks of king parrots is very inspirational and relaxing.

2 Snacking, in addition to breakfast, morning and afternoon tea, lunch and dinner, is bound to put on excess weight.

3 Whether your looking to spend hours luxuriating on a remote beach, or keen for aquatic adventures that will step up your heart rate, the Florida Quays is guaranteed to stand and deliver.

4 Observe the mist that trundles in,
   like soggy cotton balls, in waves,
   as far battalions form.
   The mist absorbs the valley,
   protects it fiercely,
   in nature's war against intrusion,

   nestling first in fertile groves,
   then nuzzling banks of silver streams,
   that feed into the river,
   under cloaks of moistured sheen.

5 Smith confessed that he had murdered the victim in court today.

6 MethoCare helps in maintaining social order in outer New London through our Community Night Patrol Service which reduces and prevents harm, associated with substance abuse, for individuals and the community.

7 McKenzie House offers elegant accommodation right on the doorstep of the old town hall.

8 With weddings that have a large number of out of town guests, it is important that there is ample accommodation within an approx. 20 mile radius of your planned reception venue as most guests will probably drive their car to the church and the venue, but will they necessarily be able to drive home at the end of the evening?

9 Simon Katich again pressed his claims as the most capable batter out of the National side to put Nebraska in command of New Hampshire on day two of the championship event at Lincoln Oval yesterday.

10 The Federal Government has issued advertisements depicting the violence and degradation wrought by the drug ice that have been classified as not suitable for children's viewing hours.

11 Wayne Bennett [the football coach] is hard to impress. After scoring a club record four touchdowns against the Packers, a surly Bennett was asked about the wingman's performance. "Pass," he replied.

12 From elegant and formal to casual and country, at Eling Forest, we can create a complete package to suit all styles and requirements from as small as 2 to as large as 200 guests.

13 Included in the tariff are generous provisions for you to prepare a hearty country breakfast for your first morning, orange juice, yoghurt, eggs from our hens collected daily, to accompany bacon and our own home grown tomatoes when in season.

Quoll

I saw an Eastern quoll last night, looking out my kitchen window.

A quoll is a cat-like marsupial, its brown body polka-dotted white. Fleet and sharp-eyed and lean. The one I saw last night was the first

I'd ever seen. She ran past my hut and around the feet of the two deciduous beeches standing there in their mosses; she was following her nose to dinner, though she found none here tonight, and then, before I could pull the camera from my anorak pocket, she was off down the drive with my syntax.

For it was I at the sink, not the quoll. You have to be careful how you make your sentences—specifically, in this case, where you locate your modifying clause. My errant sentence is an instance of loose pronoun reference; "looking" refers to "I," but it sits closer to "Eastern quoll." It's the kind of thing that happens when you let your sentences run away with themselves, as I did when I scrawled mine in my journal.

My sentence was loose; my technique let me down. You can rely on it to do that now and then. The trick is to catch yourself at your error before anyone else does.

Here are a couple of other ambiguous sentences I've encountered. Neither of them struck its reader as strange until he and in the other case she read it out loud. How easily we fool ourselves into thinking we've said what we meant.

The staff at the ANZ health clinic take care of people who are sick, like local doctors.

Between changing diapers, I wondered if you would consider writing a note to open the new issue of our baby directory.

In this last example, the magazine editor means to ask the celebrity she writes to—who is both a supermodel and a mother—if she could write something between nappies; the editor implies that the thought occurred to her—which may well be true, if I know anything about that editor—between changing her own child's nappies.

 ## Try this

1 Rework my quoll sentence and the two further examples above to avoid ambiguity.

2 "I saw an elephant, standing on my toes" is another classic of this kind; so too "I saw a car with three wheels over the

balcony." Here's another I just read: "We offer suggestions for reducing the high rates of injuries in this report." See if you can fix those.

3 I heard this on the radio the other day. See if you can fix what's loose about it: "To celebrate his two hundred-and-fiftieth birthday, PBS-FM has decided to play all of Beethoven's concertos." (If I write the pronoun "his," my readers will expect the next proper noun to be the one "his" stands in for, namely "Beethoven." Try starting the sentence with the main clause or swapping "Beethoven's" and "his.")

4 Here's a journalist, attempting a piece of new journalism a little beyond her syntax. See if you can help her. "It is 12.45am and a call comes that a man has fallen off a ladder in Queens. Hargreaves, the ambulance officer, shakes his head, putting it down to the full moon."

5 Admittedly, this is a spoof of a certain famous thriller writer, but see if you can disentangle it: "For what seemed an eternity, trying to remember his PIN, the screen mocked the famous writer."

Writing is the best kind of conversation you never heard

When you write, you talk on paper; when it's good, you sing.

"The sound of the language is where it all begins," wrote Ursula Le Guin, "and what it all comes back to. The basic elements of language are physical: the noise words make and the rhythm of their relationships."

When you write, using letters to make words, and words to make phrases, and phrases to make sentences, and all of it to make sense, what you're doing is patterning sound, as you do when you speak. You're using letters, which, as Eric Gill once said, are just signs for sounds. The signs are not silent. And the relationships among the letters and words have rhythm. Out of all of that choreographed signage one makes, with luck, a meaningful music, a score that, when the reader plays it in her head, makes the meaning one had in mind.

Whatever you create by way of art or meaning—the description you offer, the story you tell, the argument you outline, the exposition you offer, the poem you utter—you make by patterning sound. A noise is what you're making at that keyboard. The noise of speech.

The more you write as though you were *saying* something to someone, the better they are likely to understand, to be moved, to be changed, to be sold; the more likely they are to read on and still be awake at the end. Which would help.

The more your writing sounds like the best kind of *talking*, in other words, the more like the best kind of writing it will be.

Good writing is the best kind of conversation you never heard. It's talking tidied up. It's speaking compressed, clarified, enriched and heightened by thought and art, and set down on paper.

If what you write doesn't sound like someone speaking, write it again so it does. If it doesn't sound like a spoken thing, it'll probably never be heard. Or if it's heard, it will soon be forgotten. Or if your reader can't forget it, she'll wish she could.

Hear how this sounds like accomplished talking:

In the late Cretaceous and early Tertiary time, mountains began to rise beneath the wide seas and marsh flats of Wyoming. The sea-water drained away to the Gulf of Mexico, to the Artic Ocean. And, in David Love's summary description, "all hell broke loose." In westernmost Wyoming, detached crustal sheets came planing eastward—rode fifty, sixty, and seventy-five miles over younger rock—and piled up like shingles, one overlapping the another. In the four hundred miles of these overthrust mountains, other mountains began to appear, and in a very different way. They came right up out of the earth . . . These mountains moved, but not much—five miles here, eight miles there. They moved in highly miscellaneous and ultimately perplexing directions. The Wind River Range crept southwest, about five inches every ten years for a million years. The Bighorns split. One part went south, the other east. Similarly, the Beartooths went east and southwest. The Medicine Bows moved east. The Washakies west. The Uintas north . . . The spines of the ranges trended in as many directions as a weathervane . . . It is as if mountains had appeared in Ohio, inboard of the Appalachian thrust sheets, like a family of hogs waking up beneath a large blanket. An authentic enigma on a grand scale, this was one of the oddest occurrences in the tectonic history of the world . . .

The event is known in geology as the Laramide Orogeny. Alternatively it is called the Laramide Revolution.

(JOHN MCPHEE, *Rising from the Plains*)

Hear how this does not:

Several mechanisms have been suggested for the uplift [of what we call the Great Dividing Range]. One involves thermal expansion in the asthenosphere during partial melting (Wellman 1979b; Smith 1982). The second relates isostatic rise to igneous underplating and intra-plating (emplacement at various levels of the crust) (Wellman 1979b, 1987). However, these two mechanisms are not sufficient in their own right, and Lister and Etheridge (1989) expanded their earlier model (Lister, Etheridge & Symonds 1986) of upper plate passive margin develop-ment to explain the elevation of the Eastern Highlands. The uplift is supposed to have been caused by a complex interaction involving:

- negative buoyancy caused by decrease in the crustal thickness by a combination of pure and simple shear above and below an exten-sional detachment beneath an upper-plate passive margin;
- positive buoyancy induced by overall temperature rise (higher geo-thermal gradient);
- positive buoyancy induced by igneous underplating from an anom-alously hot asthenosphere; and
- the effects of flexure of the lithosphere.

(HELEN BASDEN (ed.), *Geology of New South Wales*)

This cannot engage anyone, not even another geologist, not even a reader like me, drawn to geology and keen to understand the Great Divide (of eastern Australia) and how it came to pass. It may, however, incite animosity or bring on sleep. Apart from the impossible density caused by all those technical terms, writing like this doesn't seem to come from anywhere or anyone.

This is defensive writing. It cares less about making meaning than about not making mistakes. Writing like this arises out of fear of being seen to get something wrong; fear of looking to one's colleagues like an undergraduate—or a goose. Such writing tries too hard to be exact and not hard enough to be clear; it tries so hard to allow only one meaning to arise that it generates no meaning at all. So, even when it succeeds, it fails. At least, it fails as writing. And this happens because the writer doesn't trouble to think her thoughts and speak them in a human voice. It happens because she loses sight of her readers.

There is a way of saying even the most complex and difficult things clearly and engagingly. Let's call it "the intelligent vernacular," using David Malouf's phrase. That translates as something like what Aristotle had in mind: think like a genius; write like everyman or woman. Speak, on the paper, as naturally and elegantly and clearly as you can. Charles Darwin managed it in 1859. Let his detractors try to match his grace of argument and expression:

It is interesting to contemplate a tangled bank, clothed with many plants of many kinds, with birds singing on the bushes, with various insects flitting about, and with worms crawling through the damp earth, and to reflect that these elaborately constructed forms, so different from each other, and dependent upon each other in so complex a manner, have all been produced by laws acting around us . . . Thus, from the war of nature, from famine and death, the most exalted object which we are capable of conceiving, namely, the production of the higher animals, directly follows. There is grandeur in this view of life, with its several powers, having been originally breathed by the Creator into a few forms or into one; and that, whilst this planet has gone cycling on according to the fixed law of gravity, from so simple a beginning endless forms most beautiful and most wonderful have been, and are being evolved.

(CHARLES DARWIN, "Conclusion," *The Origin of Species*)

▶ Try this

1 Take a book you like, and read a passage out loud. Note the way the writing moves, the ups and downs of it, the balance. Hear it speak. Note the passages that are particularly lovely to say and to hear. Notice, too, where it is harder to read because the book falls out of voice. The next book you decide to read, take turns with your partner or friend or child to read it aloud. Get used to hearing the way good writing goes. It will help you hear your own writing and practice it as utterance.

2 Try the same thing with a letter you receive or a report you read at work that strikes you as dull. Try it with anything that you're finding boring. Notice how the writing ain't got no rhythm.

3 If you have children around you, notice among the books you read to them which are the most pleasurable to share. I can recite *Where the Wild Things Are* from start to finish not only because my son Daniel wants it over and again, but because it sings. It's a nice example of quietly musical prose.

. . . you sing?

So, maybe you buy the idea that writing is a kind of talking, but how, you ask, does it sing? You may be wondering just how your letters and emails and business reports and essays—even your memoir or your history or your cookbook or your novel—might ever, or should ever, resemble a song. Actually, I'm stealing the idea from Louis Menand, who employed it in the introduction to *Best American Essays 2004*. "The real basis," he wrote, "for the metaphor of voice in writing is not speaking. It is singing."

The singer, unlike the talker, rehearses. What she utters she must get exactly right. Not just nearly, but just so. In song there are matters of rhythm and diction and flow that have to be spot-on. There are matters of technique, for singing is not the natural act that talking is. Song is an artificial kind of utterance; one rarely sings as one talks. Song—like writing, Menand says—is talking heightened by art. The song is performed, and its listeners will make the kind of judgments

49'er
Bar & Grill
San Marcos
San Marcos
Regional education
center
LORE | 19

one makes of a work of art. The kind one makes of a piece of writing, as opposed to a passage of conversation.

And when it works, song goes in deep and stays. Music will do that. It's got to do with the power of rhythm, the force of organized sound, to change us. I've seen photographs of what crystals in water look like after listening, first, to Bach's violin sonatas and, next, to the screaming of an angry man. You don't want your cells to look—or your readers to feel—the way those crystals looked, the way they were distressed, by the second. Bach, on the other hand, turned them into the embodiment of calm and harmony. This is what I mean by the power of rhythm.

In song, it's how you sing, not just what you utter, that counts. And so it is with writing. You do it and do it again; you're making a work that takes a finished form, that lasts, that plays again each time it's read; and it's not just what it means but the way it means that holds or loses your reader. The message is in the music. So make a beautiful noise. Still, writing isn't song exactly. If it's music, it's more Beatles than Beethoven; it's more Woody Guthrie than Giacomo Puccini.

Of all the arts writing is the most vulgar—and the least like art. It makes art out of words, out of the stuff we conduct our lives in: it makes art, not out of paint or textiles, but out of speech, out of what we use to buy the paper and scold the children and write the report. The best writing sounds just like speech, only better. Good writing is a transcendent kind of talking.

Here is an everyday piece of marketing copy. Nothing special about it. But its writer has taken care with it—to vary each sentence, to make it speak, to inflect it with humor, to make it personal and engaging. It's not a song, but it's been rehearsed.

Cherubs has been dreaming up heavenly garments for earthly angels since 1997. Its "Divine" range of baby clothes—available in Moonlight White, Starlight Yellow, Purely Pink and Celestial Blue—uses a unique layering system that makes it ideal for all terrestrial seasons and climates. In the warm months, dress your little cherub in a singlet body suit; when the weather cools, add matching long pants and a cosy hooded jacket. But *Cherubs* understands that clothes alone don't maketh the bub. On their website, you'll find stylish nursery furniture and accessories, toys, all-natural skincare products, belly mask kits for mum, books, photo frames . . . So many things, you'll think it's baby heaven on earth. But be warned: you could spend your Baby Bonus all in one hit.

Those people who write the notes on Fantale wrappers know how to do it, too. Notice how much information they cram in here, while keeping it chatty:

Born 21.7.78. When the handsome actor said he wanted to be a movie star, his father sat him down to watch old Jimmy Stewart movies to help him learn the craft. He tried out six times for TV's *Dawson's Creek* before landing a role in short-lived series *Cracker*.

Like many aspiring actors, he debuted in a slasher flick, *Halloween H20* (98) but was soon "one of the hottest young stars in Hollywood." In 2001 he proved it, using his quiet charisma to fine effect in the blockbusters *Pearl Harbor* and *Black Hawk Down*.

Guessed who that is? Read on.

 ## Try this

1 The talking cure. Think of something you're trying to write. Perhaps you're struggling with it. It may be a book, a difficult letter, a report or an essay. It doesn't matter.

   Take ten minutes, no more. Imagine you're telling a friend—someone with whom you talk about such things, or someone you admire and trust—what it is you have to write. Now, start writing as though you were talking to your friend. Describe the book (essay, report or letter) and the difficulties you face.

   Just write, and keep on writing, for ten minutes. Then stop and see what you have.

   I'd be surprised if you didn't find a better way to put things than occurred to you before. Try this whenever you find yourself stuck.

2 Begin each writing day or writing project by speaking a version of what you have to write. This often helps get your writing into a conversational register.

3 Listen to yourself. When you think you have a piece of writing

finished, read it aloud to yourself or to someone near or dear. Listen well. Can you hear a voice? Does it sound like yours? Does it have (your) rhythm? Does it sing? Notice where it works and where it doesn't; you'll notice much more with your ears than with your eyes; change whatever clangs.

4 This passage doesn't make a beautiful noise. Rewrite it so it does:

> In order to facilitate the timely preparation of six-monthly Business Affairs Statements, it is a recommendation of the Inland Revenue that businesses implement strategies and utilise appropriate software to ensure that the keeping of reliable financial records is a continuous process, not a periodic one.

5 See if you can translate that bio of Josh Hartnett (did you guess?) into the voiceless clichés of professional discourse: "Subsequent upon the discovery of his aspiration . . ." —that sort of thing.

Writing out loud

Geoff, a man who says he knows nothing about writing, a man who teaches marketing at the university where I teach writing, said to me one night at a college dinner:

"Sometimes when my students hand their essays in, I ask them, 'Did you read this out loud before you pressed the print button?' They look at me like I'm mad. But what they write often just doesn't make any sense—sentences not finished, things left in a mess, no flow to anything. What do you think about that?"

"Geoff," I said; "I've got a workshop starting tomorrow. You want to come and teach it?"

Duties of care

Writers—troubling the world with more words than the world probably thought it needed—owe the world a duty to make sure what they say is worth listening to. But to whom specifically do writers owe their duty of care?

- *The readers.* You need to remember them, for a start. The test of whether your writing works, no matter what you may think of it, is how well it works for your readers. Did they get it? Did they enjoy it? Did they nod or did they nod off? The poem, wrote Neruda, is the reader's not the poet's. Make it the best thing you can make, and give it away.
- *The cause or purpose.* You write for a reason: to achieve some result, to describe some subject matter, to give voice to some compelling notion. So, when you write, take care for the sake of the cause or purpose your writing serves. You don't, for instance, want something sloppy or shrill to harm your chances of getting a better grade, defeating the development application, winning his love, conserving the watershed, winning the job. Beware: Careless prose derails the noblest cause.
- *Society.* Writing is a social act—we share it; it grows out of and makes (or unmakes) relationships. It's a small part of a vast babble. Add something wise or useful or beautiful to the conversation we're all having, though many of us don't know we're having it, about who we are and how to live well together. Offer up the kind of language democracy and civilization depend upon—language that is original, rich, vivid, careful, accurate and true. Add something to the stock of wisdom. Speak so that everyone learns, including yourself.
- *Your people.* You might be writing a letter on behalf of a local action group, a tender for your company, or a report for your department. You might be writing a book about your grandfather or the pioneering family in the valley and the people they dispossessed. Take care of them. If you borrow a life or act as a scribe for a family, a community or an organization, they depend on you to offer on their behalf something better than a string of clichés and a suite of failed sentences. Your words speak for others, as well as for yourself. Your writing represents them. Take care for their sake.
- *The language itself.* Okay, this is lofty, but I see it as a duty as important as the others. Whenever you use the language you conserve

and replenish it; or you diminish it. Take your pick. Many of us learn the bad habits we do because so many people around us use writing to dissemble or to pose, rather than to say something. Too many people in positions of authority—people who should know better—use language carelessly or narrowly, manipulatively or defensively. We grow inured to bad language, George Orwell wrote once. It's every writer's responsibility to remember the genius of the tongue and to do what it takes to perpetuate it. Model (and copy) what is best, not what is worst from the writing around you. And take every opportunity—this email, this school report, this letter to the editor, this brochure—to practice. Language is a gift. Be grateful; honor the gift by taking care of it.

 Try this

1 Whatever you have to write this week, make it an opportunity to improve your writing, to contribute to the health of the language.
2 Ask yourself whom your writing serves. Make a list. Keep those people (and causes) in mind as you write. Ask yourself how your sentences—in the way they sing or fall apart—hobble or advance the causes they serve.

The thinking happens so fast, and the writing happens so slow

I was working the other day in my study, up in the loft of this terrace house where we live. All afternoon I could hear my two young boys talking, two floors down, to their grandparents. Speaking all the time, as though naming things were as important as drawing breath. I thought to shut the door to keep the voices downstairs. But I couldn't. When I stopped focusing on it, I realized that this was a kind of noise —the sound of people learning to make meaning—that helped me write. Until finally, up the stairs, two whole stories, came the sound of small feet on timber and a voice asking whoever might care to listen, specifically me: Who can this be coming up the stairs?

Perhaps we speak to find out who we are and how we stand in the world. We are languaging animals. We've been talking from the start; writing came much later. In evolutionary terms, we've only just begun. And still writing doesn't come naturally.

Speaking is our second nature; writing is a distant third. In abstracting—in setting down on paper—what our minds let our mouths do fluently in speech, many of us drop the thread of sense. That's not surprising; talking with one's fingers upon a keyboard or around a pencil is not all that natural an act, when you think about it. But many of us make it harder than it needs to be; we imagine writing as an enterprise with no connection to speaking, to be conducted in its own writerly tongue. And in trying to find this other language, this discourse of the fingers, would-be writers forget the lyrics they're meant to be singing; they lose the voice that, in speech, comes to them, and shape the thought, without thinking. When you write like that, you end up sounding stilted or just plain confused.

Part of the problem is that talking happens fast and writing happens slowly. When we talk, we open our mouths and a kind of vernacular music tumbles out. When we write, even if we know what we want to say and how, we have to use our fingers to say it, and this takes much longer. Then we start thinking—often too hard—about whether there's not a better way to go about it; then we forget just what it was we meant to say, and so we spiral into wordlessness or chaotic wordiness.

Because writing goes slower than speaking and a whole lot slower still than thinking, one gets plenty of time to worry. Into the gaps between the letters and the words, into the void of the blank screen, anxiety floods. And anxiety makes us all inarticulate; when we're anxious, we lose our voice. We sound, on the page as in life, like someone else, like someone we're trying to be, or like no one at all.

Some writers, when they're anxious, don't know how to start; others don't know how to stop. It's anxiety, if we let it, that will poison most of our attempts to write well.

But what is there to be anxious about?

There's the fact that writing endures, whereas spoken words pass.

Writers get anxious because they know that what they set down on the page and leave there can be read forever after—all your triumphs and tragedies of construction get preserved for all eternity. By contrast, a careless word or phrase uttered on the phone or a false note struck in conversation can be put right in the next sentence. When you speak, you can get away with umming and ahhing and losing your way and finding it again until you say what it is you discover you want to say. But when you write, no one will cut you that kind of slack. You need to say what you mean to say—and nothing else. Near enough's not good enough.

That's enough to scare the living daylights out of most of us.

But there are other anxieties—word limits; deadlines; the feeling that you don't know what you're talking about; the fear of making mistakes, of using the wrong words, of looking ridiculous; politics (more on this later); bad memories of composition classes from elementary school; grammar phobias; the feeling that you need to do more research; the certainty that you're missing the point; the fear that this has all been said before much better by someone else; the fear of offending someone, of defaming someone, of admitting something you'd rather not. Recognize some of those?

The gaggle of anxieties can induce panic, and panic spoils your prose. If you're feeling anxious when you write, anxious will be how your writing sounds. There's no end of things to fear—in writing as in life. One needs, in both cases, to get over it. And get on with it. Be alert, not alarmed! Compose yourself so that panic does not compose your sentences and put them in some hectic order. This is, of course, so much more easily said than done. You will panic; everyone does. How do you rein your panic in and put it to work for you?

Try not writing for a bit. Try thinking instead. That's what I was doing the other day when I drew myself those mindmaps before setting out on my walk. I was putting panic on a leash by ordering the mind that was meant to be writing some sentences. I was letting myself write by not writing. One reason you plan is to steady your nerves.

Trying to write like a writer—instead of writing like ourselves,

> To overcome the fear that you don't know how to write, the best thing to do is the most important writing step of all—start writing, uncomfortable though it may feel, as though you were talking. Don't think of it as writing at all—think of it as talking on paper, and start talking with your fingers. Once you've tricked yourself into trusting the words your "speaking mind" suggests, once you've stopped thinking about it as writing, you'll be surprised how much more easily the writing comes to you, and how much better it works.

caught in the act of speaking with ease—we end up writing the most stilted dross we've ever read.

And all the while the real writers are out there trying to write the way they speak (or wish they could). Try that.

 ## Try this

What do you get anxious about when you write? Looking like a fool; making some egregious mistake of grammar or fact or argument; getting yourself sued; causing problems for your family? Make a personal list. Sometimes giving names to the things that trouble us can strip them of their power.

Question everything they taught you at school

Why is it so hard to convince ourselves that to write is just to speak—on paper—with uncommon care? I think it's because we get told the opposite so early and so often; we get drummed out of us the one piece of wisdom that would help each of us write. We learn, at home, on our way through school, and then at work, that writing is supposed to be different from speaking—less personal, less plain, more circumspect, more polysyllabic, smarter, more proper all round. We learn to mistrust the way we'd say it well.

This all began the day someone told you to use the passive voice when expressing conclusions in an essay. When they told you never to write "I" in your history and science papers—in any papers at all. That day happened the other week to my daughter. It's the day you learn that you don't belong anymore in your writing.

What they were trying to teach you was the virtue of disinterested inquiry and dispassionate expression. But they may not have made that clear.

We are taught (sometimes) hastily, or we pick up the wrong

For anyone who still believes in the idea so emphatically insisted upon in some schools and academic disciplines, particularly the sciences, that "I" has no place in serious writing, consider this: Charles Darwin, who knew a thing or two about scientific inquiry and exposition, begins his great book *The Origin of Species* with "I," and he uses it liberally, and entirely appropriately, throughout. "I will not here enter on the minute details on this subject [the cell-making instinct of the hive-bee]" he writes at one point, characteristically, "but will merely give an outline of the conclusions at which I have arrived." The conclusions at which I have arrived: isn't that exactly what we want every student in an essay and every expert in a report to tell us? At the close of his introduction, Darwin writes, logically and personally: "Although much remains obscure, and will long remain obscure, I can entertain no doubt, after the most deliberate study and dispassionate judgment of which I am capable, that the view which most naturalists until recently entertained, and which I formerly entertained—namely, that each species has been independently created—is erroneous. I am fully convinced that species are not immutable . . ."

Indeed, if he had not spoken to us so carefully, so humanely and well, his work would have been far less engaging, and the theory of natural selection might never have reinvented and enriched our understanding of ourselves and our world so thoroughly. Darwin is *talking* (sagely) with us. He is considering the evidence, and he is putting together an argument. *He* is. So he writes *I.*

Now, if it was good enough for Charles Darwin, is it not good enough for the rest of us?

message. Writing doesn't need its own arcane vocabulary, its own complicated syntax; writing need not be more formal or mannered than talk. But because writing isn't, in fact, speaking, we have to take more care with it: writing lasts, and we have only the words with which to make our point and strike our tone.

Don't hunt for fancy words and erudite turns of phrase. Aim, instead, to speak, on the page. Use the same words, but choose them and order them with less haste.

Most writers spend too much time trying to write as someone else might—as they imagine they are supposed to write because they are a lawyer, a scientist, a businessperson, a professional, a journalist, a student, a mother, a father, a writer. And that's when they lose their way. That's when their writing grows dull. And the person for whom it's dullest of all is the man or woman composing it. Whenever your writing bores you, stop.

What each of us needs is the confidence to write more like ourselves; to write like one intelligent human being—this intelligent human being with the pen—speaking with care to another. That's what Charles Darwin did—who appears to have become the hero, suddenly, of my chapter. That's the simple and difficult task ahead of every writer.

Here's an example of some good contemporary writing from a psychology textbook:

As I look at the top of my desk, what strikes me is a continuous field of light, varying from point to point in amplitude and wavelength. But I see the scene neither as a continuous field nor as a collection of points, and I certainly do not see it as existing on my retinas. Instead, I see objects: a word processor, a pencil, a stapler, and a pile of books. The objects look solid, and they appear to occupy definite positions in the three-dimensional space atop my desk.

My experience is no illusion. The objects I see on my desk really exist and are located precisely where I see them. I can prove that: with vision as my only guide, I can reach out directly to the pencil and pick it up . . . Sensation entails the registration and coding of light, sound, and other energies that impinge on the sense organs . . . The ability to interpret this information, to extract from it meaningful and useful representations of our world, is called perception. (PETER GRAY, *Psychology*, 2nd edn)

Try this

The next letter or report or piece of copy you have to write, try to write it as you might speak it if you had worked out exactly what to say. Imagine, for example, that your task is to script what you would say on the matter in a radio interview. Write that. Nine times out of ten, that will be close to what you should actually write, not the gumph you usually do.

Make the complex simple

Everybody, when you think about it, writes within constraints—of time, of politics, of budget and so on. We are never perfectly free to say exactly what we might like. We are constrained, for instance, by the complexity, the sensitivity, the abstraction and the obscurity of what we have to say. We write, some of us, for an organization. There are matters of politics and confidentiality that constrain us there. And there are deadlines, frequently impossible. There is one's mood, frequently bad, and one's confidence, frequently low. There are the children screaming and all the other much more urgent things to be done. But these are just the constraints within which one must try to make something clear.

For these are the circumstances in which we all work, trying to make the complex things simple—not the other way round. And too often our writing does tend the other way, making the simple things complex. The medical center posts this notice: "Consultation fees in this practice are individually determined by each practitioner case by case. The usual fee charged for the most common consultations are as follows . . ." It might have written, instead: "Each doctor in this practice sets their own fees, but you can expect to pay something like this for common consultations . . ."

Don't let real life be an excuse for failing to write well. Clarity and stylish simplicity are not negotiable.

▶ **Try this**

1 What constraints do you work within? What do you need to be careful about? What factors place your writing under pressure and lead you to write something less than plainly, in something other than your voice? Make a list. It's good to get clear about these things. Ask yourself which of those factors are the most important; which are material; and which are personal issues. Ask yourself how you can better conform with the legitimate constraints without compromising the vernacular clarity of your prose.

2 Think of some technical task you know how to perform— changing a diaper, stripping down and rebuilding a car engine, saddling a horse, running a restaurant, mending a fence, loving a difficult man. There'll be something. Make it something, ideally, not everyone knows how to do. Now describe what you do when you perform that task so that anyone could understand. Write three hundred words.

3 You are going speed dating tonight. You've been told you have to speak about your work. You'll have a total of two minutes with each prospective partner. Write the script of what you will say tonight about the work that you do. Imagine that it will really count—there will be that one person you really want to connect with. Don't lie; don't be dull; don't imagine you can use the same kind of language I'd find in your job description.

Thrift and grace

It's the first morning of a business-writing workshop. Twenty-six students and I are sitting in a room at The Grace Hotel. Good name, I'm thinking. The air-conditioning is already too cold, and the jackets are coming out. I've spent half an hour introducing the ideas we'll be working with, and now we're going around the horseshoe, telling each other who we are, why we're here and what we hope to learn.

When it's his turn, Andrew, a young IT professional, says this: "I'd like to be more thrifty as a writer. My uncle once told me that 'thrifty' comes from the verb 'to thrive.' I think it's what you're talking about here."

Andrew's right. It's the first time I've seen the connection, though, that *thrift* makes between economy and health. Until now, I've thought of *thrift* as *parsimony*. Andrew's helped me realize that *thrift*'s a richer word than it seems.

The writing thrives if you use a little to say a lot; if you bring to each sentence just the words it needs to say the thing you have in mind— in just the way you need to say it. The writing prospers when it is not overwhelmed with syllables and abstractions. Less, in other words, is more.

Thrift is what this book's about—grace through thrift. It's most of what a writer needs. Thanks for the word, Andrew.

Listen to how this passage thrives, even if its writer does not. He grieves:

And no one ever told me about the laziness of grief. Except at my job— where the machine seems to run on much as usual—I loathe the slightest effort. Not only writing but even reading a letter is too much. Even shaving. What does it matter now whether my cheek is rough or smooth? They say an unhappy man wants distractions—something to take him out of himself. Only as a dog-tired man wants an extra blanket on a cold night; he'd rather lie there shivering than get up and find one. It's easy to see why the lonely become untidy; finally, dirty and disgusting.

(c. s. lewis, *A Grief Observed*)

▶ **Try this**

Can you write these passages more thriftily?

1 Laurie's Place provides a safe daytime drop-in centre for women and women with children who are in crisis, home-less, lonely, feeling isolated or in need of basic support. Services provided include meals, showers, laundry, medical, legal, and counseling services also a variety of activities.

2 Born amid the violent volcanic explosions millions of years ago, these mountainous islands are capped by an exotic mix

of rainforest, tropical bush, sweeping pine forests, and grassy hills.

3 Tasks

The Writer will undertake the following tasks under the direction of the contractor managing the project and under the supervision of the Project Manager:

(1) Provide input to finalizing the scope of the project in terms of: the audience to be aimed at/purpose of product; the temporal beginning and end of the "story"; the documents to be sourced (including those that might be identified as "confidential"); the people to be interviewed; the outline/chapters of the book to be written; initial book "reviewers" (likely to be "internal"); final book reviewers (likely to be external); nature and volume of final product (e.g. how "big" a book; electronic and/or hard copy; number of copies). This will be provided to the Project Manager for approval.

(2) Contribute to the preparation of a project plan that incorporates the definitions delivered in (1) including the mechanisms and timing for engaging with relevant people within the project. This may include the conduct of a workshop with the key players.

(4) Review existing documents, reports and other material and start outline of key chapter heading within book chapters covering themes identified in (1).

(5) Work with contractor to generate comprehensive list of key questions, issues, matters that require further exploration. This will be provided to the Project Manager for approval.

(6) Work with contractor to finalize detailed format for gathering required information from people identified in (2); this includes both key questions to be asked of who and mechanism by which to elicit answers to questions and to encourage more broad discussions of the experiences people had during the establishment of the National Park. This will be provided to the Project Manager for approval.

(7) Collect and collate information from people identified in (1).

(8) Complete first draft of entire text for the book/product; identify supporting images, pictures, maps, diagrams etc. that will be needed for the book.

(9) Review the book based on feedback sought from project contributors on correctness of representation of their views.

(10) Review the book and revise text based on feedback from initial book reviewers (as identified in (1) above).

(11) Provide expert input to the Project Manager in the book publication process, e.g. enlisting a publisher, ISBN number, identify a designer for book layout.

(12) Provide expertise through publication process. This includes, but is not limited to:

    a. Revision of the book based on feedback from the external reviewers.

    b. Implement final changes based upon final iteration with internal review team (1).

    c. Provide relevant input in design of product and implementation of the communication plan.

This project will use existing sources of information; the only primary data collection will be in the form of information gathered from people interviewed by the professional writer.

The genius of the tongue

We're talking English here. Things might be different in another tongue. English as a genus has almost as many species as the genus Eucalyptus (which has nearly eight hundred). All of them are alike; none of them is the same. There is Australian English, Aboriginal English, Russell Crowe English, American English, Canadian English, the Queen's English, Oxbridge English, West Country English, Cockney English, Belfast English, Dublin English, Glasgow English, Yorkshire English, Indian English, New Zealand English, Alaska English, Bronx English, Pidgin English, Outback and Veldt English, Thai English, and all the many sisterhoods and brotherhoods of English the world over. And each of them is beautiful.

But still, English is English. Like all tongues, it has its own genius, its own character. Like all language, it comes from somewhere and works after its own fashion. Something about the geography and the culture that gave rise to English loves short, grounded words. English, wherever we want to use it, works most powerfully, poetically and profitably when it uses words like *old* and *short*, like *man* and *woman*, like *now* and *ground*, like *buy* and *trade* and *miss* and *sell*, like *word* and *world* and *drink* and *child* and *time*. This is so even though English is the world's most generous language, accepting into its dictionaries more words from other languages, more neologisms, more readily and rapidly than any other language. It is large; it grows hourly; it contains multitudes. It has let in words like *minimization*, *contemplate*, *bureaucracy*, *infrastructure*, *stratigraphy*, *cartography*, *genre*, *multitude*, and *expedite*. English allows us to use those words, but it still does its best work when we write sentences made of words like *dark*, *earth*, *profit*, *grow*, *shop*, *grasp*, *fall*, *fail*, *grief*, *work*, *write*, and *wrong*.

"The short words," said Winston Churchill, "are best, and the old words, when they are short, are the best of all." In such a sentence we see the genius of English at work: words of a single syllable (short, old words like *short* and *old* and *best* and *all* and *words*) shaped into rhythmic phrases and clauses, until you get a sentence a whole lot more complicated than it seems. What you have is heightened speech. English needs to wear its learning lightly. It is inherently modest. Its music and its meaning depend on thrift.

The music of English happens more in the phrases than in the words—phrases made of short words; phrases undulant with syllables stressed and unstressed; phrases composed from the lexicon of familiar, concrete words. French, here, differs from English. Don't let anyone tell you French is more musical. French *words*, maybe. But English at its best sings an everyday music, rude with weather and the odours of the earth, robust as a conversation in the kitchen. More pastoral than rococo, for sure; more chapel than cathedral. Whatever you want to write in English, you'll write best in the vernacular, in familiar words, chosen with uncommon care and shaped into irregularly rhythmic phrases and clauses and lines. Like these:

The real world goes like this. (JAMES GALVIN)

Let us go then, you and I, / When the evening is spread out against the sky / Like a patient etherised upon a table . . . (T.S. ELIOT)

We are here to witness. (ANNIE DILLARD)

We will fight them on the beaches. (WINSTON CHURCHILL)

Grief is the price we pay for love. (QUEEN ELIZABETH II)

We have nothing to fear but fear itself. (F.D. ROOSEVELT)

Season of mists and mellow fruitfulness. (JOHN KEATS)

Workers of the world unite; you have nothing to lose but your chains. (KARL MARX)

In the beginning was the Word, and the word was with God, and the word was God. (BOOK OF GENESIS)

He was an old man who fished alone . . . (ERNEST HEMINGWAY)

The sea is flat, and across the quiet water Lion Island looms. (CHARLOTTE WOOD)

To be or not to be; that is the question. (WILLIAM SHAKESPEARE)

To everything there is a season, and a time to every purpose under heaven. (BOOK OF ECCLESIASTES)

What a piece of work is a man! How noble in reason, how infinite in faculties . . . in action how like an angel, in apprehension how like a god. (WILLIAM SHAKESPEARE)

Shakespeare understood the genius of English. That's why his works endure. So did Jane Austen and most of the many and various authors and translators of the Bible. And the others on this short and random list.

This is not to say that you can't use words like *adumbrate, amplitude, transpire, apprehension, completion, acquire, disquisition, perception, recursive,* and even—aarghh!—*minimization* or *utilization,* if each seems the best and most economical word for what you want to say, or if they speak the way you speak—or your character does. Just remember that there are always alternatives in the common tongue for what you want to say—specifically here *shadow forth, space, come to pass/happen, fear/misgiving/understanding, end/finish/close, buy, essay, sense/sight, repetitive, limit,* and *use.* And if you favor those, you'll be writing English the way it wants to be written. "He who uses many words of more than two syllables is running counter to the genius of our mother tongue," wrote Walter Murdoch in his essay "Sesquipedalianism" back in the 1930s.

But I don't want you to get the wrong impression here. This is not an argument that only the shortest words (in only the shortest sentences) will do. English likes variety every bit as much as the next language; its music depends upon a mixture of the short and the long—in words and in sentences. Shakespeare also wrote "the multitudinous seas incarnadine," and that sounds pretty cool, too. But as a general rule, what Churchill said holds true. English sentences do their best work when they're made of short, familiar words, put together in interesting ways. As for the sentences, they can be long or short or middling—as long as they stay lean and rhythmic.

And beware. As Walter Murdoch once put it, "When we wish to hide our thought or the fact that we have not thought at all, we use long words." The man who uses too many long words either doesn't know what he means or he doesn't want you to know.

Writing in short words is not dumbing down; it's smartening up. Until you can say even the most complex thing in simple words, you probably haven't thought it through. For we think most clearly in short, old, concrete terms; we write most clearly in short, old, concrete words. Never compromise the complexity of the concepts you need to relate; but find words for them that are not themselves complex, abstract or recondite.

When you make the complex simple, without stripping it of nuance or precision, you write the only kind of prose worth reading.

Take the trouble to make a difficult thing plain, and your readers will feel more intelligent. They'll thank you. They'll recognize you as someone who knows their subject well enough to know how to put it simply.

You will have contributed to the general store of wisdom. That's worth a shot, isn't it?

Here's an example of some smart writing about something fairly complicated, put in simple words:

The interesting questions about plants are not what they are called nor where they are found, but how they make a living, why they are so different from each other, how they have come to look as they do, and why they are found in one place rather than another. If we could answer these questions, we would have a good grasp of the gross ecology of a region.

(GEORGE SEDDON, *Sense of Place*)

▶ **Try this**

1 The short words are best
See if you can rewrite this passage using only short, old words:

The necessity for individuals to become separate entities in their own right may impel children to engage in open rebelliousness against parental authority, with resultant confusion of those being rebelled against.

2 A lexicon of everyday words
Find everyday words to use instead of these words and phrases:
ensue
initiate
has the capability
notify
undertake
accomplish
inculcate
legitimize
compartmentalize
validation
instigation
promulgation
publication
completion
instigate an inquiry
assist

afford an opportunity
ascertain
expedite
to effect a change
minimize
optimize
prioritize
personnel
preclude
utilize
in relation to

Bach

Ellie's Polish, but she was brought up in two languages (Polish and English). On the second morning of the business-writing workshop she raised her hand and said: "I came to this course thinking I would learn how to use words like *facilitate* and *maximization*. What I have learned is to to avoid words like that."

At the break she said to me, "Bach is what you're talking about here, no?" All that simple and beautiful intelligence, she meant.

Ellie may be, for all I know, the only student I've ever had who got hold of my meaning so well.

Bach's music, for me, is brilliant but not showy; spare but not slight. Its simplicity is deceptive but not false, for the music is complex but never opaque. It is mathematics and art in equal measure. Bach is a perfect metaphor—thanks Ellie—for writing well.

Writing is the most exact (and exacting) form of thinking

If you're writing well, if you're taking the kind of care you should take over what you say and how you say it, you'll be thinking as hard as you'll ever think.

This is why writing is so hard; this is why so few of us do it well most of the time; this is why many people choose easier paths like astrophysics, professional football, bull-riding, and school teaching. Okay, they're hard, too. But writing is about the toughest and most disciplined thinking work you'll ever do.

Writing, as Carol Gelderman put it, is the most exact form of thinking. It exacts—from those of us who want to do it well—precision, discernment, fineness of observation and detachment. By its nature, true writing practices critical thinking. *Critical* has come to mean to most people something like "negative." It also means "very important." But its primary meaning is "exacting," "skeptical," "disinterested," "discerning," "analytical." We take it from the Greek word *kritikos*, meaning "one who is skilled in judging; one who takes things apart."

The writer is the *kritikos*, but she's also skilled at putting things back together again. Good, sustained critical thinking underlies good, clear writing: you could almost say that good writing is critical thinking. It is critical thinking resolved and put down on paper— elegantly.

▶ **Try this**

Critical questions

Try asking these questions of each sentence in a piece you are writing.

1 What am I trying to say here?
2 What does that mean?
3 . . . compared to what?
4 What is the evidence for that assertion?
5 How is that fact or argument relevant?
6 Can I offer an example?
7 Can I quantify that?
8 What exactly does that word mean? Is it the right one? Will my readers understand it to mean what I intend it to mean?
9 How does this relate to my argument?
10 Will this interest my reader? How?

These critical questions should be in your mind as you write anything. If they slip as you draft, that's all right. It might even help. But make sure you ask them of your prose as you edit and redraft.

The politics of bad language

Back in 1946 George Orwell thought the language was dying. He thought that politics was killing it. Surveying public discourse—letters to the editor, print journalism, speeches, brochures, and radio broadcasts—he decided that humanity was in retreat, that sentences were losing their soul. Bureaucracy and commerce, politics and fear, he felt, were colonizing the English language, strangling it upon the page. So he wrote an essay about what he felt was wrong and what he felt might be done about it, and he called his essay "Politics and the English Language."

This was 1946, remember. There's nothing new, you see, about the decline of the language. Like the mountains of the earth, it is going up (orogeny) and going down (gravity and erosion) at the same time. It's a question of which force is winning, the generative or the degenerative. Keeping it lively and "natural," keeping it humane and democratic, is a struggle that's never won—and it will surely be lost if you and I don't keep at it. For each generation seems to invent new ways to subvert the struggle, new ways to emaciate the language for political ends (which they may be quite unconscious of).

We have become used to bad language. We've been inoculated by bad habits so that most of us are immune to the good old habits we once caught easily. We so often hear bad language—inhumane, dull, lifeless, and tuneless—from people we imagine know what they're doing, that we come to think of bad as good. After a while we stop noticing how ugly and inexact, how pompous and flabby it has all become. By then we're writing that way ourselves.

For such language is in circulation all about us—in newspapers, in government, on the television, in our workplaces. It is the currency in which much of modern life is transacted. We copy it. We take the lead from others—bosses, those who have gone before us, the style police, the newspaper editors, the newsreaders, even the politicians—on how to put things. Way back when I started work at a law firm, for instance, I found myself copying the way the senior partners wrote. It's the same for the new recruit to the government agency, the fresh academic, the young doctor, the new teacher or nurse. It was probably the same for you. But not all of them—these partners, these old hands, these professionals—were using language to make things clear.

Language is the chief means by which, as George Bernard Shaw once wrote, the professions conspire against the public. Opaque and difficult, imperious language is the best way to hold onto knowledge and power. Language, which is by nature a means of making and sharing meaning, of talking among ourselves, becomes in many places a way of doing politics. Language becomes subterfuge. It becomes the secret code of a society or profession; it becomes the conventional expressions employees and aspirants feel obliged to use, may even be forced to use, to get on in a field or a firm. It becomes a way of not making things clear, a tool for clever obfuscation, a way of hedging bets and keeping one's nose clean.

We all know when language is being used for politics. It's hard to understand if you're uninitiated. It's dense and vague. It's abstract and impersonal. It's formal and cold or it's falsely breezy. It's heavy on ideology and light on fact. It's loud and long about ends but quiet and short about means. It's polysyllabic. It dwells on processes not people. It's passive. These are all fine ways to say a whole lot less than you seem, at first, to be saying, while taking a very long time to do it. Writing like that intends not to include but to exclude its readers. It means to fend them off, not to suffer them. Such writing is caution and self-interest run amok. Its roots go down to fear and, deeper still, in some cases, to an instinct for keeping hold of one's secrets.

Good writing transcends politics. It rises above fear. Within the limits of professional care and political reality, it will speak plainly to its readers, aiming to say as much as possible, as economically as possible. As opposed to the kind of fearful, political writing we encounter too often, good writing will be humane, plain, active, informal, concrete, clear, and specific. It will have a voice. It will have a life.

Here are the things George Orwell thought writers should do to save their prose from politics.

1 Never use a metaphor, simile or other figure of speech you are used to seeing in print.
2 Never use a long word where a short one will do.

3 If it is possible to cut a word out, always cut it out.
4 Never use the passive where you can use the active.
5 Never use a foreign phrase, a scientific word or a jargon word if you can think of an everyday English equivalent.
6 Break any of these rules sooner than say anything outright barbarous.
(GEORGE ORWELL, "Politics and the English Language")

▶ Try this

See if you can mend this paragraph, a victim of politics.

> Pursuant to the recommendations of our nominated consultants, an all-departmental initiative has been implemented, effective immediately, rationalizing human and financial resources in conformity with our strategic mission statement, which I am sure you have all internalized and made operational in your teams. An organization-wide announcement on this decision will be circulated in the foreseeable future.

Or this:

> At ground level, the next issue of *Gardens Plus* would have been an informative publication for our readers, however it has been decided that *Gardens Plus* did not have the alignment for our company direction, and hence does not coincide with the bigger picture for our next five-year business plans.

Short and right and nice

At the end of a workshop, Molly, in her Glaswegian accent, summarized my message thus: "What you're saying is that you want it said short and right and nice."

It sounded better in Scots. But it's thriftily put, and it says it pretty well.

CHAPTER 2

SENTENCING

On the craft of the sentence

I take it as a basic principle that anyone who aspires to use his
native tongue professionally and publicly had better know it.
WALLACE STEGNER

Wrangling

When these boots arrived at the door in a box and I put them on and
walked them up the stairs, my wife heard me coming. She stopped me
on the way to my study at the top and pointed down. "What are these
for?" she said.

She wasn't saying how good they looked.

"They're yard boots," I explained. "They're not meant to look pretty.
They're meant to work."

"So when was the last time you did any actual work in boots of any
kind?" she said sweetly. Fairly. Cruelly.

I got the boots to carry me to the shops, to push prams in to the
park, to negotiate the sand down there, to take the pavements
coming home, and to hold me up when I walk around teaching.
That's work, isn't it? These past days by the lake, they've come into
their own as uncompromising, waterproof walking boots. But the
truth is I got them because I like boots, and I wanted these ones.

And I've been wondering down here why it is I like to sit (and to get
up and pace around) and write in yard boots, and it came to me that
I'm a wrangler. And what I wrangle is sentences. They come to me
wild from the scrub. I rope a few at the edge of the trees and lead
them to the yards. I gentle them and whisper and bully them tame.
After a little while, sometimes as short as a few hours, a few of them
let me on.

What I'm doing is teaching them manners and technique—a bit more grace than they had when they found me. I need them to carry me where I want to go, and for that to look pretty smooth. There's a rhythm, you see, that carrying me and my ideas requires. That's the kind of taming I need to perform. But I need them never to forget where they came from and who they were before they found me. I need them to remember how freedom and wildness go. For that's something a good horse doesn't lose in the yard, and it's a good part of the reason you ride her.

So, that's what the boots are for. I tame sentences; I whisper lines. The ones that break, I call poems. It's work one needs boots for.

Wrangling sentences—training them to work, each one in its own way, but all of them elegantly—that's what this chapter's about.

Syntax, sex, and synergy

A sentence is a miracle and a mystery.

A sentence is the way we move from making sounds to making sense, from naming to meaning. A sentence is the track from somewhere to somewhere else. It tells a story—of what is, of what happens, of who did what, of what is done. It carries a reader from silence to understanding, from nothing to something.

A sentence is to a piece of writing what a river is to its watershed. Namely, everything. The part serves the whole; it is what the whole comes down to.

Words alone or words laid out in no particular order mean something but not much: *table banana on a the see I.* Huh? *I see a banana on the table.* Oh, I get it. A story is told; meaning arises. How does that happen? It happens because a writer or speaker puts words into an order in which we have learned to recognize a pattern of relationships and so can derive the meaning that particular pattern makes. It happens because of the innate human avidness for story, for relationship and causality. It happens because of the human gift for seeing and attributing meaning to patterns—and for storing and repeating them in mind and body and speech. We humans make sense of our life and the world we live in by learning how things interact, what causes what. When we speak, we look to articulate patterns among our words that correspond to the way other physical forms and forces in the world interrelate: the way rivers fall and run; the way fish swim and where and how; the way trees respond when the wind blows; the way the whole water cycle works; the way the stars circle the sky; the way that the predator preys; the way every cause has its effect; the way every action has its actor, its object and its consequence.

What I'm trying to say is, watch a predator (this hawk) hunt its prey (this mouse), and what you see is a sentence. A fast one. Put a man and a woman who like the look of each other in a place together and what you'll get pretty soon, among other things, is someone doing something; and someone doing it back; and two people doing something together. What you get is syntax. Sex; a relationship; perhaps issue. What you get is sentences performed—simple, compound, complex, and compound–complex; fragments and declarations and exclamations and commands and questions.

But there may be no fathoming just how it is that sentences perform their alchemy upon words and make meaning. Just why is it that English sentences make sense of a gaggle of words by, mostly, putting the subject in front of the verb and the object after it (*I see a banana*)? It happens differently in other tongues; why is that so, and how did that mathematics evolve, and how did its speakers learn it? One can learn the patterns by which this complex symbolic system, the sentence, works; but how it came to that, and how it is we humans learn the code—that's as mysterious still as the soul of a man or woman or the origins of the universe. You can understand the whole scheme of evolutionary history, without ever knowing why a deciduous beech or a black cockatoo moves exactly, and with such intelligence, as it does—why that is necessary and how it came to pass; you can understand everything about how grasses germinate, take root and grow, but never know just why they do and why that's the way they do it. Language is another such lively mystery.

Since human lives depend upon sharing the kinds of meaning language makes, we all start learning pretty early how to make sense. We do that by learning to make sentences, and we learn to make sentences by listening and mimicking patterns of sound, accompanied by gestures and emotions and consequences.

Just three months ago, my two-year-old boy, coming home with me from watching some horses race, pulling their buggies around a paceway, could say: "Horses racing buggies come-on." Now he can say, "I saw horses racing. They were pulling buggies, and the men said 'come on' "; he can say, "Mummy gone to work," "Daddy gotta get up," "That's Mummy looking at the stephanotis," "Henry getting tired now. He has to get his jamas on and go to bed." He's speaking in sentences (listen to their rhythm, by the way, for one of the joys of sentence making is making not just meaning but music). Henry's started making sense. He's begun to narrate his world and ours. He's got hold of the mystery. It's a miracle. It happens every day, somewhere, for we are creatures who make language in order to make sense of our world and our place in it. This is what we do; this is how we live. And we start early.

When we get older and start to write, many of us lose the feel Henry has just acquired for syntax, the talent for spareness and rhythm in meaning making, and we start making sentences that are hopelessly complex and attenuated. We lose sight—and we lose the sound—of what makes a sentence a sentence. When we do, our sentences, though they may still work, lose their life and their capacity to inform, let alone delight, anyone, including ourselves, who makes them.

The more shapely and elegant one's sentences are, the sounder they are structurally, the better one's writing will be.

This chapter's about how to make sentences that work; it's about how to make sentences that are lean and clear and lively; and it's about how to make different kinds, so that your paragraphs rock and roll. This chapter's about syntax and sentence craft.

 Try this

1 Do you remember the first sentence you spoke? Or the first sentence your child spoke? What was it?
2 Go to your window or door; in three sentences of different lengths, describe what you can see going on out there.

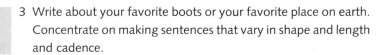

3 Write about your favorite boots or your favorite place on earth. Concentrate on making sentences that vary in shape and length and cadence.

Grammar and syntax

"Grammar" and "syntax" mean almost the same thing. But not quite. Syntax *is* sentence structure; and it's the name we use for what we know about what a sentence is and how you put one together (soundly). It also names the larger pieces (phrase and clause, independent and dependent) one arranges, this way and that, composing sentences that cohere, and "syntax" articulates the rules and conventions governing the arrangement of these pieces. Grammar is both larger and smaller than that. It names the whole system of language and its rules. Grammar is the logic and the language of the language. But *grammar* is also the word we use to talk about the smaller bits and pieces of sentences—the parts of speech (nouns, pronouns, verbs, adjectives, adverbs, conjunctions, prepositions, articles and some hybrids)—and their morphologies (the way verbs change their spellings to indicate their tense and number, mood and voice, for instance); *grammar* is used to refer, also, to some conventions of word order.

For all these small parts and their mechanics, this book has, alas, no room. Nor can it find space for punctuation. I'll stick with sentences here, their nature and personality types. There's more than enough to say about those, and I'll have to assume you've got a grammar book close by. I won't enter deeply into syntax either, for this is a book of style. I want to tell you only as much as you need to know to make your sentences strong. Beyond that, I want to offer a field guide of sentence types. For, just like an ecosystem or a local community, a piece of prose thrives on diversity—and the particular diversity it craves is a diversity of sentences. It wants them long, and it wants them short, and it wants them simple, and it wants them complicated. But at the heart of even the most elaborate sentence is a simple one that must be sound or the whole structure will give.

Whether 'tis better

In Shakespeare's time, grammar, as a rubric, was much looser than today. And so was spelling. Shakespeare himself never seems to have written his own name the same way twice. In his day, no one had codified spelling; no one had fixed grammar, either, with as much rigor as we have come to want. These days, grammar has settled, and it's been written down in books, which no one seems able to find. Reviewing two new Shakespeare biographies in *The New York Times Book Review*, John Simon regrets that both books contain some sloppy grammar:

I cite only select examples . . . Ackroyd, the distinguished British author, writes "comprised of," "central protagonists," "wracked" for tortured and "Beaumont's and Fletcher's" . . . Shapiro, the noted Columbia English professor, writes "neither lives nor history come sliced," "Wart, whom even Falstaff admits is unfit," "any soldier could be hung," "disinterested" for uninterested, "every male . . . were required" and "transpired" for happened.

Could their love of Shakespeare elicit a desire to return us to his colorfully chaotic grammar and usage?

(*The New York Times Book Review*, October 25, 2005)

Depending on your take, this is pedantry or it is stewardship of the language. It reminds me that anyone can write a bad sentence; and anyone can slip up in his or her grammar and usage. In days past, we had astute editors to save us; some of us, if we are lucky and find good publishers, still do. But this is much less reliably the case than it was once. In this respect, too, our times are perhaps becoming Shakespearean again.

 Try this

Can you say what's wrong in each of the cases Simon points to? You may have to check a dictionary and style manual. But none of them is too arcane. I confess I had always understood that "happens" worked as a good translation for one of the meanings of *transpires*.

Sound sentences

Grammar hasn't been taught in most schools in Australia, where I live, for over a generation. It's a good thing it's not important! It's nothing more, after all, than the way we describe the way our language works—that complicated system of sounding signs we use every day of our lives. So I guess there's no need to teach it beyond elementary school.

They stopped teaching grammar, it was once explained to me, because too much emphasis was being put, it was thought, on the formal aspects of language and not enough on the creative ones. That may have been right. And anyway, the argument went (and it's true, as far as it goes), we pick up 80 percent of what we need to know about sentences by listening. My boy is proof of that.

But writing is both creativity and discipline; it is freedom within bounds. You need to know the constraints in order to know how to be free within them. And then there's the other 20 percent (that you can't pick up just by listening)—the finer points. How were we going to learn those?

So we let grammar slip from the curriculum. And forty years on we live with the consequences. The teachers who might teach it know too little to even begin. Though it's true that you learn most of what you need by living inside the language, still, you don't know what it is you know. You have no language to speak of the system and its parts. You cannot name your mistakes when you feel you have made them; nor, therefore, can you fix them. When your car with its fancy engine—which is to say, when your sentence—breaks down, there's not a thing under its hood whose function you understand, whose name you can name. You couldn't even talk usefully to the mechanic who came when you called, if there were such a person.

Even if you learned at school more grammar than most of my compatriots, it pays not to forget it. Making sentences is most of what writing is about, and grammar's going to help you make them sound and true and various. Without grammar on your mind, you fall out of the habit of thinking structurally about sentences. You think about what they're trying to mean, but not enough about how well each of them and all of them hang together. You stop working at the infra-structure of what you're trying to say—or sing. A footbridge badly made will fall, and so will a sentence. The consequences of the second may be less deadly than the first. But still: neither, shoddily con-structed, will carry the traffic it's made for—the people or the message.

The other thing that happens in the absence of grammatical wisdom is that we hold fast to the few syntactical half-truths we vaguely recall from somewhere or someone.

▶ **Try this**

Can you say what's wrong with these sentences? Can you then fix them?

1 The plentiful streams and rich farmland of southeastern Pennsylvania has given the region a legacy of watermills larger than any other part of the United States.

2 He has a style so unique it just may carry him to the champi-onship.

3 Neither the software nor the hardware have been thoroughly tested.

4 Three double bedrooms (one with study), lobby, eat-in kitchen, south-facing sun room, separate dining room, reno-vated bathroom, and balcony comprise the accommodations.

5 Two paperback copies should be mailed to every contributor, not the hardbacks.

6 The voracious opposition of the Iraqi insurgents had so far resulted in a thousand deaths among the US-led coalition.

7 The winner of several prizes for poetry, Ashley's books include *Pine* and *The Problem with Prose*.

8 Advice to seniors; ask the driver to wait till you sit down; and sit down as fast as you can.

9 She tells me she saw you and I at the play last night.

10 These are the advantages of the new printer:
   • high efficiency
   • high speed

- low waist
- low noise
- and have no toxic fumes

Deep law and shallow law

Let's out those false gods of grammar.

Why is it everyone can remember what they needn't—never start a sentence with *and* or *but*, never ever start one with *because*; never end a sentence with a preposition; never split an infinitive? My theory? They're easy to spot—most of them occur at the start or the finish of a sentence—so they're easy to police. Easier by far to insist on these few *shouldn'ts* than teach a young writer the thousand ways to make a sentence right.

Moreover, each of these so-called rules, painfully remembered by so many adults, is, if not an outright error, merely a nicety—a piece of fashionable usage—elevated to the status of a rule. Grammar isn't interested in the kind of manners you can enforce with a red pen or a ruler on the knuckles. It is a deeper kind of lore.

So here's how these "rules" stand (and always did).

1 *You may start any sentence you like with an* and *or a* but. Check your Bible sometime. It's harder to find a sentence that doesn't start with a conjunction, especially in those early Old Testament books, than to find one that does. Reread your Virginia Woolf. *A Room of One's Own* even begins with "But." Look at any accomplished writing —novels, poems, essays, reportage, reports, textbooks—and you'll find more initial conjunctions than you can poke a stick at.

   The grammar of it goes like this, I guess: conjunctions may be used to join words or phrases or clauses; since a sentence is a clause (or a number of clauses), conjunctions may join sentences.

   The real rule is *don't overdo it.* Like anything. Starting a sentence with a conjunction is unexpected and, therefore, striking. If you do it every other sentence a reader stops being so struck.

2 *You may start a sentence with* because. If *because* is the first word in an introductory phrase or clause, it belongs there perfectly well—as

long as there's a main clause following after. Here are some good sentences that start with *because*:

> Because her book was so unlike anything else, she had trouble finding a publisher.

> Because of all this rain, we've had to call off the game.

> Because this is a complex sentence, I can start it with "because" if I want to.

Don't feel obliged to replace *because* with something awkward or roundabout or vague like *due to* or *due to the fact that*, *as a consequence of* or *as*, don't turn the sentence around, so that it ends with its causal clause. It's fine to start a sentence with *because*, as long as it's a good sentence. Why were we ever told otherwise? When mum asks you why you're playing with the football in the house again, you may have told her, "Because!" or "Because I want to!," each of which is a sentence fragment; each of which is rude.

3 *You may end a sentence with a preposition.* "A preposition is a bad thing to end a sentence with," we were all once told, though not in those words. (". . .with which to end a sentence," the injunction ended, practicing, thus, what it preached.) It can still feel clumsy to place the preposition where we frequently place it in speech—at the end of the sentence, detached from the word it really belongs in front of (oops!). But English word order is loose and generous. It allows you to delay a preposition in this way, often when you're forming up a question or writing a periodic sentence (one ending with a subordinate clause), as in "Whom should I give the book to?" or as in the sentence I put at the start—or just because, as in the third sentence of this paragraph, a verb–preposition combination comes at the very end. All the style guides these days say just forget it; end your sentence with a preposition if that's the way you do it in speech. If you want to tidy the sentence (up), shift the preposition, but watch you don't end up with something like this: "Ending a sentence with a preposition is something up with which we will not put." (That was Churchill's sarcastic reply to a pedant who wrote to tell him he'd put a preposition at the end of a sentence in a speech.)

4 *You may split your infinitives.* Like atoms, you always could, but we didn't always know it.

A split infinitive looks like this: *to boldly go, to thoroughly deserve, to absolutely deny* or *to lightly tread*—a verb in its infinitive form with an adverb lodged between its *to* and its *go* or whatever.

It happens all the time. It's a way of modifying a key verb right at its heart. Nothing was ever really wrong with it. Nineteenth-century grammarians, who looked to Latin for their precedents in most things, used to argue that since one could not split an infinitive in Latin, one should not in English. But then the infinitive form in Latin was a single word (*ambulare*: "to walk") that could only be split with a heavy iron tool.

There's also a sense that the usage is sloppy. Sometimes it does sound untidy. If it does, change it: *boldly to go* or *to go boldly* are always available.

Let's stop worrying about the silly things none of us seem able to forget and start worrying about the one thing none of us seems able to remember: how to build sound sentences of every kind. Let's do syntax, not pedantry.

Twenty-four troublesome words and phrases

- *about.* Use this lovely and functional preposition in place of all other falsely eloquent alternatives, such as *with regard to, regarding, as to, in relation to,* and so on. For instance "I write to you about the job I saw advertised." Sometimes *on* will be what you really mean, as in "The government's policy on insider trading."
- *advice/advise.* See *practice/practise* and *licence/license,* below.
- *affect/effect. Affect* is a verb that means to influence, change, alter. *Effect* is a noun and a verb. As a noun it means result (of the cause). As a verb *effect* means to bring about, as in "He effected the touchdown in the corner."
- *among,* not *amongst.* The *st* is a resistant and redundant

archaism. In some ears (mine, for instance) it sounds sibilant and unnecessarily formal. *Amongst* means among. Write *among*. See *while/whilst*, below.

- **as, in place of *because***. "As this provision is not in force yet, we haven't taken it into account" uses *as* where it means *because*. I suspect because there is a growing allergy to naming causes unequivocally these days, *because* is falling out of use. *As* in place of it is vague. Whenever you mean that one thing caused (in part or wholly) another, write *because*. Not *as*, nor *due to the fact that* or *as a consequence of the fact that* or anything else of that nature.

- **as to**. Favor *about* in sentences like "We had some questions as to the suitability of this product for our needs." *As to* is bureaucratic and oblique.

- **as yet/as such**. Two horrible and unnecessary expressions. *Yet* alone will do for *as yet*: "We don't know the reasons yet."

- **being**. Not needed in "He was regarded as being the main culprit." Another common usage is "It is especially hot today. The reason being is that the air conditioning is off." *Being* isn't needed after *reason*.

- **comprise/constitute**. *Comprise* means embrace or include. A company comprises all its parts and people. But the people don't comprise the company. They constitute it. Similarly, a book comprises all its chapters; the chapters constitute the book. *Constitute* means to make up.

- **disinterested/uninterested**. *Disinterested* means impartial, objective or detached. It does not mean "not interested in"—at least, not yet. That's what *uninterested* means. Alas, it's probably time to avoid *disinterested*; you're likely to be misunderstood, one way or the other.

- **due to, in place of *because***. See *as*, above.

- **enormity**. *Enormity* means horror, monstrous wickedness; not just bigness. Journalists are fond of using enormity when they simply mean size or significance. Avoid this one.

- **fewer vs. less.** *Fewer* means a smaller *number* of people or things; *less* means a smaller *quantity* of a single thing. So it should be (but never is in supermarkets) "Twelve items or fewer." It's *fewer words, fewer hours, fewer books, fewer friends,* and *fewer hairs.* It's *less verbiage, less time, less paper, less love,* and *less hair.*
- **hopefully.** *Hopeful* is an adjective meaning full of hope. *Hopefully* is an adverb, indicating that the person does something full of hope. It's not accurate, though it's common, to use *hopefully* to mean "I hope" or "one hopes" as in "Hopefully the Board will accept the proposal." Doesn't matter much if you do, but try not to.
- **personalize/prioritize and other verbalizations.** These are pretentious, lazy, made-up words. Avoid them by rephrasing. Instead of "Personalize your stationery," use "Get letterhead" or "Put your name on your letterhead." Instead of "I have prioritized the issues," say "I have ranked the issues [in order of importance/urgency]." (Strictly speaking, one can have only one priority, anyway.) The other slang meaning of *prioritize* is to make a priority of, as in "The president has prioritized tax reform." This is vague.
- **practice/practise.** In British (and Commonwealth) usage, there's a pattern that's been lost in the United States. It goes like this. *Practice* is a noun; *practise* is a verb (meaning to perform or to carry on a practice, such as law or dentistry or Buddhism). The *c* indicated the noun and the *s* or *z* the verb; and this was the case also for *licence/license* and *advice/advise.* US style now— confusingly, perhaps—favors *practice* and *license* for both noun and verb; whereas it upholds the British distinction between the noun *advice* and the verb *advise.*

    So, in British usage you would expect "We need to practise writing to become good at it"; "The practice of writing is good for the soul"; "She is a Certified Practising Accountant." And "James Bond has a licence to kill," but "I license you to kill James Bond". This is, also, why it would be, in London,

"Licensed Restaurant" not "Licenced Restaurant." In the US, those examples would go thus: "We need to practice writing"; "The practice of good writing"; "James Bond has a license to kill"; "I license you to kill James Bond"; and "Licensed Restaurant." Confused? Check a dictionary near you. Don't trust your ear, your memory or your instinct. And probably not your spell-check program.

- **program/programme.** *Programme* used to be in wide circulation in Australia, New Zealand, and possibly in other parts of the old British Commonwealth. In the UK it is still used except where a computer *program* is concerned. The *mme* ending was essentially a nineteenth-century affectation. Such frills are rare in English and tend to fall away in time. It's time for this one to go, too. *Program* has always been the usage in the US.

- **rest assured.** Many people have taken to using this as though it were an adjective requiring the verb *to be* or *to feel* in front of it, as in "Customers can be/feel rest assured". It's a silly expression anyway, but if you use it, remember that *rest* is already the verb here. So, you'd write "Customers can rest assured".

- **secondly, thirdly.** The old rule was *First . . . secondly . . .* I'm not sure why. But, really, the *ly* is equally ugly and quite unnecessary, whatever the number. Just go for *First . . . second . . . third . . .* or use bullets or the numerals themselves.

- **unique.** Means one of a kind anywhere in the world. Much overused to mean special. Something cannot be *absolutely unique*, *fairly unique*, *one of the most unique* or *more unique*. It's either unique, or it's not. Try to avoid it. When you use it, do not qualify it.

- **utilize.** Write *use*. For *utilization* utilize *use*.

- **while, not whilst.** *While* is better than *whilst*, which is a bit of a throwback, though some people tell me *whilst* sounds nice. To me, it sounds quaint. Each means the same thing. Use *while* sparingly in place of *although*, as in "While the governor has done a good job on the economy, there are many who feel his style is aggressive." The principal usage of *while* is as a preposition, meaning "during," as in "While the orchestra played, the people slept."

- *-wise*. As in *clockwise*. It means "in the manner of." Avoid it everywhere, except as a joke: *people-wise, music-wise, tax-wise*.
- *z* or *s* in **minimize, computerize, pasteurize, analyze, recognize, emphasize, and so on**. Once upon a time, Cambridge-educated teachers and their pupils learned to spell all these with *ss*; Oxford souls got *zs*. Both habits coexisted for a long time. *Z* has always ruled in the US, which favors spelling things the way they sound (like, also *color* and *favors*).

Who does what

Every sentence names something and says something about it. This is the secret life of the sentence—the short story it tells. If that story is clearly told, the sentence will work; if not, it will not.

Naming things and telling us a short story about them is what readers, whether they realize it or not, expect every sentence to do. Naming and telling is how we talk with each other. It's how we think and how we make sense of things. It's the way we experience reality: plants and elements and people and organizations doing things, often to others. *The bison graze the prairie*; *the check bounces*; *the Yankees beat the Red Sox*.

The first sentence in this section, for instance, *named* "every sentence." That's its *subject*. *What it said* about it was that a sentence "names something and says something about it." That's its *predicate*. So, the part of the sentence that *names* is called the *subject*; the part that *tells* is called the *predicate*.

Sometimes the thing we name is, indeed, a thing: *orange, book, antelope, stone, tooth, gun, pen, watch, chair*. Sometimes the something is a some*one*: "*I* just wrote a sentence," "*You* just read a sentence," "*Mark* writes poems," "*The president* spoke sense last night." (We give the noun a capital when it is someone's name or a title, but not when it's a common noun like *president*.) Sometimes the thing named is an inanimate entity: *the government, the school, the company, the department, the team, the nation,* in which we all know real live people are breathing and speaking. These are collective nouns. Sometimes the thing we name is a concept (an abstract noun): *death, grief, writing, syntax, ecosystem, inflation, love, risk minimization.* Sometimes, again, the thing we name is a place: *Southeast Asia, Europe, Iowa, the Mojave Desert, the Caribbean.*

As a part of speech, the subject will be a noun or a pronoun, such as *I* or *we* or *the man* or *the government* or *Peter* or *the managing director* or *the river*; or it may be a whole mob of words, like *the tendency for economies to atrophy over time* or a shorter phrase like *economic reform* or *the purpose of all writing* or *all of us.* Predicates, too, come in all shapes and sizes—but they always include a verb.

What a sentence says is:

- what that person or thing *does* (active voice)
- what they *are* (linking or defining sentence) or
- what *happens to them* (passive voice)

Some sentences name things and ask questions about them. These sentences are called questions!

Sentences (or, strictly speaking, their verbs) have moods. Some grammarians say that moods are old technology. But mood is a feature of many languages. It is a way of understanding what sentences set out to achieve. So let's say it exists. You'll find a sentence in one of three moods:

1 Indicative (*Mark writes books.*)
2 Imperative (*Write that book, Mark; Look at me!; Romans, go home; Lodge your forms here; Come, my beloved, let us go forth to the field.*)
3 Subjunctive (*If I were you, Mark, I wouldn't write that book; She would lie down in the field beside me as though she were my beloved.*)

These eight sentences show you the variety you can achieve using only simple sentences.

1 *The rain falls*; *The sun also rises*; *Jesus wept*. (Who does—intransitive verb, which has no object: the rain just falls, the sun just (also) rises, Jesus just wept.)

2 *Lucy leaves home*; *The river floods the town*; *McCarthy writes great novels*. (Who does what—verb is transitive this time; the action described in the verb carries on to a second part, the object)

3 *Roland Hemmert is a fine writer*; *This is the place*; *You are the one*. (Who is who; what is what)

4 *God sent me her*; *I give you this ring*; *I wrote this book for Emily*; *We make this promise to the people of America*. (Who does what to whom)

5 *The sky is grey*; *I am a faster kind of sandstone*; *I am sorry*. (Who is what —where what, this time, is a describing word, or adjective)

6 *The book was read by millions*; *The recommendations will be implemented*; *The plane was recovered*. (What is done—passive voice)

7 *Why is Graham Greene a fine writer? Why did he never win a Nobel Prize? When will the rain stop falling? Whom does this book belong to? Which of these animals belongs to Lyle? How long has Jim lived in the valley?* (Question)

8 *See the child*; *Call me Ishmael*; *Ask not what your country can do for you*; *Let us go then, you and I*; *Vote early and vote often*. (Imperative mood)

Every sentence, no matter how long or short, how simple or convoluted, must do the basics soundly. No matter what else it attempts, a sentence must say plainly who does what (and variations on that theme listed above). If it does that well, we have a conversation on our hands—we have a walk in the woods. If it trips up, if it makes heavy weather of this short simple story, it's over. Forget the woods; forget the walk. It will have nothing much to say; we will have nothing much to learn.

Good style is grounded in—even if it is not constrained by—sound syntax. So concentrate, before you do anything else in a sentence, on these three matters: the agent of the action; the action; the recipient, if any, of the action. Get them straight; leave no confusion about what word or phrase in your sentence plays each of those roles. And be brief about it.

Where you can, choose for those key parts of every sentence words short and clear and vivid. Wherever it's possible, make the who—the agent of action—somebody, rather than some kind of abstraction or process, some great cluster of words. That is, as often as you can, make your subject (and your object too) human or animate entities (such as *I, we, she and I, the writer, President Lincoln, the black deer*). And make your verbs recognizable actions like *change, leave, regulate, make, diminish,* rather than the verb *to be* or something effete like *seems, facilitates, tends, suggests, indicates, implements,* and so on.

Why? Because every reader wants a (short) story—she wants something named and something said about it—and this is how stories go best. What we understand fastest is a sentence that describes some people doing things. What a good sentence needs is some action, some human beings, and some particular things being affected or performed or whatever. Put in some beat and color and texture and poetry, by all means, if they belong; qualify what you're saying. Beat around those kinds of bush. But if, instead of people, the sentence alludes to abstractions and processes, then it will also, very likely, have nothing much by way of a verb, and nothing will be happening and no one will be doing anything at all, and the poor reader will be left to conjure an image of what the hell is really going on out there beneath the sentence's cloudy abstractions, all on her own.

Let me show you what I mean.

Recent changes in the insurance industry, whereby insurers are refusing to cover schools for injuries to students on excursions beyond the school grounds or on school grounds outside normal hours, except where specific insurance has been taken out to that effect, make it incumbent upon us to curtail such activities until a review of our insurances is completed.

Here, all the words from the start to *effect* constitute the subject—the who. *Make* is your verb—the does. And *it*, believe it or not, is your object—your what.

How much clearer is this?

The school has canceled all excursions and events such as sports practice, carnivals and concerts until it knows whether its insurance covers staff, students and visitors on such occasions. Recent cases give us cause for concern about this, and we're not prepared to take any risks.

If this is any better, it's because it puts *school* in the role of subject and makes the verb *has canceled*, and makes the phrase *all excursions and events such as* . . . its object. Making the sentence this way, and putting other matters into other sentences similarly made, manufactures meaning more economically. Not to mention more humanely. It works like speech—only better.

Not so good:

It is a requirement of the relevant legislation that business tax documentation be lodged by all business entities by 30 June each year.

Better:

Every business must lodge its tax statement by 30 June each year.
or The law requires every business to lodge its BAS by 30 June each year.

Life sentences

Listen to this:

The fundamental principle for the efficacious elucidation of meaning in documentation is the minimization of abstraction of expression and the abandonment of convolution of construction and, instead, the utilization of quotidian diction and the employment of syntactical simplification.

Okay, it's a spoof. And it's meant to be absurd—it practices the very thing it preaches against. But in its diction and in its structure— which is what I want to dwell on—this is a characteristic sentence of our times. It makes an important but simple point complex; it's plain hard work. If we can see where this sentence goes wrong, we can start writing sentences that get it right.

Notice these things about my deathly sentence. First, it feels incredibly long. In fact, if you only count its words, it isn't. Thirty-eight words isn't short, but it's not a monster. It's not the number of *words* that's the problem; it's the number of *syllables*. My sentence mutters eighty-nine of those. This sentence assaults you with syllables. They make so much clangor it's hard to make out what message they amount to.

So, it's a moderately long sentence made of way too many words made of way too many syllables. In English, as a general rule, the more syllables a word has, the more abstract it is—and the less efficient. This sentence proves that rule pretty well.

Second, you'll have noticed that many words my sentence uses are not the kind you'd use in conversation. Its diction is obscure, stuffy and formal. In fact, this writer goes out of his way to choose fancy and longwinded ways of saying everything. The sentence is pompous. It poses. It's intended to impress rather than inform. And it's pretty much guaranteed to lose anyone who wanders in it, wounded by its polysyllabic ordnance, angered by its pretension and bored by its ugly, exacting diction.

Notice, too, how often my sentence uses the construction "the abstract noun of the abstract noun": *the minimization of abstraction of expression* (which takes this one step further), *the utilization of quotidian diction*, and *the employment of simplification of syntax*. This device is called nominalization; and it's ugly (and all too common, especially in bureaucratic and professional discourse), especially repeated like this. You could translate each nominalized phrase, using essentially similar diction, like this: "to minimize abstract expression," "to use quotidian diction," and "to employ simplified syntax."

But that would be to use some actual verbs. And the almost complete absence of verbs in this piece is its most important failing, and a characteristic of too much bureaucratic writing. This passage takes every opportunity to turn verbs into abstract nouns. This not only strips the sentence of activity, it also strips it of actors. No one is doing anything here. It is abstract from top to tail.

Ask yourself who's doing what here, and it's very hard to say. There's only one verb, and it's *is*—the verb *to be*, which describes no action at all. (This is a *what-is-what* kind of sentence.) If nothing is being done, nobody's likely to be doing it. And so, here, the subject of the sentence is not a person or even a government agency but a great string of words from *The fundamental principle* down to *documentation*. (And the *what*, which in this sentence is not the object but the subject–complement, is all the words that follow *is*.)

Most of the difficulty in this sentence, in other words, arises from the inelegance of its structure or syntax—from the poverty, specifically, of its *who-does-what*.

To translate this sentence into the intelligent vernacular you need to find some people to enact it and some verbs for them to perform, and you need to make the whole thing concrete—you need to describe something actual actually going on. It might go something like this:

If you want to make your meaning clear when you write, choose simple sentence structures and favor familiar words. (This uses the imperative mood.)

Writers who make their meaning clear use everyday words and make elegant sentences.

The best writers use the common words and simple structures.

Writers, especially in business, political, academic, and professional settings, steer clear of such simplicity and humanity in writing, if I may be generous for a moment, because they are trying to be dispassionate and objective. Those are worthy aspirations, as far as they go. But if they lead to writing stripped of its humanity, they have failed a more important test of communication. Be objective; there's no need, though, to be pompous.

Here are some more sentences made in this characteristic contemporary style:

ABC's implementation of the SAP system is the culmination of extensive negotiations and strategizing between our organization and ABC Inc. Our capacity for delivery of innovative solutions for clients, specifically the deployment of integrated infrastructure, is dependent upon ongoing proactive strategic engagement with relevant industry organizations.

Thus, some anomalous empirical result can always be conserved by a redistribution of predicates or truth-values across the entire existing fabric of beliefs.

These are typical sentences, too. What's wrong with them, again, is how poorly they communicate who does what. What's missing from them is humanity, action (or animation) and slender particulars. What's missing from them is the stuff of life. They don't seem real. They fail as talk; they don't make much meaning happen, and they don't do it very fast.

Too many authors of too many modern sentences shy from people and verbs and particulars, as though they were afraid of, or embarrassed by, or unfamiliar with the real world. As though writing had to be abstracted from the world, even the world of business or governance or professional expertise they transact in writing: scholarship and science and law and commerce and banking and diplomacy and healthcare. And what the experts model, as Orwell explained, the rest of us copy. So that the average modern sentence sounds like a cranky and awkward simulation of living, breathing sentence; there is no heartbeat in it.

So the secret of bringing your sentences to life is this.
Make sure you:

- put *people* in—particularly in the role of performing the verb (*Who*)
- use strong clear *verbs*—particularly the verb performed by the subject (*Does*)
- be very clear and *concrete* about exactly what is going on (*What*)

Bearing those points in mind, you might recast the last of those sentences, for instance, like this:

If we encounter a result that doesn't fit our thesis, we can call that an anomaly and reassert our broad and well-founded belief.

 Try this

Breathe life into these sentences, making sure there's a *who-does-what* in there somewhere.

It was apparent from discussions held with various parties during the course of the investigation that there are differences of opinion among them as to whether or not some of the more entrepreneurial activities currently undertaken by the country's universities were compatible with their current mandates.

The mechanization and commercialization of agriculture along with the globalization of commodities markets are the chief reasons for the deterioration of social and cultural integrity in rural North America.

It is the conclusion of this study that the orthodox view that all species were independently created and are immutable is unsustainable.

Throughout my lifetime, my ethnicity has played a significant role in my existence, being of mixed race. Or maybe it's not so much this as it is my attitude towards this world and what combining two divergent cultures has produced.

Unhappy sentences

My local paper arrives and reminds me there are as many ways to write a bad sentence as there are people to write them.

Sentences know a thousand ways to die in the telling; every unhappy sentence, like Tolstoy's unhappy family, is unhappy after its own fashion. But most failed sentences are loosely strung; they get away from their writer, who never listened hard enough to notice. Like these:

Work on the foreshore trail should commence soon after tenders were put out for the job late last year. (Tense shift; the writer may have meant us to hear a comma after *soon*, but *soon after* makes the sentence try to mean something else, in two incompatible tenses.)

Work will include landscaping, mangrove planting, excavation, lighting, creating pathways and boardwalks, and sea wall repair, and should be finished by the end of the year. (If you're going to make a list, structure every item on it in the same way—all single words like *landscaping*, or all phrases like *sea wall repair*, not three or four different ways; and it might have sounded better as "The work, which should be finished by year's end, will include . . .")

Meanwhile, the possibility of traffic mayhem in small streets behind Bellevue mansion which sits near the east walkway was one of the issues raised late last year at a consultation with residents in Town Hall on the Black Bay Park Draft Management Plan. (Hellishly long subject followed by a verb *to be* plus wordy subject complement *was one of the issues raised*; nonrestrictive relative clause—about Bellevue mansion, which probably should be *Bellevue Mansion*, if that's its name—without commas fore and aft; concluding with four prepositional phrases, the last of which includes an horrendous noun cluster.)

Then there's the accidental ambiguity of a sentence somebody shared in a class the other night: "I haven't seen the sandy-haired guy wearing the brown overalls lately". (Have you seen him wearing other clothes, or haven't you seen him—wearing overalls or any other sort of clothes—at all?)

Tame those sentences; train them; rein them in. Help them step out elegantly.

 Try this

> Fix the sentences from my local rag (and from my class). Some may need breaking into more than one sentence. Make them smooth and unambiguous and elegant.

Verbs

A magazine editor said to me once, "You'd think there'd be a book of verbs; they're so important." She meant something more than a thesaurus. She meant something that might be called *Two Thousand Verbs to Use Before You Die*—a book organized by activities with lists of verbs under each.

It's a good idea. Verbs make sentences go. They are where and how a sentence lives. They are where a sentence moves, where it gets up and runs or walks or means or elopes or ignites or loves or hates or talks or recommends or concludes or surrenders or speaks its mind. The verb is the breath of the thought; it's the heart that pumps the blood that keeps the sentence alive. If your verbs are good, your sentence has a chance.

Recalling my editor's idea, I took a break from writing this chapter and walked out into the rain and wind to the top of a mountain. I went into the field to gather some verbs, like a naturalist stalking butterflies. When they came to me I wrote them in the margin of my map. But the rain seeped into my backpack and flooded my list and swept twenty verbs or more away. A few hundred survived the drenching, though, and by the time I lay down in my bunk and slept, I had blackened five pages of a foolscap pad with their names. Verbs spawn. Open your mind, and in they flock; write a hundred on a page, and in an hour you'll have a thousand. Here are some of the verbs that dawned on me and multiplied.

fledge	wail	muster	sow
fleece	grieve	pine	raze
hoist	surrender	overwhelm	reap
absolve	cradle	school	harness
infest	baffle	enfold	saddle
hedge	fathom	besiege	subdue
harvest	cohere	comb	loom
unhinge	harass	slough	compel
reprise	tilt	limn	engage
redeem	pool	wrestle	marry
exhaust	blanch	excoriate	tarnish
deride	leach	shear	craft
forage	temper	hustle	vary
thrive	loose	attenuate	knead
degrade	thrum	belittle	ache
dread	harrow	humble	grimace
heal	hasten	grub	mourn
lope	rein	grind	weather

dwell	couple	rank	plumb
infer	parrot	plunder	constrain
hide	flood	wonder	congeal
contend	beguile	steep	rally
crowd	bewilder	covet	rope
swarm	calm	tamp	forfeit
mob	seep	ransack	soothe
team	condemn	outlaw	suffer

Good writing enlists splendid verbs—muscular and apt and vivid. Here are two plainspoken examples:

The road ahead tapered to infinity, in stages. Hill led to hill led to hill, and at each summit the road abruptly shrank to half its width, then half its width again, until it became a hairline fracture in the land, then a faint wobble in the haze, then nothing. From out of the nothing now came a speck. It disappeared. It resurfaced as a smudge, then as a fist-sized cloud. A while passed. Finally, on the nearest of the hilltops, a full-scale dust storm burst into view. The storm enveloped a low-slung pick-up truck, which slowed and came to a standstill beside the car, open window to open window. (JONATHAN RABAN, *Bad Land*)

After we had spent a couple of hours going through the book of images, using them to narrow my choices and refine our idea of the building, Charlie took out a roll of parchment-colored tracing paper, drew a length of it across his drafting table, and began to draw. He worked in ink to start, sketching rapidly in rough, scribbly lines, discarding a drawing and tearing off a new length of paper any time he didn't like what he was seeing. If there was anything in a sketch worth saving, he'd start the new drawing by loosely tracing over that part of the rejected one; in this way a process of trial and error unfolded . . . the good ideas getting carried forward from one generation of drawing to the next, the bad ones falling by the wayside.
(MICHAEL POLLAN, *A Place of My Own*)

Including present participles like *sketching*, I count over twenty verbs in that second passage, only one of them the verb *to be*. Think how that animates the paragraph. Keep an your eye on your verbs.

Take a highlighter and mark the verbs in your sentences. Are too many of them *is* and its siblings? Have you written "There was a letter on the desk" when you might have written "A letter lay on the desk"? Are too many of your verb forms passive? Are enough of them good, lean, useful verbs like those in my list? Are too many of them effete, vague, and lifeless, like *facilitate*, *indicate* or *optimize*? Are there many verbs at all, or are there mostly nominalizations like *lodgment*, *facilitation* or *utilization*?

Collect verbs. Husband them. Breed them. Fledge them lovingly. Keep the best and make them ready and, when the time comes, set them to work. You're going to need at least one per sentence, so start your collection today. Don't let the thesaurus suggest them. Go out and find your own. Then they'll sound like yours.

Listen for verbs on the radio and in the conversations on the bus. Steal them, adopt them, share them—they're yours.

▶ Try this

1 Think how many other verbs you can use in place of these overused and underperforming verbs: *facilitate*, *take*, *have*, *do*, *manage*, *project-manage*, *implement*, *prioritize*, *minimize*, *optimize*, *indicate*, *instill*,

2 Rewrite these sentences to avoid giving the hard work to the verb *is*. Do whatever else you think they may need to smarten and tighten them up.

Our underlying aim is to support individuals and communities to strengthen and increase their capacity for independence.

UCA's aim is to be regarded as the leading provider of adult and continuing education in the northern hemisphere and one of the top twenty providers in the world.

This role is responsible for the oversight of a range of marketing support functions.

Vocab

Good writers know plenty of words. And they know where to find more. They never stop collecting.

Verbs may be the most vital parts of speech, but you're going to need words of every kind—nouns, pronouns, modifiers, prepositions, participles, the lot. The more you know (or can uncover fast when a deadline presses) the more likely you are to be able to say what you have to say with clarity and brevity and verve. And the more words you know, the more likely you are to understand and care for the distinctions between them. The likelier you are to shape the perfect phrase now and then.

English is one of the richest language systems on the planet—it contains multitudes of words. But don't be fooled into thinking those longish, abstract, professional-sounding words are where the richness or intelligence lie. It is a kind of pretension to favor the long over the short, the unfamiliar over the familiar, the fancy-pants over the plain, unless that practice is leavened with wit and made palatable by self-awareness; and the habit, whose name is *false elegance* when it is unaware of its absurdity, abounds these days, especially in workplaces and faculties; it abounded in Orwell's day; it has always abounded among the educated and bureaucratic classes. It does so because users learn to imagine that unfamiliar and polysyllabic diction is a mark of rank or intelligence or expertise. An idea wanting in humility and subtlety.

And in our times, writers inherit a thin lexicon of overbred and largely vacant words, which many uncertain writers feel obliged to use to build their sentences—eschewing the teeming universe of language going on all around us in playgrounds and libraries, churches and paddocks and bedrooms and running tracks and forests and trawlers and stages and football fields. Particularly on the sidelines.

This kind of polysyllabic constipation, this dedication to a long-winded and emaciated English, is part of a campaign, largely implicit, but perfectly real, to wrestle English into submission, to cow and diminish it. Resist! Use the whole language—especially that great stockpile of little words, where the genius of English dwells, where the range of choice is widest.

And where do you find words? Open your ears and listen in all those places I listed and all the others they are meant to imply. Just listen; they're out there. People doing work (or play) they love and excel at—truck drivers, rangers, farmers, teachers, accountants (I think), barristers, chefs, dancers, drovers, flyfishers, geologists, electricians, engineers, foresters, IT nerds, musicians, even writers—talk the language richly when you catch them talking shop. Ignore the expletives. Don't bother with a farmer who thinks you need to hear that she's in agribusiness. Cut through the kind of hip talk that will be gone in a year's time. Listen for the verbs and nouns, in particular. The words people use to describe their craft and tell their lives.

Where else do you find words? Have you heard of the dictionary? Big book that sits on your desk, or someone else's, and you rarely use? Well, let me tell you something: a dictionary is not mostly a book for checking your spelling, so it hasn't been made obsolete by the spellchecker. It's a field guide to words—a book that tells you what words mean (the many things they mean, in many cases, in different contexts), where they came from, how you can use them properly. The writer is hamstrung who doesn't have a dictionary at hand. She needs it to test the words that offer themselves up to her. To prove they mean the thing she thinks they mean, and, if not, to set her thinking up a word more apt. At this point you might want to open a smart thesaurus—a book of synonyms. But start with the dictionary; do most of the thinking and the conjuring, yourself. The writer may even stumble on words, looking for one in particular, that take her fancy. She may, now and then, just mine it to see what she can find. Dictionaries teach you words; they school you in precision and verbal dexterity.

So have a dictionary. Have many. Use them to master words. Use a good thesaurus to build up your repertoire; but don't let it prompt you too soon; write your own script.

If you're going to deploy a thesaurus, make it one like *The Oxford American Writer's Thesaurus*, which gives you little essays by writers like Zadie Smith and Francine Prose on the past lives and personality traits of words; on morals versus ethics; on *who* versus *whom*. Get profitably lost finding your way.

Try this

Make a place at the back of your diary or journal where you write down words that come to you, gifts from living your life with your ears open. Write down anything that catches your attention. You might even open a file of words in your filing cabinet or on your computer. And don't forget to write down what the word means, too. That might help.

Learn words. Lure them. Keep them close.

A democracy of sentences

Lively sentences come long and short; they come compound and complex and simple.

I mention this because word has got out that the only good sentence is a short sentence. As Ursula Le Guin comments, that's only true for criminals. There are many ways to write a sentence, and one ought to try most of them. Some of your sentences ought to be short; some ought to be long; some might even not be sentences at all (as long as they get that way by design, not accident). The point is: mix them up. Like an ecosystem or a local community, a piece of prose thrives on diversity.

Here's a passage rich with different kinds of sentence. We'll talk about sentence styles pretty soon, but for now notice the myriad lengths and shapes; observe the confederacy of clauses.

With my pencil point I crawled over the mitt's topology. I slithered over each dip and rise; I checked my bearings, admired the enormous view, and recorded it like Meriwether Lewis mapping the Rockies.

One thing struck me as odd and interesting. A gesture drawing took forty-five seconds; a Sustained Study took all morning. From any still-life arrangement or model's pose, the artist could produce either a short study or a long one. Evidently, a given object took no particular amount of time to draw; instead the artist took the time, or didn't take it, at pleasure. And, similarly, things themselves possessed no fixed and intrinsic amount of interest; instead things were interesting as long as you had attention to give them. How long does it take to draw a baseball mitt? As much time as you care to give it. Not an infinite amount of time, but more time than you first imagined. For many days, so long as you want to keep drawing that mitt, and studying that mitt, there will always be a new and finer layer of distinctions to draw out and lay in. Your attention discovers—seems thereby to produce—an array of interesting features in any object, like a lamp.

By noon, all this drawing would have gone to my head. I slipped into the mitt, quit the attic, quit the house, and headed up the street, looking for a ballgame. (ANNIE DILLARD, *An American Childhood*)

In there you have simple sentences like the first and the second last. You have sentences like the second in the second paragraph, in which two independent clauses, two opposites, are beautifully juxtaposed. You have a question and two sentence fragments by way of an answer. You have the elegant symmetry of the two long sentences—each of them itself internally balanced—in the middle, beginning at "evidently". You have the smart use of the clipped aside set within dashes and following the lovely phrase "your attention discovers" in the last sentence of the second paragraph. You then have the jump back from the intellectual to the bodily, from complexity of structure to simplicity. And throughout, a nice array of verbs.

Just to show that she's a master (mistress?) of all manner of sentence, here's Annie Dillard again elsewhere in the same book:

In 1955, when I was ten, my father's reading went to his head.

And shorter and plainer still:

Amy was a looker.

Here is good long sentence about long sentences:

At times a writer may indulge himself with a long sentence, but he will make sure there are no folds in it, no vaguenesses, no parenthetical interruptions of its view as a whole; when he has done with it, it won't be a sea-serpent with half its arches under the water; it will be a torch-light procession. (MARK TWAIN, quoted in Earle, *English Prose*)

Here's another about a morning and a city and a party and a woman's state of mind:

And everywhere, though it was still so early, there was a beating, a stirring of galloping ponies, tapping of cricket bats; Lords, Ascot, Ranelagh and all the rest of it; wrapped in the soft mesh of the grey-blue morning air, which, as the day wore on, would unwind them, and set down on their lawns and pitches the bouncing ponies, whose forefeet just struck the ground and up they sprung, the whirling young men, and laughing girls in their transparent muslins who, even now, after dancing all night, were taking their absurd woolly dogs for a run; and even now, at this hour, discreet dowagers were shooting out in their motor cars on errands of mystery; and the shopkeepers were fidgeting in their windows with their paste and diamonds, their lovely old sea-green brooches in eighteenth-century settings to tempt Americans (but one must economise, not buy things rashly for Elizabeth), and she, too, loving it as she did with an absurd and faithful passion, being part of it, since her people were courtiers once in the time of the Georges, she, too, was going that very night to kindle and illuminate; to give her party. (VIRGINIA WOOLF, *Mrs Dalloway*)

Sentences: a field guide

Composition is the name we give to the work of making sentences grammatical and various, each apt in its form for the story it tells and the way it needs to tell it. Composition, further, is the labor of building paragraphs out of these sentences, varying their form to keep the paragraph lively, to keep the reader awake, and to advance the story as it ought to be advanced. (More about that in the final chapter.)

What follows is a short guide to sentence styles and stylish sentences.

A writer may use all—and a good writer will use many—of the sentences that follow. Each has its virtues and vices. Each is good in its place—for different effects and genres, for different purposes and tones. But each is equally worthy and proper.

Most of us unthinkingly favor one or two sentence styles. They suit us somehow; or else, we've come to accept them as the kinds of sentence serious people—like writers and professionals—make. Most of us write in too narrow a band. And there's nothing so dull as a piece of writing made of the same kind of sentence from start to finish.

Good writers—again, usually without stopping to think too long about it—cover the whole range.

Of the twelve styles of sentence, the first six employ no subordination; they are what you can do using simple and compound sentences. The next five are varieties of subordinating sentences, including the frighteningly named compound–complex. At the tail comes that mongrel, the fragment.

[A] SIMPLE AND COMPOUND SENTENCES

1 Segregating sentences

A segregating style lays down short, uncomplicated, (generally) grammatically simple sentences one after the other.

This is a style that the plain English movement has encouraged. It's good for being clear in narration or description. It concentrates a reader's attention on the content—often a series of steps or actions, or the elements of a scene—and it keeps the narrator detached from what she narrates. It is one of the devices of the detached narrator (see Chapter 4). It seems to leave no room for comment, sympathetic or otherwise, from the teller. If not overdone, it's good for literary prose, it's good for thrillers, and it's good for reports and papers.

Doctor Plarr opened his eyes. The raised edge of the bed became Clara's body set against his own. It was dark. He could see nothing. He put his hand out and touched her . . . He put his fingers up to her face. Her eyes were open. He said, "Are you awake?" but she didn't answer [this one is a compound sentence]. He asked, "Is something wrong?"

(GRAHAM GREENE, *The Honorary Consul*)

William Maxwell uses the segregating style here to make a doleful recitation. His sentences are at the long end of this style, but nearly all are grammatically simple.

My grandfather, spending the night in a farmhouse, was bitten on the ear by a rat or a ferret and died three months later of blood poisoning. My mother's only brother was in an automobile accident and lost his right arm. My mother's youngest sister poured kerosene on a grate fire that wouldn't burn and set fire to her clothing and bore the scars of this all the rest of her life. My older brother, when he was five years old, got his foot caught in a turning carriage wheel . . . My younger brother was born on New Year's Day, at the height of the influenza epidemic of 1918. My mother died two days later of double pneumonia. After that, there were no more disasters. (WILLIAM MAXWELL, *So Long, See You Tomorrow*)

David Quammen describes here the panicked calm after a shooting accident in Montana:

The woods were silent. The gunshot still echoed awesomely back to the boy but it was an echo of memory, not sound [compound]. He felt nothing. He saw his father's body stretched on the snow and he did not really believe he was where he was [compound]. He did not want to move: he wanted to wake. The snow fell as gracefully as before.

(DAVID QUAMMEN, "Walking Out," *Blood Line*)

There is so much clean space and silence in that passage, a function of his diction as well as his syntax.

In this passage from *The Sun Also Rises*, Ernest Hemingway uses the segregating style for a narrative moment much more homely:

I heard Brett and Robert Cohn come up the stairs. Cohn said good night outside the door and went on up to his room. I heard Brett go into the room next door. Mike was already in bed. He had come in with me an hour before. He woke as she came in, and they talked together [compound]. I heard them laugh. I turned off the light and tried to go to sleep. It was not necessary to read any more.

The segregating style can also help you make an argument.

The starting point might be to recognise that the problem starts with us non-Aboriginal Australians. It begins, I think, with that act of recognition. Recognition that it was we who did the dispossessing. We took the traditional lands and smashed the traditional way of life. We brought the diseases. The alcohol. We committed the murders. We took the children from their mothers. We practised discrimination and exclusion.

It was our ignorance and our prejudice. And our failure to imagine these things being done to us. With some noble exceptions, we failed to make the most basic human response and enter into their hearts and minds. We failed to ask—how would I feel if this were done to me?

As a consequence, we failed to see that what we were doing degraded all of us. (PAUL KEATING, "The Redfern Address," December 10, 1992)

The virtues of the segregating style are power and clarity; its vices are monotony and disjunction. It's jumpy; it doesn't differentiate one piece of action or argument or information from another. It may sound detached, sometimes cold. In corporate writing it can lead to what one of my clients calls "bureaucratic staccato." It's weak at linkage and, consequently, not much good for sustained and subtle argumentation. Musically, too, its dynamics are poor, and it all goes at pretty much the same pace.

In unpracticed hands it can sound like the worst kind of baby book: *Sally is a puppy. She loves to run. Feel her fluffy coat.* That sort of thing. As though children didn't need a little more music than that.

▶ **Try this**

1 Write a description of an incident you observed or were involved in using sentences of no more than seven words each. Write a hundred words.

   Then try this on a letter you have to write complaining about something or asking for something. Or try it on a report you have to write at work.

2 Rewrite this passage in a sequence of simple sentences.

   After the necessary provisions, blankets etc., had been collected and stowed away, and my Indian crew were in their places ready to start, while a crowd of their relatives and friends on the wharf were bidding them good-by and good-luck, my companion, the Rev. S. H. Young, for whom we were waiting, at last came aboard, followed by a little black dog, that immediately made himself at home by curling up in a hollow among the baggage.

   (JOHN MUIR, "Stickeen," *The Best American Essays of the Century*)

2 Freight-train or run-on sentences

These are long compound sentences, main clauses strung together, coupled by conjunctions, running on and on into the night. As opposed to the segregating style, which favors small sentences in sequence, the freight-train is one long sentence made of many small main clauses linked with conjunctions or semicolons.

The Bible favors them:

And God said, "Let the waters under the heavens be gathered together in one place, and let the dry land appear"; and it was so. And God called the dry land Earth, and the gathering together of the waters He called Seas; and God saw that it was good. (BOOK OF GENESIS)

Not pure freight-train, admittedly, for new sentences start here and there, but most of them start with a conjunction *and*, which links the whole thing as though it were a single sentence. God likes freight-trains, apparently. Run-on sentences are, after all, litanies; they have a liturgical gait.

Marilynne Robinson starts her novel *Gilead* with this freight-train (including a subordinate clause "that I might be gone sometime" early on):

I told you last night that I might be gone sometime, and you said, Where, and I said, To be with the Good Lord, and you said, Why, and I said, Because I'm old, and you said, I don't think you're old. And you put your hand in my hand and you said, You aren't old, as if that settled it.

Here, from Hemingway, a master of the craft, is a relatively short instance:

Nick and his father got in the stern of the boat and the Indians shoved it off and one of them got in to row.
(ERNEST HEMINGWAY, "Indian Camp," *In Our Time*)

Cormac McCarthy's readers will recognize the freight-train as his stock-in-trade:

There were a few last warm days yet and in the afternoon sometimes he and his father would sit in the hotel room in the white wicker furniture with the window open and the thin crocheted curtains blowing into the room and they'd drink coffee and his father would pour a little whiskey in his own cup and sit sipping it and smoking and looking down at the street.
(CORMAC MCCARTHY, *All the Pretty Horses*)

Like the segregating style, the freight-train is insistent. It strikes only one note, but it flows. It makes what it narrates run like a film in front of a reader. As well as action sequences, landscapes and journeys, the freight-train lends itself to descriptions of the activities of the subconscious—dreams, in particular. It is a good vehicle for what is now called stream of consciousness.

But don't try the freight-train (too often) at work; outside literature, it can scare the horses. And sometimes the boss. It's not going to work for policy and business writing—too stylized for that. Nor is it particularly good for the exposition of ideas and the making of arguments. One thing it is good for, though, is getting creative writing students writing, and keeping them writing, delving into self and subject, keeping minds and memories and fingers moving. Try it if you're stuck; it might draw some thinking, even some writing, from way down deep, where you didn't know you had any.

In character, though not in form, a simple sentence with a single subject performing many verbs (joined by conjunction) reads very much like a freight-train:

He closed the bag and redid the fasteners and shoved it under the bed and rose and stood looking out the window at the stars over the rocky escarpment to the north of the town.
(CORMAC MCCARTHY, *No Country for Old Men*)

The old dog came out from its rug in the garage and wandered into the fenced yard and sniffed the boys' pantslegs and sniffed the baby and licked its hot red tongue across the baby's forehead, and then it scuttled up to the women on the porch and looked up at them, and looked all around and turned in a circle and lay down . . . (KENT HARUF, *Plainsong*)

When performed by a semicolon instead of a conjunction, the linkage of independent clauses is called parataxis. Paratactic freight-trains run less fluently.

And now he knew that it was the waiting and that night he crept out; he had not heard them but he knew they were there and in the dark he could smell their fear too; he stood erect then, shouting at them in the darkness: "Yao. Come and take me. Why are you afraid?"
(WILLIAM FAULKNER, "The Bear," *Big Woods*)

Faulkner mixes parataxis with conventional compounding in that freight-train. Here's some straightforward parataxis.

> But for herself she had done nothing wrong; she had loved Septimus; she had been happy; she had had a beautiful home, and there her sister lived still, making hats.
>
> He strained; he pushed; he looked; he saw Regent's Park before him.
>
> (VIRGINIA WOOLF, *Mrs Dalloway*)

▶ Try this

1 Write a run-on sentence starting with this clause: "I just want to go home." Keep going for five minutes or at least two hundred words. Alternatively, take as your subject, "The thing I have to write."

2 Using the freight-train style, write a journey you once took. Again, two hundred words.

3 Identify the kinds of sentence Joan Didion uses in the opening of this paragraph from "The White Album":

> On this evening in 1968 they were gathered together in uneasy symbiosis to make their third album, and the studio was too cold and the lights were too bright and there were masses of wires and banks of the ominous blinking electronic circuitry with which musicians live so easily. There were three of the four Doors. There was a bass player borrowed from a band called Clear Light. There were the producer and the engineer and the road manager and a couple of girls and a Siberian husky named Nikki with one gray eye and one gold . . . There was everything and everybody The Doors needed to cut the rest of this third album except one thing, the fourth Door, the lead singer, Jim Morrison.
>
> (JOAN DIDION, "The White Album," *The White Album*)

3 Triadic sentences

A more shapely version of the freight-train, apt for business, professional and academic, as well as literary uses because of its elegance and order, is the triadic sentence. In one version, three independent clauses are simply split by semicolons. In another, you split the clauses with commas (plus *and* ahead of the final clause). The virtue of triads is balance. Three is a holy number in many religious systems. Beyond its spiritual clout, three has an appealing geometry. For the Greeks, and for Cicero the Roman orator, three was a sacred rhetorical number, too. Listing three items in this way, to make a sentence, is memorable and powerful. A thing that Julius Caesar knew:

I came; I saw; I conquered.

Here's a lovely triad by Kim Stafford:

We live many things, we remember some, and we die.
    (KIM STAFFORD, *The Muses among Us*)

In the prologue to *Killing Mister Watson*, Peter Matthiessen uses a triad in description:

A clothesline flutters in the trees; thatched roofs are spun onto their poles like old straw brooms; frame buildings sag.

You might write something like this at work:

We have finished our quantitative research; we have run our theoretical models; these are the conclusions that we draw.

Or at home, something like this:

My son has attended this school for five years; this is the first time I've ever had cause for complaint; I hope you'll take that into account.

This way of organizing your thoughts won't work for everything, but it has a magic and elegance about it.

These days one might write triads differently, employing an introductory phrase or a heading, and then bullet-pointing three items (phrases or clauses). Where there are more than three items on that list it becomes one of the other kinds of sentence—the cumulative. But it's worth recalling the particular power of three. Four can be one too many.

4 Cumulative sentences

The cumulative sentence lets a writer develop an argument, an exposition, an idea, a character, a landscape, a scene, a moment, a mood, a description, by the steady accretion of detail. In its pure form, the cumulative sentence is an independent clause, with a long tail—an aggregation of subordinates (phrases and clauses). But sometimes the tail wags the dog: the detail gathers itself toward a summary; the main clause comes last. It matters less which way they run than how they run, which is long and slow. The detail, while structurally subordinate in a cumulative sentence, is in many ways the point; these sentences build by slow degrees, and they want us to understand that the reality they describe was built in such slow and subtle degrees, too. Cumulative sentences are almost geological (specifically, sedimentary, I guess) in their steady deposition of strata—and data. The cumulative sentence gathers and builds in teeming increments.

Danielle Clode, starting with the main clause, uses a cumulative sentence to gentle us out of the present into the past:

We must step back to a time before Buffon had noted the consistent geographical differences between species on different continents, before Jussieu and Linnaeus had developed systems of classification and nomenclature, before Lamarck had developed his evolutionary theory and before Cuvier had established the "fact" of extinction.

(DANIELLE CLODE, *Voyages to the South Seas*)

You can see how the main work of the sentence is done in the subordinate details, not in the main clause, which really just opens the door on the journey to her point.

Jeffrey Eugenides uses a sustained cumulative sentence in the opening paragraph of Book 2 of his novel *Middlesex*. In this case the phrases accumulate in increasingly complex units, heading further and further back in time, ahead of the final main clause, which repeats the opening sentence of the paragraph:

Detroit was always made of wheels. Long before the Big Three and the nickname "Motor City"; before the auto factories and the freighters and the pink, chemical nights; before anyone had necked in a Thunderbird or spooned in a Model T; previous to the day a young Henry Ford knocked down his workshop wall because, in devising his "quadricycle," he'd thought of everything but how to get the damn thing out; and nearly a century prior to the cold March night, in 1896, when Charles King tiller-steered his horseless carriage down St. Antoine, along Jefferson, and up Woodward Avenue (where the two-stroke engine promptly quit); way, way back, when the city was just a piece of stolen Indian land located on the strait from which it got its name, a fort fought over by the British and French until, wearing them out, it fell into the hands of the Americans; way back then, before cars and cloverleaves, Detroit was made of wheels.

(JEFFREY EUGENIDES, *Middlesex*)

Eugenides uses the cumulative style to fashion a kind of historical and rhetorical panorama—to flesh out, almost ridiculously, his poetic main point. The cumulative sentence is particularly good for setting a scene or for panning, as with a camera, a place or critical moment, a journey or a remembered life, in a way not dissimilar to the run-on. It is another kind of—potentially endless and half-wild—list.

Virginia Woolf accumulates phrases about Clarissa in her youth before finally getting to her verb:

Clarissa once, going on top of an omnibus with him somewhere, Clarissa superficially at least, so easily moved, now in despair, now in the best of spirits, all aquiver in those days and such good company, spotting queer little scenes, names, people from the top of a bus, for they used to explore London and bring back bags full of treasures from the Caledonian market —Clarissa had a theory in those days . . . (VIRGINIA WOOLF, *Mrs Dalloway*)

And here is this writer Kent Haruf, writing a cumulative sentence, opening his novel with it, panning the smalltown western landscape of his story:

Here was this man Tom Guthrie in Holt standing at the back window in the kitchen of his house smoking cigarettes and looking out over the back lot where the sun was just coming up. (KENT HARUF, *Plainsong*)

Near the end of her memoir, looking back over everything, Annie Dillard uses the cumulative style like this:

You may wonder where they have gone, those other dim dots that were you: you in the flesh swimming in a swift river, swinging a bat on the first pitch, opening a footlocker with a screwdriver, inking and painting clowns on celluloid, stepping out of a revolving door into the swift crowd on a sidewalk, being kissed and kissing till your brain grew smooth, stepping out of the cold woods into a warm field full of crows, or lying awake in bed aware of your legs and suddenly aware of all of it, that the ceiling above you was under the sky—in what country, what town?

(ANNIE DILLARD, *An American Childhood*)

True to the structure, but not to the spirit, of the cumulative sentence, and over-familiar to us all from the powerpoint presentation, is the long list of bullet points introduced by a main clause.

 Try this

1 Write about a favorite place using a long cumulative sentence or two. One hundred words.

2 Describe a person you know well, using this same sentence style. One hundred words.

3 Do the same thing for the work that you do or the best book you've ever read. This time, though, use a cumulative, a freight-train or two and a couple of segregating sentences.

5 Parallel sentences

Parallelism is another way to shape sentences that have a number of moving parts. The idea here is to give to two or more elements of the sentence (words or phrases) the same grammatical form. This symmetry gives cadence to the sentence.

A writer wants his writing to change himself and to change his reader.

My belated discovery—inside this wind, inside this shaking house, inside this other book of Lopez's—of that passage from Montaigne moved me with a sense of calling confirmed.

People go by; things go by. (JAMES AGEE, "Knoxville: Summer of 1915," *The Best American Essays of the Century*)

Aldous Huxley uses parallelism at two levels in this passage to guide his readers through complicated philosophical territory:

Philosophia Perennis—*the phrase was coined by Leibniz*; but the thing—*the metaphysic* that recognizes a divine Reality substantial to the world of things and lives and minds; *the psychology* that finds in the soul something similar to, or even identical with, divine Reality; *the ethic* that places man's final end in the knowledge of the immanent and transcendent Ground of all being —the thing is *immemorial and universal*.

(ALDOUS HUXLEY, *The Perennial Philosophy*)

I've italicized the elements (the coining of the phrase and the age of the metaphysic; and the three elements of the philosophy) Huxley sets in parallel. Can you see how the syntax lays bare the bones of the thought? It represents his thinking visually.

By contrast, parallelism can be as simple as a sentence with two subjects—but if the first is a single word, so should be the second; if the first is a phrase of three words, so should be the second. There is grace in such order:

Peter and Emily skated happily around the lake.

A decade of economic chaos and a century of political unrest have left the country in ruins.

The agency exists to ensure safety in the skies and confidence on the ground.

The revolution was the inevitable result of a century of decadence among the ruling classes, anger among the working classes, and ambition among the bourgeoisie.

The more things change the more they stay the same.

Among literary writers these days, parallelism is used mostly by essayists and upmarket journalists. It lends itself to argument and exposition better than it does to lyric evocation of place and character. The novel, that mirror to society, is in a loose-fitting and casual era, with which the formal tone and look of parallelism are out of keeping.

It doesn't have to sound nineteenth-century, though. Here's Annie Dillard giving it a run:

A gesture drawing took forty-five seconds; a Sustained Study took all morning. (ANNIE DILLARD, *An American Childhood*)

Susan Sontag makes use of parallelism in a lovely, brainy sentence at the start of her essay "Notes on 'Camp' ":

Many things in the world have not been named; and many things, even if they have been named, have never been described.
(SUSAN SONTAG, "Notes on 'Camp,' " *Against Interpretation*)

And here's a classic example from George Orwell:

So as long as I remain alive and well I shall continue to feel strongly about prose style, to love the surface of the earth, and to take pleasure in solid objects and scraps of useless information.
(GEORGE ORWELL, "Why I Write," *The Penguin Essays of George Orwell*)

For the same reasons the parallel sentence puts off the modern novelist—its grace and order—it's a smart play in policy and professional writing. (I should note, in passing, that if the sentence I concocted in "Life sentences" (p. 61), as an illustration of the sins of abstraction, had one virtue, it was the parallelism of its structure. Read it over, and you may pick it up. But, of course, in that case the parallelism only underscores the pomposity.)

Parallelism—where each item is structured identically—makes bullet-point lists work, too.

Shorrick & Associates must do four things this year:
• grow its professional staff numbers to twelve
• improve its people's writing skills
• place more research publications in the relevant journals
• raise its corporate profile in the government sector

Three factors have led to our poor profit result this financial year:
• the upward pressure the drought placed on grain prices
• the decline in sales because of the extortion campaign against Weeties mid-year
• the entry into the market of Uncle Tom's Organic Weet Flakes

6 Balanced

A looser kind of parallelism, more common in contemporary writing, is the balanced sentence—a sentence made of two parts, each about the same length and weight and divided by a pause (a comma or a semicolon—or a dash). Here are three such sentences in a row in a John Updike paragraph:

Inhabiting a male body is much like having a bank account; as long as it's healthy, you don't think much about it. Compared to the female body, it is a low-maintenance proposition: a shower now and then, trim the fingernails every ten days, a haircut once a month. Oh yes, shaving—scraping or buzzing away at your face every morning.

(JOHN UPDIKE, "The Disposable Rocket," *More Matter*)

Here are two more—one short, one long:

The passage was cool; a telephone sat on the lino.

(HELEN GARNER, *The Children's Bach*)

This immense process had begun in the United Kingdom and western Europe by 1815; it was soon to spread, with increasing impetus, eastward to Germany, Italy, and eventually Russia.

(DAVID THOMSON, *Europe Since Napoleon*)

One might also balance one sentence against another, shaping each one much the same. This works best when the two sentences point up a contrast:

Full, the reservoir looks all right: a mirror Sheep Creek dies in, timber straight and still along the edge, and sky swimming through its face. Drained of water, the reservoir that used to be a hayfield is a barren gravel pit with the dead creek laid out in the bottom of it.

(JAMES GALVIN, *The Meadow*)

A good writer is trying to do more than just make sense. Balance, like all these devices, rewards readers by giving them a pattern and a large-scale rhythm. Those things are engaging in themselves, but they also underscore one's message, giving it a form a reader can get hold of.

Try this

Make an argument about something that concerns you right now. Write a paragraph, and use some balanced sentences in it.

[B] SUBORDINATING SENTENCES

But there's a limit to what one can do with simple sentences, and we've reached it. The complex sentence brings an extra dimension to composition, a whole new bag of tricks. Because it lets a writer stress one part of a sentence over another, subordination brings nuance to writing. It allows modulation and subtlety of connection, especially useful in dealing with psychology and character in a story and with exposition and argument in other narratives. It introduces to the sentence the gearshift and the key change, the piano and the forte.

There are, believe it or not, four species of subordinating sentence, each an instance of the complex sentence. Then, beyond those, we have the compound–complex sentence and all the incredible variety it introduces.

7 Loose sentences

Here you start with your main point, and then add something more about it, often an explanation or justification, in a subordinate clause. The more subordinate phrases you add, the more the style approaches the cumulative sentence we looked at above (the difference coming down to the often irrelevant question of whether the bits that accumulate are phrases or, as here, clauses). Like the cumulative sentence, the loose sentence feels relaxed (hence its name). It feels like talking. Kept trim, it's good for explanation. At length, it suits description.

I am standing for this high office because I feel I have no other choice.

I stumbled on this idea when I first went to the desert.

These changes strike us as essential if the agency hopes to bring its financial accounting in line with best practice.

Here was a place that I could come to now and then for the rest of my life, that would no more stay the same than I would, and that would express its love by having me stay and ignoring me exquisitely.

I haven't seen a soul since I got back from overseas.

8 Periodic

Periodic sentences end with their main clause. Here's a different music. Such sentences set a stage and put someone down on it; they pose a problem and suggest an answer; they make an exception and state the rule; they excuse themselves for what they are about to say —and then say it. They are a plain or a series of foothills and then the main range. They feel artifactual—a little more like oratory, a little less like speech. They have an elegance about them, when they are well handled; and they are probably more commonly encountered than loose subordinating sentences. They ask a reader to wait, though. Watch that you don't try your reader's patience too often or too long.

Here are some (successful) examples:

Early in October 1975, when the first rains had already come but were still deciding what sort of season to create . . . a small plague of two missionaries descended upon us.

(ALEXANDRA FULLER, *Don't Let's Go to the Dogs Tonight*)

On the bay shores and down the coastal rivers, a far gray sun picks up dead glints from windrows of rotted mullet . . .

(PETER MATTHIESSEN, *Killing Mister Watson*)

If much later the Germans again fell behind their western neighbours, if in the seventeenth, eighteenth and even in the nineteenth century they were still in a sense imitating the more advanced West, the explanation is not to be sought in their barbaric origins.

(GOLO MANN, *The History of Germany Since 1789*)

If you can think of life, for a moment, as a large house with a nursery, living and dining rooms, bedrooms, study, and so forth, all unfamiliar and bright, the chapters which follow are, in a way, like looking through the windows of this house. (JAMES SALTER, *Burning the Days*)

In the morning, when the sea was still white and calm, as if with the concealed heat of molten metal, when among the fishermen the general movement was away from the sea to land, to wife, to bed, or tavern, the fisherman Sebastian Costa untied his boat and pushed off from the shore.

(NORMAN LEWIS, *The Day of the Fox*)

> ▶ **Try this**
>
> Take this passage from Hemingway's *The Sun Also Rises*, written in his most limpid segregating style, and rework it using only loose and periodic sentences. With apologies to Mr. H.
>
> > In the morning I walked down the Boulevard to the Rue Soufflot for coffee and brioche. It was a fine morning. The horse-chestnut trees in the Luxembourg Gardens were in bloom. There was the pleasant early-morning feeling of a hot day. I read the papers with the coffee and then smoked a cigarette. The flower women were coming up from the market and arranging their daily stock. Students went by going up to the law school, or down to the Sorbonne. The Boulevard was busy with trams and people going to work. I got on an S bus and rode down to the Madeleine standing on the back platform. From the Madeleine I walked along the Boulevard des Capucines to the Opéra, and up to my office.

9 Centered sentences

After you set down first a subordinate clause, you put down next your main clause, which you follow up with another subordinate clause (or two)—this is the centered sentence. Some books assure me this is common and handy. I don't think I use it much, and I've found it hard to turn up many examples. Ah, but here's one at last, in Montaigne, where, perhaps, I should have started:

If one book wearies me, I take up another, applying myself to it only during those hours when I begin to be gripped by boredom.

(MICHEL DE MONTAIGNE, "On Books," *The Complete Essays*)

It's a sophisticated way, I guess, to order a sentence with three (or more) related things on its mind.

10 Convoluted sentences

The convoluted sentence, if you use it deftly and only now and then, makes an elegant change-up. I guess it's a kind of wrong 'un, for the cricketers among you; a curve-ball, for the baseballers. You take a main clause ("the convoluted sentence makes an elegant change-up"), and you split it, often between its subject and its verb, and there you put a subordinate thought ("if you use it deftly and only now and then"). The convoluted sentence lets you splice an afterthought between your subject and your verb, or your verb and its object—an interpolation, an apology, an aside. Then you pick up your clause where you left it and carry it to its end. Convolution, despite its name, is elegant; it's also conversational. The very definition of *talk tidied up*.

The clause you insert is sometimes called a parenthetic expression because you notionally ask readers to take it out of the sentence if they wish. Generally the best way to punctuate around the parenthetic remark is with commas—or with dashes, if you want to emphasize the thing a little more. Not with actual parentheses.

This structure holds readers in suspense while you sidetrack from the sentence for a bit. Watch that the interpolated clause doesn't go on too long—or you'll lose them. And don't do it too often—or it will sound like you're absent-minded.

Greed, if that's what you want to call this force that drives enterprise, is good.

The first thought he had upon waking—if he had any thought at all—was how nice it would be to go back to sleep.

The political revolution of November 1918, which accompanied the armistice and the abdication of the Emperor, was made by none and wanted by none. (DAVID THOMSON, *Europe Since Napoleon*)

The geese, which had wintered by the lake, took flight at the first hint of spring.

11 Compound–complex sentences

Combine a compound and a complex sentence, and this is what you get. When you marry, in other words, (at least) two independent clauses with (at least) one dependent clause, you've made yourself a compound–complex sentence. A subtle and sophisticated thing—and tricky to get right. They make you think hard, for instance, about your commas. But they offer up the same kind of pleasure as a walk through woods over undulant ground.

He felt no lust, and when she moaned and tightened, he felt no sense of triumph. (GRAHAM GREENE, *The Honorary Consul*)

I knew I was quite drunk, and when I came in I put on the light over the head of the bed and started to read.
(ERNEST HEMINGWAY, *The Sun Also Rises*)

I was born free, and that I might continue so, I retir'd to these solitary Hills and Plains, where Trees are my Companions, and clear Fountains my Looking-glasses. (MIGUEL DE CERVANTES, *Don Quixote*)

Here is a beautifully balanced example from Cormac McCarthy's *The Crossing*. Because McCarthy eschews commas, it's not till you look closely at his conjunction-rich sentences that you see how many dependent clauses he uses. (I've highlighted the dependent clauses. Apart from those, there are two independent clauses, each with a compound verb.) Hear its irregular but orderly rhythm.

They crossed through the dried leaves in the river bed and rode *till they came to a tank or pothole in the river* and he dismounted and watered the horse *while Boyd walked the shore looking for muskrat sign*.

Here's one from Tim Winton (who doesn't go for conventional commas either), doing its musical work:

On the long grassy bank beneath the peppermint trees and the cavernous roots of the Moreton Bay figs, they lay blankets and white tablecloths which break up in the filtered sunlight and they sprawl in their workclothes and stockings, rollers in, buns half out. (TIM WINTON, *Cloudstreet*)

And just to show that they don't have to be long, here are two more from *Cloudstreet*:

His hand was between her breasts and she left it there as the river went by and by.

When he turned into Cloudstreet the sun was on the rooftops and a man stood alone across the road from the big house.

And an essayist's compound–complex from George Orwell:

[A writer's] subject-matter will be determined by the age he lives in — at least this is true in tumultuous, revolutionary times like our own — but before he ever begins to write he will have acquired an emotional attitude from which he will never completely escape.

(GEORGE ORWELL, "Why I Write," *The Penguin Essays of George Orwell*)

 Try this

1 Write a couple of compound–complex sentences describing the best holiday you ever took.
2 Write another couple about the route you take to work.
3 Write another about your favorite river.

That's it for, as it were, legitimate sentences. But there is still one kind to go: that uncultivated child, the fragment.

12 Fragment sentences

If you put a full stop (or a question mark) at the end of anything less than an independent clause), you've written yourself a fragment. An unsound sentence. Such as this one. And the one before it. And after. In other words, you cannot make a grammatical sentence using just a word or a phrase or a dependent clause. Microsoft Word will tell you that what you've written is a fragment; and so it is. And in certain settings — the legal brief, the board paper, the headmaster's letter, the audit report, the academic paper, the insurance contract — you'd better follow Word's lead. To be honest, most of us write them by mistake. Whenever that's the case, fix them; and whenever the formality of the occasion demands it, write your sentences out in full —find yourself a subject and have it perform a finite verb; make yourself at least one main clause.

(A related offence is the joining of two independent clauses with a comma. That won't make a valid sentence either—what you make is called a comma splice. *She's not a boy, she's a girl.* Which should be *She's not a boy; she's a girl.* Or *She's not a boy—she's a girl.* Or *She's not a boy. She's a girl.* A splice is two sentences rolled into one: a super-fragment, if you like. But they're not what I have in mind here.)

Strictly speaking failed sentences, fragments belong, nonetheless, in the best writing. They only work, though, when you use them sparingly. They work because they're striking; they're striking because they're different. They're emphatic; they're bold. If you use them too often they stop being different and start looking sloppy; they imply that you can't be bothered, or don't know how, to write a sentence that goes the distance. They have become a bit of a fetish in contemporary fiction. But they work best, like alcohol, I'm told, in moderation.

These are the varieties of the fragment. The subject alone. The sentence without a verb. The verb without a subject—*Goes on and on.* The verb in a participial or infinitive form—*Going on and on.* The lone noun —*Noun.* The lone adjective—*Alone.* Not lost. Just alone. And emphatic.

In short, a sentence is a fragment if it lacks a subject or a finite verb or both.

In this passage, which begins with some other sentence types, Cormac McCarthy ends with number of fragments, each participial, but each of a different length. The fragments catch the coldness of the air; they articulate the boy's fear and excitement; they choreograph the coming of the wolves.

He was very cold. He waited. It was very still. He could see by his breath how the wind lay and he watched his breath appear and vanish and appear and vanish constantly before him in the cold and he waited a long time. Then he saw them coming. Loping and twisting. Dancing. Tunneling their noses in the snow. Loping and running by twos in a standing dance and running on again. (CORMAC MCCARTHY, *The Crossing*)

James Agee writes a sentence, here, that is a string of fragments. "People go by; things go by," goes the sentence before, setting it up.

> A horse, drawing a buggy, breaking his hollow iron music on the asphalt; a loud auto; a quiet auto; people in pairs, not in a hurry, scuffling, switching their weight of aestival body, talking casually, the taste hovering over them of vanilla, strawberry, pasteboard and starched milk, the image upon them of lovers and horsemen, squared with clowns in hueless amber.
>
> (JAMES AGEE, "Knoxville: Summer of 1915,"
> *The Best American Essays of the Century*)

The fragmentation of the list implies disconnection and contemporaneity; it is a shifting mosaic—a kaleidoscope

Delia Falconer writes almost as many fragments as complete sentences in her spare poem of a novel *The Lost Thoughts of Soldiers*. Her fragments capture the voice, as it were, of a mind at its asyntactical work of memory. Her fragments are shards of an old man's recollection, stabs of indecision, intrusions of landscape. It seems right that they are incomplete, their subjects or their verbs lost.

> The others dead:
> Sumner who said once that no one in all his life ever posted him a letter.
> Madden who ate grass when he was nervous.
> A dash into the big nothing, the mystery of air behind them.
> Custer's legend still growing even now . . .
> A crawfish he had seen once in a market in New Orleans . . .
> History another battle.
> How to explain it to the boy.
> Outside, the bright sheen of the river passing and repassing.
>
> (DELIA FALCONER, *The Lost Thoughts of Soldiers*)

▶ **Try this**

1 Name the sentence styles McCarthy used in that paragraph I quoted on p. 94.
2 Write a passage using five different sentence styles, including the ones he's used and one or two others, describing someone you love or admire doing something they love.

3 For one or all of the following, write a paragraph or two using the sentence styles I name in brackets.

- What is the worst fight you ever go into? (Segregating and run-on)
- What is the best late breakfast you ever had? (Compound–complex and other subordinated sentences)
- What is the scariest swim you ever made? (Cumulative)
- What is the most frightening flight you ever took (Segregating and balanced)
- Did you ever cheat death? Write about it. (Mix)

Wishful thinking

About this far through the final rewrite of this book, I came down the stairs to find the newspaper.

"Daddy's finished his book," said Henry. A declamatory sentence, disguising a wish.

"I wish I were," I said. Subjunctively.

CHAPTER 3

GRACE

On style, economy, and poise

All good things come by grace and grace
comes by art and art does not come easy. NORMAN MACLEAN

Timepiece

Old watches are my weakness. Old watches and old fountain pens. Okay, old watches, old pens, books of any age, and cowboy boots. But that's it; and most of all it's watches.

Time—what it is, how it felt to other people, why it goes so fast, what it does to memory and perspective, how to handle it in a piece of work—time is the great mystery a writer grapples with. This one, anyway. So a good timepiece, in which the mystery is caught, ordered, and beautifully expressed, is a comforting thing to wear. And when a deadline looms as it always does, I want to be able to find out in the most beautiful way just how little time I've got to go.

I don't go in for fancy things; I believe in style, not fashion. I'm with whoever it was who said that beauty is simplicity in perfection. The most beautiful things work—and go on working—elegantly, without drawing attention to themselves. A nice watch, like a good pen, is a beautiful tool. And I believe in beautiful tools. Such as poems. Such as books.

I like my tools—especially my pens and watches—*old* because I'm drawn to original things; I like to feel connected, physically, to other lives and other times and places. When I wear my favorite wristwatch, this 1930s Lord Elgin, I feel I'm carrying on a story that began seventy years back. People, long gone now, designed and manufactured this watch to look good and keep the time in the 1930s, and here it still is on my wrist, looking good and keeping time in a new millennium, as it's done for others in between. Wearing it, I get to live in other people's older moments and right up to the minute in my own. In a small way, it makes my life and world a little larger than they seem. It keeps me humble.

To live as much in other lives and time zones as one's own, to feel humble and to inhabit stories—this is the writer's fate. This, and poverty, and the agony of how to make the next decent sentence.

I believe in traditions, in keeping alive the (good) things that have worked well from the start. I'm not sold on much that's new (I make an exception of my laptop). And I'm allergic to the faux. It's authenticity I admire most in a book or a person or a pair of boots or a pen. I want the real thing, if I can afford it, and I want to put it to work for me.

Here's another thing: it feels right to have to wind a watch. It establishes relationship, a benign kind of co-dependence. It lets me take part in the passage and articulation of time.

There's an inscription on the back of my favorite watch: HWN 11/12/39. I've always imagined that the watch was a twenty-first birthday gift to a boy who went to war soon after. I have no idea what happened to him, but his watch has come to me, and not long before I found the watch, my wife had a boy, and we named him Henry William—HW. These are the loops and buckles in time, the recursions and continuities, that fascinate me.

I like the form and size and quiet ornamentation of my watch, which is small for a man's timepiece. It's restrained. I like the separate orbit of the tiny second hand. I like the gold deco numerals on the off-white face. I like the way my watch bows out a little from its rectilinear form, its pretty face caught in parentheses, and I like the way its glass arches elegantly over it like the sky over the ground. Now that I think about it, my watch is much less straight than it seems. Like the earth; like time; like a good line; like style.

I fell for the watch the day I first saw it in Bill Newman's shop, where most of my pens and watches have come from. I'd bought another watch from Bill not long before, and I couldn't think what I'd done, particularly, to deserve, let alone afford, another so soon. But it wouldn't leave me alone. It ticked away. A month later I took

Maree to see it and to recite the many reasons I shouldn't get it. A week later, I was dressing for my doctoral graduation, when Maree came in and made me shut my eyes and strapped the Elgin to my wrist.

Did I list my wife earlier, among my weaknesses?

So this is a watch I plan to keep winding and wearing and, every other year, servicing. If I ever write anything that sells and makes me half famous, I may auction the watch and set up a fund to do the kind of good my books and poems will never do on their own. Until then, I'm keeping it, and it's keeping me, and I suspect it's me who'll wear out first. Before I do, I'd like to pass it on; I have the boy in mind. That's what I think you should do with traditions: make them new by making them your own and pass them on.

This chapter's about that kind of tradition and that kind of style. It's about what this watch is about: old-fashioned grace and cool and the techniques for achieving them, sentence after sentence in the face of time and fashion.

 ### Try this

1 Do you have something like my watch—a beautiful tool, an elegant, timeless, serviceable thing you love to use? Write a few hundred words about it.
2 Are you still wearing anything you bought more than ten years ago? Write about it in three hundred words. Try to write about it in a style that becomes that stylish garment.

Down with fashion

If it's in fashion today, it'll be out tomorrow. Or one day soon. That's how fashion works. So, you don't want to write the kind of sentence—worse still the kind of book—that you'll look back on, as you look back on that dress or that beard or those shoes or that song you waltzed to at your wedding, and think, "What was I thinking?"

Resist fashionable turns of phrase (like *pushing the envelope* and *going forward*), vogue words (like *segue* and *morph*, like *marginalize* and *validate* and *resile*, like *holistic* and *outcomes-based*), and hip expressions (like 24/7). Any day now, they'll be very yesterday.

Write the kind of prose that's never quite in fashion, and never out of style. Write a book that belongs today but lasts a little longer. Maybe a hundred years. Write clear, elegant, resonant sentences like "To be or not to be; that is the question"—four hundred years old and as good as new.

Or write a blockbuster in worse than pedestrian prose, and perhaps become very, very rich! I guess it depends what you're looking to do with your words and your time.

▶ Try this

1 What do these mean?
   - Morphs
   - Moving forward
   - Pushing the envelope
   - 24/7
   - Keep me in the loop
   - Get across it
   - Just touching base
   - Take a raincheck
   - A benchmarking exercise
   - How does this impact the economy?
2 This paragraph from a design magazine is a victim of fashion. See if you can tighten and smarten it up.

   She stood on the podium accessorized with her own design trademark sunglasses, silver bracelet-like watch and nifty trainers.

Here's a little piece of travel narrative, at once so reckless and so fashionable, it puts on the first things its author's hands fall on:

   The seeds of grass-is-greenerism were starting to germinate. It was only a matter of time before the first shoots poked up through the ground and demanded my attention.

Can you make sense of—and restyle—these examples from the business world?

> Much work has gone into the building of the 08/09 Roadmap. Our aim yesterday was to work through how we realistically link our objectives to our departmental and individual roles and responsibilities, and our personal performance planning. This was an extremely productive exercise and highlighted further steps for us to take to ensure we get this right. What we achieved yesterday was clarity and agreement around our Vision and Purpose and a clear pipeline of activity for 08/09.

> The scope of this project is to provide a robust and scalable production environment that will minimize production system downtime.

Up with style

Style is personal—but that's not all it is. For me style is, for example, my watch; for you it's yours. But each of us could find expressed in the other's timepiece—if it's a well-made thing—the same disciplines of design and craftsmanship. Style in writing is like that, too. It's about sound design and craftsmanship. It's also about humanity and good manners—matters more than merely personal.

> Style in writing is how each of us masters a universal code of writerly conduct. Each of us essays that in our own way, but it's the same code we're trying to enact.

Clarity is next to godliness

"Be clear," commands E. B. White. It's rule number sixteen of "An Approach to Style," a section he added in 1957 to William Strunk's classic, *The Elements of Style*, after Strunk's death.

Is this, perhaps, the primary rule of writing? Since the purpose of writing is to make meaning, one had better make sure the words don't get in the way. The words are meant to be so clear that, having uttered their plain and unambiguous truths, they disappear. Clarity has two dimensions.

1 *What do I mean, exactly?* That is sometimes the hardest part. I see too much writing that is either an unsuccessful search for what its author means, or an effort to avoid expressing it.

2 *How can I say it clearly?*

When our readers are left in two minds or more about what we mean to say, we've fallen at the first hurdle. And so have they. Sometimes a writer wants a certain obscurity as part of a literary strategy—a poet or a fiction writer particularly. That's fine in its place (see Chapter 4). But even then—especially then—let your *not* saying, let your withholding, let your wild and figurative language be limpid. Be beautifully unkempt. Be deftly and lucidly opaque.

Just exactly where Clarissa and her thoughts are going, at the start of *Mrs Dalloway*, is not certain (see the passage I quoted in the last chapter on p. 74. But every word and image Woolf selects is, in itself, clear. And Rachel Carson acknowledges lucidly the darkness that veils her subject matter in *The Sea Around Us*: "Beginnings are apt to be shadowy, and so it is with the beginnings of that great mother of life, the sea."

Your political or your aesthetic project or your profession or your anxiety may ask you to say something indirect, unspecific, mysterious or guarded. Go right ahead, if you think you must. But don't trip over your words doing so. Don't mumble into your beard.

Make sure that you've said what you set out to say. "The chances of your having said it," concluded E. B. White, "are only fair." That is always the case; it is especially the case when you're trying to be clever or evasive.

"I see but one rule: to be clear," wrote Stendhal. "If I am not clear, all my world crumbles to nothing."

 Try this

1 In this passage from his sad, wise book *A Grief Observed*, C. S. Lewis writes with wonderful clarity about something it is hard

ever to be clear about; and he is writing at a time, sunk in grief, when it is almost impossible to be clear about anything:

> No one ever told me that grief felt so like fear. I am not afraid, but the sensation is like being afraid. The same fluttering in the stomach, the same restlessness, the yawning. I keep on swallowing.
>
> At other times it feels like being mildly drunk, or concussed. There is a sort of invisible blanket between the world and me. I find it hard to take in what anyone says. Or perhaps, hard to want to take it in. It is so uninteresting. Yet I want the others to be about me. I dread the moments when the house is empty. If only they would talk to one another and not to me.

Imagine or recall a difficult time in your life—a loss, a dread, a disappointment—and try to write with that kind of self-effacing honesty about exactly what it felt like.

Try the same thing for a dispute you find yourself involved in, about which you feel particularly heated.

2 I'm not sure I will ever understand exactly what Jim Galvin means by this sentence in *The Meadow*: "He lived so close to the real world it almost let him in". But I'm very glad he wrote it. And every word in it is plain and clear and deliberate. It's just that it concerns itself with a mystery.

Buy or borrow the book and see what you think he might mean.

3 This passage is not as clear as it might be. It falls into the trap of favoring expert and bureaucratic language over plain old everyday diction. It's not trying to fool anyone, but it probably does. Can you guess what it means and rewrite it so it says so?

> The service operates within a harm minimization approach with the objective of assisting clients to re-establish their independence and facilitate reunification with the community. [Some clues: This refers to a bus that goes out at night, picks up people on the city streets affected by drugs and alcohol, finds shelter for them, dries them out and tries to set them straight.]

Avoid clichés like the plague

After "be clear," the most important thing anyone can tell you about writing is this: express your thoughts in your own words; write each sentence originally, in a voice and in diction native to yourself. Write; don't mimic. Refuse phrases you've read or heard too often before. They are someone else's.

A cliché is an expression, some kind of metaphor usually, clapped out from overuse. You may know how *to ride roughshod over* translates, but what the phrase literally meant and how it came to denote *reckless disregard* are matters as arcane to most of us these days as farriery. Recently, I heard journalists and politicians speak of a particular electoral seat as a *bellwether seat*, as though the phrase referred to the prevailing weather. They knew what they were trying to say—that it has always gone with, and therefore predicted, the government—but there's some absurdity in employing an obscure pastoral metaphor in a profoundly post-pastoral era. Only the other day, watching *Thomas the Tank Engine* with my children, did I learn what it really means to *build up a head of steam*, a phrase still in common use, long after steam trains themselves traveled our daily lives. Now, I have nothing against old things; and these expressions, in their way, are charming. But they are obsolete in modern sentences. And more to the point, they mean nothing—literally—to most of their users.

As a rule, then, don't use a word or phrase you can't explain. Even then, ask yourself how apt and transparent your borrowed and exhausted expression may be for readers who are not, for instance, engineers or shepherds or horseriders. Ask yourself what you're *really* trying to say, and say *that*. In your own words, in other words.

Unless, when you write *fully fledged*, you realize your metaphor refers to a young bird's making ready to leave its nest, you should probably enlist another figure.

Write every sentence your way. Keeping every phrase vernacular, make it, at the same time, striking. In the way that your own speech is striking in its particularity. Don't waste a single word, let alone a sentence, on the kinds of expression you hear on run-of-the-mill (now, there's a nice early industrial adjectival compound) television documentaries, in tourist brochures, in courtrooms or advertise-ments, monographs or tabloids. Be strong. Listen carefully to your writing. If it sounds like something you've heard before, strike it out. Without going crazy, without being anything other than conversa-tional, make every sentence original. Say it freshly, wrote Orwell.

So, not *It's raining cats and dogs* but *Rain falls on the roof like it means it* or *Rain falls hard and keeps at it all day.*

There's a funny thing about good writing: it is both unprecedented and familiar. It gets that way by refusing clichés.

Here are some tired expressions I've found reading through a brochure in my cabin: *meander* (when people and boardwalks do it; maybe it's okay for rivers, for whom it was invented); *beckon*; *greater scheme of things*; *precious times*; *pressures of daily life*; *back in touch with nature*; *fresh perspective.*

Something about travel writing seems to call forth whole sentences of cliché:

Or maybe you'd prefer floating above a myriad of colorful corals, swim-ming languidly in the shallows off a deserted beach of pristine white sand, or watching exotic birds flit through the tree canopy whilst bush-walking through lush rainforest. [Are the exotic birds flitting as they bush-walk?]

A box of clichés

Generic clichés

It's high time	Guests were treated to
It doesn't get any better than this	This is a dream come true
How good was that?	Fact of life
What the?!	Harsh reality
This day and age	At this point in time
The young people of today	At the end of the day
A cleansing ale	On a regular/daily basis
Extol the virtues	The time of her life
Wend your (weary) way	The tools of the trade

Caresses (except for what
lovers do; and even then)
Punctuates (except for what
commas do)
Ambience
Milieu
Rat race
Time heals all wounds
Just have to wait and see
Wind whispers/whistles
Holistic approach
Shipshape
Sea change
Wipe the slate clean
The grass is greener
Mother Nature
Time catches up with us
Road to success
Climbing the corporate
ladder
Just take it one day at a time/
play one game at time
Look at each case on its merits
Backs to the wall
Family and friends
Words are inadequate
Cool, calm and collected
Hook, line and sinker
Whole nine yards
Whole box and dice
Happy as Larry

Corporate clichés

Proactive approach
Strategic initiatives

Synergies
Convergence
Time is money
Value chain
Buy-in
Ongoing basis
Rationalization of resources
Change agents
Think outside the box
Drivers of change/strategy
Push the envelope
Core competencies
Scope the problem
Run it up the mast
Walk the talk
Client service
Refurbish (just about anything)
Going forward
Service delivery
Deliverables
Integrated (solutions, etc.)
Outcomes orientation
Runs on the board
Key (as in "This element is
key")
Commercial reality
Touch base
Steep learning curve
Executive (anything)
On a case-by-case basis
Keep me in the loop
Sign-off
Ball is in your court

Some popular expressions seem fine, used sparingly and with a hint that you know you're using a colloquialism. (One place where clichés belong, of course, is in the direct speech a creative writer gives to her characters. Even there, be careful. Make sure you use clichés that characterize your man or woman; choose colorful, memorable clichés, and authentic turns of regional phrase. See Chapter 4.) *Big smoke* for the city is a good Australian usage, I think. And I quite like *take the gig*, though my interest is waning, a sure sign . . . unless those, too, are clichés.

Write everything from scratch. Don't strain for novelty, though. Make yourself write exactly what you see and what you mean, without the help of any conventional phrases. Many aspiring writers imagine they must affect a kind of literary—or professional—patois; they write how they imagine a writer should write. This produces a stilted, sing-song, Romantic kind of prose; or it leads to the kind of hackneyed hip and derivative cool, out of which good writers finally graduate into their own voice. Or, unreconstructed, it results in banal bureaucratic blah like this:

This is a pragmatic commercially based and tested set of realistic alternatives . . .

We comply with the highest ethical standards.

Should you have any queries regarding the abovementioned, do not hesitate to contact the undersigned at your convenience.

Try something more like this (but after your own fashion, of course):

At the back of deserted cafés, women behind the bars yawned between their untouched bottles; the newspapers lay unopened on the reading-room tables; in the laundresses' workshops the washing quivered in the warm draughts. Every now and then he stopped at a bookseller's stall.

(GUSTAVE FLAUBERT, *Sentimental Education*)

Nothing flashy; nothing fashionable; just plain and authentic prose.

A certain kind of borrowing is fine, of course. Just be careful whom you choose. I wouldn't recommend Dan Brown particularly. Go to school on the writers who move you. You find your voice and broaden your vocabulary and tauten style by apprenticing yourself to the masters. Purloin from them words that sing; plunder sentence structures and devices. Borrow and steal—not to write the same things their way, but to enrich the way you say your things in yours.

And, please: it's a long time since *anything* has been *pristine*—not even a beach in what we like to think of as the wilderness. Especially not anywhere they're trying to sell you real estate. A village can no longer *nestle* anywhere. And no more *myriads* and *plethoras*. All these are examples of false elegance and conformism.

So shoot me! I know I'm being tough. But do you think any writer ever got to be any good using other people's turns of phrase? Write like yourself and yourself alone, but do it in language that anyone might use.

 Try this

> The director of a client organization once sent me a nice letter after I'd run a course with them. In it he cleverly spoofed the kind of writing we had spent two days unlearning. Here's his sentence. Try rewriting it.
>
> > There is a general consensus amongst the attendees in relation to the way in which the course was delivered that it was likely to provide ongoing guidance and facilitate the optimization of our corpus of verbal product both written and oral.

Bureaucratic tics

You know the kinds of thing I mean: *prior* and *prior to* and *prior year*; *further to* and *in relation to* and *with reference to*; *with regard* and *regardings* and *in regard to*; *find attached* and *herewith*; *above* and *as discussed* and *effective immediately*. They have their defenders. But the best you can say for them is that they come in handy; they save you thinking. They're instances of antiquated good manners become bureaucratic habits.

I remember the first time I encountered a *further to*. Fresh from law school, I began work with a big city law firm. Reading *further to* in a partner's letter, I thought it just about the strangest phrase I'd ever met. Remember when these expressions seemed strange to you, too? Then you start using them because they're an easy way to sound professional; you imagine certain readers demand them (if anyone ever really did, their numbers are thin these days); they're a kind of shorthand. Soon you're using them without knowing it.

I was going to write that no one uses these figures in conversation; then I thought of one or two people I know who do; then I heard the woman in the shopping center say into her cell phone "Someone rang in regard to the horse." Still, these are stuffy phrases that don't— outside business affairs—come naturally to our mouths. And they never come happily to our ears; they clang. They are lazy habits; they are hangovers. They are discourteous because they let you avoid treating your reader as a real-life human being.

Drop them. Come on, you can do it. Please. They do no one any good. They are small things, but it's in small ways one sometimes makes the biggest change.

Technical words and verbal profundity

I have clients who insist on *intermodal* in the reports they write on the economics of ports and shipping lines and warehouses, on the distribution of goods by road and rail and sea and air. They tell me they need *multimodal,* too, which means something a little different, though they find it hard to tell me what. When I suggest they find a plainer way to say such things, they say they feel obliged to because these terms have taken on specific meanings in the industries where they consult. The terms have become, my clients say, industry idiom. Meaning may be lost, my clients say, if they tried to translate these terms into commonly understood language. They ignore my raised eyebrows; I wait for the apparent absurdity of what they've just said to strike them, and it doesn't. So I say, "define them in a glossary." And still they resist. There are just some expressions the industry expects of us, they say. And I take their point.

The man who runs that organization is a careful and passionate writer; he's a smart man. He stands up and tells people, for instance, that the purpose of economics is to make people happy. So I let them get away with *intermodal.*

Sometimes you just have to use a technical word or phrase; it's the only way you can be sure that you've said exactly what you meant. I've used a few in this book. You might have to speak of *waste minimization, dispatchable capacity, network constraint issues, kilowatts, LV reactive compensation, takeovers provisions, interconnectivity, accountability,* and *Other Statutory Matters.* Explain them, though, as clearly as you can. Make them the exception; put everything else in everyday language.

The sparing use of apt technical expressions is no sin. But its cousin, verbal profundity, is. Verbal profundity is the unnecessary use of long words and obscure phrases for things that might be simply expressed. This fallacy grips many people in many professions and walks of mercantile and bureaucratic life; it seduces many beginning students and senior academics and writers of doctoral theses. False elegance is the assumption that the long way around—the polysyllabic, the mannered, the abstract and obtuse—is the right way to go—the proof of one's competence, one's seriousness and seniority. The fallacy, as Thomas Kane turns it, is that words and phrases that "look impressive must mean a lot." This endemic misunderstanding leads to everyday abominations like *keep the client apprised of the situation, subsequent upon the discovery of, comprising/comprised of, it is recommended/noted, has responsibility for, facilitation of desired outcomes, in certain respects, facilities, capabilities, core competencies, alignment, environmentality, infrastructure, expiration, hermeneutic, assistance, incommensurability, aforementioned,* and *take cognizance of the fact.*

 Try this

Find everyday ways of saying each of those falsely profound phrases.

The concrete particulars

There are two different but closely related rules of style.

- Make the abstract concrete.
- Make the general particular.

Abstract words (such as *economy, policy reform, administration, financial management, demand, leadership, minimization, style,* and so on) point to things that have no actual existence. You cannot touch or see or hear or smell or taste them; they have no form; they are concepts, processes, systems. We understand them through conceptual thinking. One needs to talk about such things, of course, as love and economics, management and grief, law and order and syntax and quantum physics. And humans are good at processing concepts. But we can only, it seems, understand abstractions fully when we can translate them into an image of someone somewhere doing something.

Concrete words point to things that have form and life in the actual world—things one can see or touch or hear or smell or taste. You can walk outside and pick one up, or kiss one, or carry it back inside or take it, or drive it, home to meet your parents: *a pen, a car, a woman, a man, a boy, a watch, a hen, a quoll, a ripe pear.*

General words contain multitudes and allude to them all together: *furniture, stationery, assets, facilities, constituents, consumers, fruit, staff, habitat, literature, landscape.*

Find a way to write in concrete and particular terms about even the most abstract and general topics: this is the principle of style I offer you now. It's not mine, though. You'll find it highlighted in all the style manuals; and you'll find it broken in almost every corporate and government brochure, every financial pronouncement, every academic paper, every letter from your lawyer or accountant you ever read. It is Strunk and White's second rule of style because it always has been a chief failing of most of the writing that happens.

Good journalists know how to observe it, though. When they're taught to write every story so that they tell the who, what, why, when, where, and how, they're being trained to write concretely and specifically.

Consider how clear a picture these two journalistic paragraphs offer:

The Black Hawk helicopter that crashed off Fiji in November 2006, killing two soldiers, was a flight destined for disaster. That was the assessment yesterday of counsel assisting a military board of inquiry into the tragedy.

For six years, an Amtrak engineer, Saed Marcos, quietly awarded air-conditioning contracts to family members, landing him at least $710,000, the corruption watchdog has found.

The mind and the soul—like the body—love the particular; readers need to *grasp* what you say, not just listen to your exquisite abstractions. Readers want examples, images, quantities, names, times and places. Outside our particular field (and even within it), most of us struggle with abstraction. If you write abstractly, you ask your readers to transpose what you say into the sensible world; you ask them to conjure an image of what you intend them to see. There's a risk, increasing as the abstraction of your subject matter deepens, that something may be lost in translation—what you mean exactly, for instance.

How many different things might these sentences mean?

An allocation has been made for the refurbishment of various major assets and facilities.

We are in agribusiness.

I'm a relationship manager/team leader/consultant.

The company strives for continuous improvement in delivering effective and efficient client service.

A number of exogenous factors have been responsible for the situation the company finds itself in.

Various innovative approaches are under investigation.

 Try this

Have a go at translating those abstract and general statements into something concrete and specific. You'll have to imagine some plausible particulars. (There were some; the writer just forgot to mention them.)

It's hard, of course, to write concretely when your subject matter is, itself, abstract: if you are a philosopher, say, or an IT professional, a policy writer or a financier; if you want to write about services, ideas, structures, policies, economics, strategy, politics, and human relations. But that's the challenge, and there's no shirking it. I can think of practitioners in all those fields, and others, who succeed in writing elusive, ethereal stuff like that plainly and humanely.

Look warily at any word in your work that ends in *ism* or *ology* or *ality* (as in *environmentality*) or *tion* or *ment*. Ask yourself if there's not another way to say it. Interrogate, similarly, every word longer than three syllables. "A man who makes use of a host of long words," wrote Walter Murdoch in "Sesquipedalianism," "is like a man who stirs up the mud in a pool in which, he tells you, he has dropped a pearl of great price." Ask yourself, "What would this thing I'm trying to say actually look like; what would someone see if they were looking at what my sentence has in mind?" Which is pretty much what they will be trying to do, translating your sentence. "How would they know if the thing I am describing had occurred yet? Who would be doing what? What would my statement look like in the real world; how would it be observed; how would it be measured?"

Cultural and literary theorists, art historians, and contemporary philosophers, along with management consultants, are particular offenders here. Many of them have fallen under the spell of a certain diction, abstract to the core, if abstraction can be said to have a core. Some people, I have heard, don't believe anything original can be said unless it is said in a language next to no one can understand, in a polysyllabic discourse resistant to any kind of translation into real time and the actual world. The irony seems lost on such practitioners that in seeking originality this way, each of them conforms to a narrow rubric, and parrots an equally narrow diction, thus closing the door on originality before they've even opened their mouths. But how could anyone tell if they were being original, anyway?

I sat once through a paper on—I think—environmentally aware architecture at an academic conference, and I swear I understood nothing from start to finish. (Others, I should add, seemed to quite enjoy it.) I can tell you why I learned nothing. What I heard was language severed almost entirely from humanity, almost from sense. Every sentence concerned itself, in sinuous abstract words, with abstractions; with other people's ideas about other people's ideas about abstract notions about—I think—public versus private space. There was scarcely a human being and scarcely a human action to be found. The closest we got to verbs in which any action transpired was *constructed, read, can be accounted for, privilege, mediate,* and *marginalize.* Nouns went like this: *paradigm-incommensurability, modalities, construal, implication, perceptivities, subversion, paradigm* and *alienation.*

Here's an instance of the kind of thing I heard:

If one concedes, with Levinas and Blanchot, that Heidegger's version of this twist of language upon itself, *Dichtung,* does not eschew vestiges of phenomenology (namely in Heidegger the transcendental element of language is still being determined, however subtly, by way of certain phenomena *in* the world) then Heideggerian *aletheia* and disclosure must be reconceptualized as a mobility or dislocation of/in language and this syntactical twisting itself is alone the peculiar (non) essence of language as a form of non-phenomenal spacing.

(TIMOTHY CLARK, *Derrida, Heidegger, and Blanchot*)

A sentence like that, impressive though it is, is a parody of itself. It does what so much of this discourse—to steal one of this field's clichés—seems helpless to avoid: it drops names; it uses opaque technical jargon (*"aletheia"*), litotes ("one concedes . . . does not eschew"), nominalization, the passive voice ("must be reconceptualized"), and common words put to uncommon uses ("spacing," "disclosure," "mobility").

The writing I have in my sights is often urbane, like Clark's, and impressive; it's also often self-satisfied, abstracted, conforming and jargoned. If it doesn't outsmart itself, it outsmarts most of its readers —and that seems to be part of its (absurd) purpose. "When you hear a man deal too much in long words," Murdoch went on in "Sesquipedalianism," his fine defence of plain thought and speech, "it is as well to count your spoons—ten to one he is a fraud . . . The general rule holds good; long words are a sign either of muddled thinking or of sham erudition."

Clever, abstract theoretical writing seduces some readers. Not me. Gail Gilliland in her book *Being a Minor Writer* draws a distinction between two lines of theory she encountered at writing school. One line comes down from Aristotle's *Poetica*: literary theory "by and for the literary theoreticians." The other line descends from Horace's *Ars Poetica*: writing about writing "by and primarily directed toward practising writers." I'm with Horace, for reasons I hope this book of mine makes plain. But I'm grateful to Gilliland for helping me see that thinkers about writing form two tribes; part of my animosity toward the abstraction of the other tribe could, I'd have to admit, be tribal.

The stylistic problem with the pieces I've quoted and pieces like them is their intractable abstraction. A reader looks for miles around each such passage for any sign anywhere of anyone doing anything visible, tangible, audible, actual. In vain.

A good writer doesn't aim to reject abstract expression entirely; she aims, instead, to ration it, to embed it in writing that is as full as she can make it of particularity, of actors, actions, and images.

Compare:

Certain adjustments have been made to the operational activities and resource base of the department due to fiscal restraints flowing from the new government's election mandate.

with:

To respond to a $40 billion reduction in our funding this year, we have transformed the department—reducing staff by 140, redesigning structures of work, and introducing new computer systems, to allow us to meet our clients' needs with fewer resources.

 Try this

Rewrite these samples of abstract writing. Make them more concrete and specific. You may have to invent some plausible facts.

The role is responsible for a range of sales support functions.

I am the Assistant Procurement Fulfilment Manager at a major educational institution.

Fraud control is an important consideration in the public sector, due to the responsibilities that flow from the management and utilization of public funds.

> In the discourses of globalization the categories "consumer"
> and "consumption" are privileged over those pre-modern
> concepts "citizen" and "living"; economy is substituted for
> geography; abstractions are reified and the obsolescence of
> time and place and cultural particularity are all presumed.

Sentences should be written in the active voice!

You want to sound like a bureaucrat or a cheat? Go ahead; write in the passive voice.

Everyone who writes books like this will tell you: ration the passive voice; favor the active. The vitality is leached from prose, if I may say so in the passive voice, by overindulgence in the passive voice. But the passive voice has its uses, as the best style gurus have always conceded.

Most of us write in Word these days and are prey to its grammar checker, which is implacable in its enmity for the passive voice and dependable in finding it. As a result, many writers have deduced that to write passively is to commit a mortal grammatical sin. But it's not a grammatical lapse; it's a lapse of style. It's a gaffe. A sin grave but not mortal; a want of virtue, specifically of grace and economy. But not a syntactical train wreck.

What is the passive voice?

Verbs have two voices—active and passive. When the verb is active, the subject of the sentence acts. When the voice is passive, the subject is acted upon. In the active voice, the subject is also the actor (the agent of the action). What it performs is the verb. In passive-voiced sentences, the subject is not the actor. It is the recipient of the action—a kind of object, if you like. And the actor may not even get a mention.

Here's the difference—active voice first. *I wrote this sentence in the active voice.* Now the passive: *This sentence was written in the passive voice.*

So, in this sentence—*In this document, we propose changes to the law on gambling*—the subject (*we*) acts (*propose*) upon the object (*changes*).

In this sentence, by contrast—*In this document, a number of changes to the law of gambling are proposed*—the subject (*a number of changes to the law of gambling*) is acted upon (*are proposed*) by an unnamed but implied agent (presumably the writers of the document).

Some examples of passive-voiced sentences

- The proposed policy *was discussed* and issues arising from it *were debated*.
- A meeting of the PTA *will be held* on Tuesday night at 8.
- The measures *were approved* by the board.
- The ball *is passed* to Beckham.
- The trees *were planted* in 1934.
- Your application *has been turned down*.
- Pursuant to the recommendations of our consultants, a number of changes *are to be instigated* at Atlantic Pictures Inc.

What does the passive look like?

In the passive voice the verb takes a specific form: a combination of the verb *to be* in one of its tenses and the past participle of the verb. It is from the tense of the verb *to be* that the form takes its tense. It follows that verbs can be passive in every tense. It's from the construction that the verb takes its voice.

So: *have been achieved, is achieved, will be achieved, are given, were given, am overwhelmed, will be overwhelmed, was overwhelmed, were being overwhelmed, will be performed, will be controlled*. All these are verbs in the passive voice.

The (im)personality of the passive voice

A sentence in the passive voice downplays agency; it subdues the subject, rendering her inactive; it leaves out the actors or delays their appearance. It speaks like an official affecting disinterest; at best it sounds calm and objective; at worst, officious. And it's what it sounds like that's the biggest problem. Its voice implies that things have occurred by force of preordained necessity, at the hand of some god. It suggests the speaker takes no responsibility, invests no particular interest, and couldn't, perhaps, care less.

It is above all objectivity that too many writers have been trying for too long to affect by writing in the passive voice. Objectivity is good as far as it goes; and the passive voice is one good way to essay it. By leaving oneself or any other (human) agent out, you make your sentences sound impersonal. But the passive voice, particularly when it becomes a habit, strips sentences of humanity, personality, and life—qualities they could do with.

So what's wrong with writing passively?

1 *It's sneaky.* Well, it can be. The closest Richard Nixon got to taking responsibility for Watergate was to say "Mistakes have been made." If dodging the blame is your game, don't use the passive voice—that game is up; we're onto you.

   Even if you're not trying to be shifty, you run the risk of sounding like it.

2 *It's stiff.* Except in skilful hands, passive sentences sound pompous, lofty and stiff. Passive-aggressive, even, or defensive, because the writer withholds a key element of the truth—who's taking responsibility? Passive sentences make readers nervous and suspicious. Two examples of unnecessary and all too commonplace stuffiness:

   A license will be issued upon receipt of a correctly completed application form.

   Please ensure that taps are turned off due to water restrictions.

3 *It's dull.* It bores us. How can it fail to? Where are the people doing things? Where is the action? Nothing's doing when the voice is passive.

4 *It's vague.* The passive voice leaves a reader in the dark. Unless it sneaks them in at the end, a passive sentence leaves out the actor, a piece of information without which a reader cannot compose a clear picture of what the sentence tries—or tries not—to depict. The

agent; the who. It's not that we care exactly who the agent is. It's just that if you don't put someone in that role, we'll have to guess. And guessing grows dull pretty fast, and then it grows aggravating.

5 *It's inefficient.* In the passive voice, you either leave the agent out, conveying, in this way, less information than you would in the active voice while using as many words; or you add the agent in a prepositional phrase at the close, using, by comparison, many more words than you would in the active voice to say the same thing. The passive voice is less efficient than the active. It may not seem much, but such inefficiency annoys and and the annoyance accumulates:

The following are key components that were noted during our investigation.

Why not, "We noted the following factors" or "Our study uncovered the following points"?

And what's right about it?

Turns out the language did have some uses in mind when it dreamed up the passive voice.

1 *Coherence.* The passive voice comes in handy when knitting together sentences, or phrases within a sentence, trying to make them flow and cohere. Here's an example:

In Oregon, there is a group of friends who call themselves "The Homeless Waifs Holiday Club." The group was formed in the 1970s when a generation of college students realized they weren't going home for Thanksgiving . . . (KIM STAFFORD, *The Muses Among Us*)

Starting the second sentence with "the group" keeps our attention on it, and opens out into some more information about that topic. This is gracious composition. We hardly notice it's passive at all.

2 *Emphasis.* I may want to emphasize the person acted upon and not the actor. Like this: "The pilot was found in the crashed plane. He was taken from the wreckage by Bedouins." Or like this: "Charles Wright was born in 1935." It just wouldn't make much sense, at

least not in a short biographical note on the poet, to write: "In 1935, Charles Wright's mother gave birth to a son and named him Charles." This suggests the next point (which is almost the same thing only more so) . . .

3 *Irrelevance*—of the actor, I mean. Just as, in the Wright sentence, the identity of the agent of the action is irrelevant, so it is in "The government has been defeated." We know who's responsible for that— or do we?—if we live in a democracy, or indeed most other kinds of polity. What's most relevance, rhetorically, is the government and the fact of its defeat. When it's someone's death I mean to tell you about, it may also be wrong (because immaterial at this point) to begin with the manner of the dying or the identity of the killer: "Denys has been killed" says it about right when Denys Fitch-Hatton died in a plane crash. Mind you, one could write "Denys has died," though that implies, curiously, less violence than was in fact the case.

4 *Ignorance*. It could be we don't really know who killed Denys or who started the fire or who sank the boat and drowned the refugees. If not, one might write a sentence about it in the passive voice: "A fire has been deliberately started"; "The boat has been sunk." Notice, though, that one could write "Someone has started a fire . . . " in the active voice.

5 *Inactivity of the subject*. Rhetorically, for reasons of accuracy or poetry or politics, I may want you to understand that the subject of my sentence was inactive. Rendering your subject passive is exactly the trick the passive construction performs on a sentence. So it may be the way to go: "The King Billy pines had been stained and stunted by two millennia of bad weather"; "I was encouraged by my senior colleagues to stand."

6 *Variety*. If you set out to write mostly in the active voice, the passive can be a pleasant change-up. Paragraphs thrive on diversity—of style and structure, length *and voice*.

7 *Objectivity of tone*. Although there are other ways, the passive will help you write objectively. It overdoes it, really. "The National Parks Act protects every form of life within the park" sounds just as objective as "Every form of life in the park is protected (by the Act)," but

slightly less stuffy. "Guests are requested to vacate cabins by 10 am. Your assistance in leaving the hut clean and tidy would be appreciated" sounds not just objective but plain awkward to me. How about: "Please vacate cabins by 10 am. And please leave them clean and tidy"?

"The world is made of rock and music"

That sentence came to me on the bus today. We were passing through all these cuttings, and I began to notice how many different kinds of rock we were cutting through—dolerite, folded quartzites, sandstones (I think), maybe some basalt. I wrote: "The world is made of rock and music." It may be the start of a poem. We'll see.

But tonight, writing this section, I notice that my sentence is passive. Will I strike it out? I don't think so. To name an actor in that sentence would cause me to cover some contentious theological and scientific ground, and in doing so, I'd miss my point. Thinking about it, I see that I could make rocks my subject, thus: "Rock and music compose the world." But that's not the music of the thing I had in mind.

▶ Try this

1 Write a paragraph in your journal. Write for five minutes about the last meal you made. Take a look back at it and find your verbs. See how many of them are passive. If any, see if you can rewrite those sentences actively.

2 Convert the following sentences from passive to active. First spot the passive verbal forms, then rewrite the sentence, making it active. One way to do this is to ask who, in real life, would have performed the verb. Make that person the subject of the sentence. Another way is to keep the subject of the passive sentence as your subject, but make it do something. ("The staffer is learning writing skills" in the example that follows.)

Example:

The staffer is coached by a writing teacher.
A writing teacher is coaching the research officer.

- It is recommended that suitable training be implemented across the department.
- The Commission was established by legislation enacted by Congress in 2002.
- As soon as the Sydney Opera House was finished, it was adopted by Sydneysiders and lovers of good design the world over.
- Your inquiry has been received and will be responded to soon by one of our client service officers.
- The coastal township had been struck by another tropical cyclone.
- Our hospital in Harrisburg was refurbished during the year.
- This sentence should be written in the active voice.

3 Every time you meet the passive voice in your writing try to make it active. Going cold turkey on the passive helps you kick the nasty habit, if you had it, of writing in the passive voice without meaning to.

Less is more—or, why this section ought to be half as long as it is

Be generous with the truth and economical with how you tell it. Most of us do it the other way round; that is the art of politics. Instead of doing politics with words—just write. Mean as much as you can in the fewest syllables; that is the art of writing.

Less, they say, is more. And yet, although this is a central orthodoxy of English prose style, particularly beloved of editors, I only half believe it. Under another hand, this little book might have been littler still; but it would not then be this book; it would not be itself; it would not be mine. Sometimes less is simply less. I believe in economy and grace and clarity; I believe in short words and tight phrases; but I don't believe that half as long is always twice as good.

For one thing, it's no good trying to be short before one has worked out, and articulated, what one is trying to be short *about*. Sometimes the long way around is the shortest way home. What counts is not how short a piece of writing is, but how useful and how good and how true. You want it trim, but not so trim it begs more questions than it answers; not so trim it's oblique; not so short it's blunt.

This much is true: if a thing can be said in ten words, you should try not to use thirty-five. Be thrifty, in other words. But didn't I say that, already?

You could write, for instance, "Fold the pastry over to the other side so that it forms a semicircle"; or you could make it "Fold the pastry to make a semicircle." Tighter. You could write "Up to 2 percent of our body weight is made up of calcium, which is about 1.2 kilograms for a 60-kilogram individual"; or you could trim it to "2 percent of your body weight is calcium—that's 1.2 kilograms if you weigh 60 kilos." You could write, very loosely, "The courses denoted in italics mean that they cover the key concepts specifically recommended for aspiring book editors"; or you could make it "The courses in italics cover concepts book editors need to master."

And think how apt it might have been to have written a leaner sentence than this in the department's house style manual: "A considerable amount of departmental resources are consumed in producing our published reports so it is important that we are able to produce them in an efficient manner"—efficiently rationing, for example, our syllables.

 Try this

Trim that sentence. Think, for instance, of neat replacements for *a considerable amount of resources*, *it is important that we are able to*, and *in an efficient manner*.

There may be more than one path to the end of the equation, mathematicians and physicists know, but the best path will use the least chalk; the elegant equation is usually the best equation. The machine that burns the least fuel, moves the fewest parts, leaves the smallest mess, will—leaving aside a few sometimes significant matters of taste and habit and fashion—be the machine you want. The dancer we most admire expends the least energy performing her impossibly effortless leaps; the greatest tennis player you ever saw hits the ball sweet and true and hard as hell, without a wasted gesture. We're talking about elegance here. The absence of anything inessential. What's true for mathematics and farming and driving and dancing and sport, for instance, is also true for writing.

So, keep it lean. Leave no words in a sentence that do not pull their weight. Don't qualify a statement unless you must. But be specific and particular, even if it costs you a word or two more. Say *orange*, even *Valencia orange*, not *fruit*; say *poet* not *writer*; say *machinist* not *worker*. The measure of trimness isn't the straight word count; it's how much meaning you generated with how few words. "Make every word tell," intoned old Will Strunk.

Be clear, and use as many words as you need to do so—but not one syllable more.

Here are some ways to write more with less:

- Write *orient* instead of *orientate* and *specialty* instead of *speciality* and *rain* instead of *precipitation*.
- Lose unnecessary prepositions and adverbs: write *retreat* instead of *retreat back*, *repeat* instead of *repeat again*, and *conjure* instead of *conjure up*.
- Drop *that* wherever you can: write *there are three lines of strategy we should pursue* instead of *there are three lines of strategy that we should pursue* (and while you're at it, write *we should pursue three strategies*).
- Cut *field of* from *field of study* and *try to* from *try to write the best book you can*.
- Write *because* instead of *due to the fact that* and *about* instead of *in relation to*.
- Write *apply* instead of *make an application* and write *repainted* instead of *undertook the repainting*.
- Drop *it is noted that* or *we observed that* or words to that effect from your reports. Once you start using such expressions, it's hard to stop.

You'll be surprised how much waste there is in writing you thought was tight. A thing poetry has taught me. Clear the clutter. Replace the falsely eloquent clangor with some splendid particulars.

E. B. White writes that Professor Strunk so earnestly enforced his own nostrum "omit needless words" that he often finished his lectures early—even having repeated each austerely pruned sentence three times.

Don't worry, though, that this exacting principle might stunt literature as we know it. There will be plenty of books, and many of them will be long. Concision is a discipline, you see, best practiced on one's phrases; it gives rise not to short works but to works in which every word is apt, every phrase tight, and every sentence taut. Economical writing produces reports and novels and essays and memoirs made of deftly chosen and striking words, of dour and heartbreaking phrases, of pithy and elegant sentences, and of wise and shapely paragraphs. How long each of them is depends on one's nature and one's voice and one's purpose and one's audience and one's deadline and one's editor and one's word limit. But every good piece of prose feels about as long as it needs to be. And sometimes just a little shorter.

Be careful, though: one word is not always better than five. *Computerize* is not a shorter way of saying *install the computer systems we need*; nor is *implementation of diversified logistics infrastructure* a shorter way to describe in a full and decent sentence or two (with examples) exactly what that means. Concision is a bastard virtue. Short, in other words, isn't always best; clear, on the other hand, is. Clarity and brevity are nearly always at war. Make sure clarity wins, but do it without wasting a word.

Intelligent readers will go for long and pellucid prose ahead of short and turbid prose just about every time.

Beware useless modifiers like *actually, somewhat, virtually, almost, just,* and *really.* And in the same vein, watch out for *tends to* as in "He tends to write sentences that run on too long." If the truth is "He writes long sentences," write it.

Watch out, too, for *would.* People fall into using it, particularly

---

Some elongating usages to watch out for

the way in which [she spoke]	Try	the way [she spoke]
to the extent that [this matters]	Try	if [this matters]
as a result of the fact that	Try	because
owing to the fact that	Try	because
this is a [matter] that is important	Try	this matters
to make an application	Try	to apply
the refurbishment of the building	Try	to refurbish the building
to effect a tackle	Try	to tackle
it is recommended that training be instigated	Try	[the department] should start training
he acted in an outrageous manner	Try	he acted outrageously
the writing of the book took him ten years	Try	the book took him ten years
in the most efficient manner	Try	efficiently
I am going to go to bed soon	Try	I am going to bed soon
I am going to sit and try to start to write	Try	I'm starting my book *or* I sit to write my book
she was tall in height	Try	she was tall
the question as to whether	Try	whether
at this point in time	Try	now

---

when reflecting on times past, on childhood and lost love. We use it thus to generalize, and that rarely makes compelling reading. Ground your reflections (or whatever they are). Write, "Most mornings we went . . ." and "I remember the time we . . .". Cut out dead *would*.

And instead of vague modifiers like *several* and *many* and *a multitude*, try to state the number.

▶ **Try this**

1 You won't believe me, but this passage is real. In fact, only the names, as they say, have been changed. See if you can think of a style principle it does not breach. In particular, notice how wasteful it is with words, how stiff and passive and excessively formal. Can you recast it so it's shorter and more lively?

> Welcome to the website of the Diagnostic Ultrasound Practice of Drs. Peter Rabbit and Beatrix Potter. We have designed the layout and content of the site in such a manner so as to provide useful information to both referring doctors and patients attending the practice.
>
> Information is included about our newsletter topics.We plan to release a newsletter to referring doctors on a twice yearly basis in which we will attempt to provide information about current topics of interest in obstetric and gynaecological ultrasound. We are also including patient information pages on obstetric ultrasound examinations and also pelvic examinations. We hope that this will help patients to prepare for examinations that they are soon to have referred. We are also providing information regarding prenatal diagnosis and the different types of tests available that are of interest to patients. We are also including a copy of our request form such that details may be entered to assist in booking an examination. We hope that the website provides some useful and interesting information and we plan to update the site on a quarterly basis, hopefully adding some more interesting features.

2 Can you write these sentences more concisely?

> I'm going to ask you to try to start to teach the kids to make an effort to try to finish their food.

> I am delighted to have the honor of being asked to assume responsibility for the oversight of the day-to-day running of this wonderful secondary educational institution.

Conjure an image in your mind of someone caught up in the throes of first falling in love with someone else.

There has been notification from the board of MAG Publications, that there will be a restructure within the company: and therefore our internal resources will now be focusing on the core titles within MAG Publications, not including the gardening directory we first published last year.

In the family in which I grew up, one of the things we were always taught was that there was no material difference of any kind between the disciplines involved in the business of fly fishing and those involved in leading a good Christian life.

Near enough ain't nearly good enough

"What would you call those?"

I meant the long metal troughs drawing water from the stream as it came down from the mountain. Once, these channels had carried off enough water to inundate cane fields. These days they are doing older, slower work, feeding a jerry-rigged irrigation system to sustain a crop of taro.

And then, from somewhere, the word came to me: "Flumes."

"That would do it," said Kim, who was walking with me to the spring. "A word that seems so well made for the thing it describes."

We stopped by the flume and talked about the hard work and the virtue of finding just the right word for what one needs to say. "Mark Twain said something about that once," said Kim. "He said, 'The difference between the almost-right word and the right word is really a large matter—it's the difference between the lightning bug and the lightning.'"

"If Twain had stayed longer in Australia," I said, "he might have said it was the difference between the dunny bat and the dunny."

I had to explain that.*

---

* *Dunny* is a colloquial term for "water closet" or "toilet" in Australia, particularly an outside toilet. A *dunny bat* is a large brown moth often found in such a locale in early summer in subtropical centers such as Brisbane, drawn there at night by the light.

Up to the point where I just can't follow any more, and even slightly beyond, I like listening to people speak unselfconsciously about a thing they love. I mean the way shearers and carpenters, horse-women, chefs, poets, cellists, gardeners, and fitters and turners name the tasks they enact, the moves they make, the tools they wield, the processes they set in motion, the responses (the rising cake, the can-tering horse, the blossoming plant, the humming motor) they engen-der; I like the fitness and particularity of the verbs and nouns they utter when they're not thinking too hard about it.

Whatever you're writing about, use the vernacular that belongs to it. Favor it to all-purpose words like *cuts*, *makes*, *puts*, *takes*, *prepares*, *produce*, *vehicle*. Avoid, too, the generic and anaemic diction of man-agement—unless, perhaps, business is the actual work we are describ-ing. And even then, beware. We owe the language the courtesy of deploying the right words for exactly the right things; we owe a duty to the tasks we describe to get them right and tell them in the lan-guage in which they are, as it were, performed. The same is true for the words we need for places—use the words the locals use for their trees, flatlands and ranges. We owe the places and their people that kind of care.

So listen up. Study the field you're writing about. Teach yourself the words for the tools and tasks; make sure you know their mean-ings. Remember your readers; explain what you think needs explain-ing. But don't explain too much. It's okay to offer readers some words they've never heard before used in the right places to mean what they're meant to mean. Writing can educate in this way, too. Send your readers off to the dictionary now and then. It might remind them to keep one handy.

And clearly I'm not talking about those falsely eloquent generaliza-tions like *utilization*, *beverage*, *competencies*, *methodology*, *configurable item*, *deliverables*, *aquatic leisure centre*, and *modality*. Nor do I have in mind the kind of ultra-multisyllabic words doctors (*coronary infarction*) and engi-neers, for instance, often use. Use those if you must, but define them, preferably first. The kinds of word I mean are the ones I've been trying to use here: words like *flume* and *flange*, *grade* and *class*, *enjamb* and *broil*: humble, fitting, and precise, not oblique or grandiose.

Try this

Write a hundred words about the work you do, or the work someone you love does. Try to use the kind of language I've been talking about here. If it's too hard to do that for your day job, do it for a task or hobby you love.

Let's contract

We contract many words in speech: *don't*, *can't*, *won't*, *didn't*, *hasn't*, *wouldn't*, *what's*, *it's*, *they'd*, *you're*, *they're*, *we'll*, and many more. Australians do it, I notice, more commonly than North Americans. But everyone who speaks English contracts and contracts often.

A contraction, to explain, is two words collapsed into one. The apostrophe indicates that (and roughly where) some letters are missing—letters we mean but don't utter.

We contract in speech to make words fit our mouths; we recalibrate the words to suit our tongues. What we do in speech we ought, on the whole, to do on paper. So, it's perfectly acceptable to contract in writing. It always has been. Shakespeare did it; Jane Austen did it; Abraham Lincoln did it; judges do it; contracts do it; let's all do it.

If you spell out all your contractions you sound stuffy. Bossy. Awkward. And it's not likely to help.

The more formal a document, though—a piece of legislation being more formal than a board paper, which is more formal than a marketing brochure, which is more formal than an email about a date—the fewer the contractions you'll use. But even the most formal documents will, quite aptly, contain *can't* and *won't* and *isn't*.

So don't feel obliged to spell those words out. Save yourself some syllables; relax your tone; contract.

Try this

1 What is the contracted form of each of these phrases?

I am; it is; she is; you are; they will; there is; shall not; will not;

do not; cannot; should not; ought not; what has; we would; let us.

2 Use each of those contractions in a sentence.

The three *theres*

They're *They are*
Their   Possessive form of they: *This is their land.*
There   A noun (*We live there*), pronoun (*There is a house at the top of the hill*), adjective (*That book there, So there, There you are*), adverb (*Let's not go there*), and other things

The two *yours*

Your   Possessive of *you: Have you finished writing your memoir?*
You're   Contraction of *you are: You can look as long as you like, but sooner or later you're going to have to leap.*

The two *itss*

Its   Possessive of *it: The dog chases its tail.*
It's   Contraction of *it is: It's a shame you have to go.*

But let's not abbreviate

When writing words, just write words. When writing text, write the text and nothing but the text. Abbreviations (such as *e.g.*, *i.e.*, *NB*, *p.a.*, *K*, *kW*, *mph* and *mg*) don't belong in finished documents. Write down the words you want your readers to hear; it's one of the courtesies.

Spell out an abbreviation or leave it out. Never write *etc.*; complete your list or say that your list includes these things, or, at worst, write *et cetera*. Write *for example* for *e.g.*; write *that is* or insert a dash for *i.e.*; write *each year* or *a year* for *p.a.*; write *thousand* for *K*; write *kilowatts* for *kW*; write *miles per hour* or *miles an hour* for *mph*; write *milligrams* for *mg*. It really doesn't take much longer. Is your time so precious and your regard for your readers so slight you couldn't spend a few moments writing whole words? Save time elsewhere: for instance, say only what you mean, and choose short words over long ones.

It also follows that you ought to avoid symbols like numerals and % and @ and #. They aren't words either. Just write words and punctuation marks. That's it.

Exceptions? Dollar signs, because, hey, money does talk and because it gets dull writing *one hundred and sixty-seven million dollars*. And numerals, as long as you spell out small numbers (usually those below 10 or 100) and whenever they open a sentence (not a great place for a number, anyway). Between one and ten million (and billion), this rule kicks in again—if you can round your number out. So *$1,500* and *$9,999* and *17,567* are all fine (in non-technical writing you need the comma when the number has four or more digits); but then make it *seven million, two billion*, and so on.

Any more exceptions? Whenever you have to name something often, and its name is made of many words, you're allowed to abbreviate. But spell out the full name first; then put the abbreviation in parentheses beside the full name and move on. (So, *General Motors Corporation (GMC)*.) Spell it out again in each new chapter. You might use the odd acronym for organizations you'll be referring to a lot: *DoCS* for the Department of Community Services, *CASA* for the Civil Aviation Safety Authority, *ASLE* for the Association for the Study of Literature and Environment. In cases where an acronym has become an organization's name, you must, of course, write it that way: *AMP*, *GE*, *NBC*, *CSR*. And you can get away with abbreviating (by acronym or otherwise) longwinded names of processes, legislation and so on—I've abbreviated *The Adventures of Huckleberry Finn* to *Huck Finn* in this book, for instance. You could name the piece of legislation *the Act*, or the State Department *the department* or *State*.

Apart from that, don't abbreviate. Ever. Except perhaps on the label of a medicine bottle—but even there, if you have room, spell it out.

And write *percent*. That's what one says.

Avoid strings of nouns

Functional writing has issues with verbs. We spoke of this in Chapter 2. Government, academic, technical, scientific, financial, and business writing focuses on processes; it abstracts then it nominalizes things that people do; and then it leaves the people out. This results, among other things, in noun clusters. Watch for them—they are horrible to behold and hard to unravel. Spell them out where you can; you'll need to add some verbs and articles and prepositions. Translate noun clusters first, if you can't avoid them.

An example or two: *network constraint issues*; *estimated future after-tax cash flows*; *home loan interest declaration*; *committee action effectiveness*. Every word (except for the past participle *estimated* and *after* in the compound adjective *after-tax*) is a noun.

Sometimes noun clusters pop up in the most ordinary circumstances; often, for example, in signage or headings, where a writer is trying to be clipped. This one was on the wall of a room I where I was teaching recently: *end of year function lottery ticket sales*.

Bottom line: noun clusters make bad reading. Use them sparingly, if you must use them at all. They are one of the ways the anxious or pompous parade their expertise.

Consider the ambiguities within

- [he is an] English history teacher
- Little Penguin Safety Steering Committee
- oyster cellular heavy metal distribution
- enterprise resource planning system implementation
- demand management investigation methodology

▶ **Try this**

Write down some noun clusters you see around you at work. (Often they are terms that get turned into acronyms.) Spell them out and translate them into clauses that would make sense of them to a child or an outsider.

CHAPTER 4

POETICS

On creative writing

All my writing is plagiarized, but not from books.
KIM STAFFORD

Creative writing is communication through revelation—it is the Self escaping into the open. E. B. WHITE

Warning

This chapter's about writing as an end, not a means; it's about writing when the point is not really the point. It's about writing as art, not craft. It's for the writer as artist.

If that's not you, you might want to turn to the next chapter. I say some things here that might shock. Some, even, that pretty much contradict things I've said so far.

Writing as an art, like all arts, puts familiar materials to strange uses. It breaks rules (though not all of them, not if it's any good). In particular, it should not try to make itself perfectly plain; it should come at things from an angle; it should leave a lot of things unsaid and unseen. In common with functional writing, however, creative writing must observe the disciplines of syntax and style. It must have voice and rhythm. Music, now, is even more the point. In a word, like all writing, creative writing needs technique. A fancy story, a hip subject, a fashionable attitude, some crazy characters, sex, and a sting in the tail won't be enough.

This is a chapter for essayists, memoirists, novelists, short-story writers, and poets. It won't cover everything, but it shares some thoughts that have saved my writing life. "Give thy heart to letters," wrote an Egyptian father to his son on papyrus 3,000 years ago. If that's you, this chapter's yours. (So are all the others.)

Reasons for writing about nothing at all

Write—about the wind tonight, your bright and terrified child, the intelligence of the darkness, the opacity of grief, the shape of her breast—because these are small, good things and they need to be witnessed. Write them because writing them reminds you—and whoever may listen—why we live at all. Write because it's a practice the world wants and civility depends upon. Write to stay in the habit of telling the truth. We may need people who are good at that; it seems to be going out of style.

Write because it seems like a better thing to do, in every possible way, than blowing yourself or someone else up, than rioting on a beach, than dropping democracy on a Middle Eastern country from a B-52, or telling a bunch of lies and calling it politics or business. Write because, who knows, you may hear and speak a phrase that just may save a life or change a mind or start a worthwhile rumor.

Write well and write often because it's a way of playing the instrument you've been given—that voice of yours. Of keeping it alive and humming.

Write most quietly when the politics are shrill. That's when quietness and calm and inconsequential beauty are most exquisitely needed. Give them to whoever may be listening. Give them back to the world, which gave them to you.

Write because writing is a proof of civilization. Someone had better do it. And it might as well be you.

▶ **Try this**

1 Write for ten minutes, starting like this: "The work I want to write . . ."

2 "Small, good things" is a phrase from a Raymond Carver story. Write about a small, good thing a violent, hasty world needs—that you need, anyway.

3 Think of something huge and troubling in the world, like the culture of death that's taken hold in some parts and the culture of fear in others; then think of some inconsequential thing that

pleases or saddens you close to home (my old watch was such a thing for me). Now try to write about the small thing with the large and hopeless thing in mind. Allow the thing you can hardly bear to think about to focus your mind on why the small thing matters (at least to you).

Write the near at hand with the hopeless and distant, the intractable, in your mind. Three hundred words.

What's writing for?

What makes writing worth writing—and reading—is what the story or the poem achieves beyond the tale it tells: its music, its form, its wisdom, the way it makes the ordinary world beautifully strange. A good tale is only good, in other words, if the telling is sound and memorable. It's the voice and mood, the arc and flow, the poetry of the writing that endure when the storyline fades.

Literature doesn't aim to *tell* anybody anything. To tell a story or make a poem that makes sense, you're going to have to convey some information. But that's not what the piece of work is for. Creative writing makes art out of the stuff of life—of human lives, of places, of the work we do, and the words we speak. It's for whatever art is for.

How a piece of writing becomes a work of art—a plain but unforgettable thing—has everything to do with the integrity and humanity of its voice and the elegance of the work's composition.

Barry Lopez has written that the storyteller is the one who creates the space within which wisdom may arise. The writer, I think, creates an imaginary space—the shape of the story she tells and the form of the remembered life or locale or moment—and invites a reader into it. There—in a space the reader participates in shaping, since she makes it in her mind out of the words the writer uses—the reader will find not just a plot or a bunch of information and images; she will, if she's lucky and the telling is good and beautiful and true, discover something, more shapely but less exact than a thesis, about the nature of grief or love or time or land or desire or memory or childhood or death, something she seems to recall once knowing.

And why do we read? To know we are not alone, C. S. Lewis thought.

We read to join our lives, our joys and troubles, our questions and answers with those of other people. We read to link our stories with others'—to remember, in fact, that our life, like all lives, has a story, which we may find repeated or obliquely mirrored in this book or that. I am at once most utterly myself and not myself, wrote Lewis, when I read. We read to grow and deepen and console ourselves. We read to contain multitudes. We read to find out how others live, and how we live ourselves. We read to find out how we might hope and forgive and act. We read to make meaning of our lives and days, and of heaven and earth. To find out about sex and grief and landscapes and gods. We read to break our hearts and to heal again and again.

"Why are we reading," Annie Dillard wrote in *The Writing Life*, "if not in hope of beauty laid bare, life heightened and its deepest mystery probed?"

Well, some readers don't think they're after so much. But that doesn't mean we shouldn't give it to them anyway.

So, if these are the reasons people read, a writer ought to know it. Very likely what we must write is what broke our heart or woke us up or unmade us or distracted us or taught us wisdom or transported us or mystified us. And we need to write it so that what moved us moves a reader in a similar way. *How* we write, even more than *what*, is why and how the reader will be stirred.

 Try this

1 Why do you read? Explore that for ten minutes, without pausing. See what you discover.
2 Why do you write? Explore that for ten minutes.

From a deep place

Writing comes from way down deep—I don't mean the ideas, which come from everywhere; I mean the sentences themselves, the way things want to sound. You write best when you are most utterly yourself. You bring, somehow, everything you are to the page. The voice of the writers work expresses the whole man or woman—their undivided, unregenerate, original and naked self.

If you want to write, be prepared to hurt, wrote Natalie Goldberg. You can't write well unless you're ready to write out of that wounded, imperfect, brave and fearful, eternal soul that you are deep down. And sometimes that's going to hurt. Everything you are, everywhere you've been, and every significant other you've been there with: it is out of the true story of yourself that you must write. Whatever you write *about*.

Poetry, said Wordsworth, is emotion recalled in tranquillity. You need, first, to have been possessed; then you need to take quiet imaginative possession of what possessed you, so that it lives again in your calm words.

Rilke put it this way to the young poet:

Then try, like some first human being, to say what you see and experience and love and lose; describe your sorrows and desires, passing thoughts and the belief in some sort of beauty—describe all these with loving, quiet, humble sincerity, and use, to express yourself, the things in your environment, the images from your dreams, and the objects of your memory . . . Seek the depth of things.

(RAINER MARIA RILKE, *Letters to a Young Poet*)

 ## Try this

1 Recall a moment of high passion from your life—a birth, a death, an awakening, a loss, a love found or a heart broken. Whatever. See if you can write it in tranquillity. Out of everyone you are. Three hundred words.

2 List some things you'd rather do than write. Why aren't you doing them now?

Write to say something beyond what you say

You need to know what you think you're trying to say, of course, and you need to mean it. But the creative writer is writing the poem beyond the poem, the story beyond the story, the line inside the line.

Good writing is a falling short of the real nature of the moment it sees over its shoulder, or the grief or the doubt or the joy or the disappointment or the course of the river it wants to sing. If there's anything good about it, it's the dignity and humility and grace of that reaching and falling—its own recognition that its prey has eluded it.

I like writing that tells me more than it tells me. Writing that thrums with much more than what it merely means. But one must not (at least not overtly) strain for significance or effect. Rather, let your writing stumble upon mysteries it can barely find words for. Let it abide with the particular things—with the proverbial blade of grass, for instance, in which eternity is lodged. Here's an example:

When the others went swimming my son said he was going in too. He pulled his dripping trunks from the line where they had hung all through the shower, and wrung them out. Languidly, and with no thought of going in, I watched him, his hard little body, skinny and bare, saw him wince slightly as he pulled up around his vitals the small, soggy, icy garment. As he buckled the swollen belt, suddenly my groin felt the chill of death.

(E. B. WHITE, "Once More to the Lake," *One Man's Meat*)

▶ Try this

In this passage White has returned, with his young son, to a lake White knew as a boy. The writer's father took him there once when White was about the age his own son is now. In this essay, White explores the way he feels, at the lake, like many people at once: himself (the father of this child); the boy White once was here; the father whose age White has now reached; and this boy, White's own son. The place plays tricks on time; tenses congeal; memory and perception intergrade.

Has something like that happened to you? Have you ever, like me, found yourself reading to a son or daughter a book you once read at about their age? And have you then felt that you were three people at once—yourself now; the child you were then; the child you're reading to now? If you have, write that. If not, just write about a place you used to go as a child.

Without trying to write any kind of allegory, write the aspect of the place itself or your memory of it that is most deeply personal, but not merely private. That is the realm from which writing comes that speaks to—and for—everyone. Out of singular human experience, the only kind any of us can really know, personally narrated.

Poetics and politics

Writers trouble themselves, rightly, about the usefulness of writing in troubled times—and times are always troubled. Sometimes in some places, just staying out of trouble and keeping food on the table while leading a moral life of some kind is as much as a man or woman can manage. Other times, one lives in comfort and sees others swamped by the ocean or buried by the movements of the earth, or poisoned by angry extremism or patronized and diminished by the cynicism of the rich world's response. One sees a whole planet corroding. One sees civil liberties eroding, fear and terror made gods of.

Does anything I write, you ask yourself at your laptop, make a blind bit of difference—to the state of the world's happiness, to global warming, to levels of poverty, to wildness and the preservation of the earth, to sanity, to immigration policy, and to the water crisis? If not, what use is it? If not, how could my writing engage politics? Or should it not? These are the questions serious writers ask themselves, and should, and often.

I said this once at a conference, and I still believe it: the most profoundly political act a poem—and by extension any work of literature—can perform is to refuse the language and strategies of politics. Write to protest, by all means. Condemn evil wherever you find it. Show the world the world you think it needs to be. But watch your language. Offer the world a language in which what needs to be known can be; model the kind of talking upon which change and true democracy depend.

Do the kind of politics that poetry performs. Make a work of literature the best work of literature it can be. Then go out and paint and chant slogans, march on Washington, lie down in front of the bulldozers or the tanks.

Try this

Write a poem or a short piece of prose about something that you care deeply about. See if you can write it calmly and poetically without for a moment forgetting how important this issue is and how much you want to change the world to see it your way.

The art of lunch

What I was trying to say to Frank Stewart in a café in Honolulu was this: to be a writer is to transcend the here and now, your self and family, your tribe and nation, your gender and your creed. Not to shed those clothes but to be more than they would, on their own, allow you to be. To write is to practice the large and long perspective, while noticing and speaking of the "slender particulars," to reuse James Agee's lovely phrase, of where you are.

And what Frank Stewart was saying through his gray moustache and in his quiet river-gravel Nebraskan drawl was this: to write is to practice thinking new thoughts you didn't anticipate thinking and it is to take your reader with you into that thinking, and in this way to encourage in oneself and others the capacity to go beyond fixed ideas.

We were talking ahead of a conversation we were about to have on stage in two days' time, part of a small festival of Pacific writing. We were talking to find out who we were, what we thought, and who the other was. We were having just the kind of conversation writing invites and perpetuates.

Each of us had had just one glass of red wine. That'll be about the right amount for such a conversation. Any more and conversation turns into the long lunch. And we know where that leads.

Try this

Pour a glass of red wine. Or white. Take a worry or an idea or a problem or a phrase that's in your head; write for ten minutes about it, trying to think exactly and freshly about it, as Frank Stewart was suggesting, and from the kind of standpoint I was talking about. Let your writing lead you.

In case you can't think of anything, try one of these:

- What is terrorism and how can one wage war upon it?
- Why I live where I live.
- People who don't seem to understand that you're only meant to drive in the fast lane if you're overtaking someone.
- One thing I could do better as a parent or a spouse or a child.
- If not now, then when; if not you, then who?

The Yelp

In his introduction to the Modern Library edition of *The Adventures of Huckleberry Finn*, George Saunders writes:

Art, at its best, is a kind of uncontrolled yet disciplined Yelp, made by one of us who, because of the brain he was born with and the experiences he has had and the training he has received, is able to emit a Yelp that contains all of the joys, miseries, and contradictions of life as it is actually lived. That Yelp, which is not a logical sound, does good for all of us.

Writing as art doesn't work on us as argument. It works as half-wild (but only half) speaking. It speaks for—and to—all of us because it speaks authentically from deep inside one of us.

 Try this

1 Make a list of books that yelp for you.
2 Write for ten minutes on this: "When I was younger I used to believe . . ."

Write what you don't know

Everyone is writing a kind of memoir. Directly or indirectly, everyone is writing out of what they know and who they are.

You write a memoir—*as* memoir or in any of these indirect modes (the short story, the novel, the poem, the essay)—not to parade your wonderful life. You write your life because it is the life you know best; it is the way and the place you look life's mysteries in the eye. From where else am I going to draw the material for anything I write if not from what I have dreamed and what I have read and what I have lost and what I have thought and what I have suffered and what I have been curious about and what I have tried all my life to fathom or avoid? One writes out of what one has been given.

It won't always be your own life you tell; often it will be other lives that have come your way, unmade and remade you.

What makes a writer is not an extraordinary life—that can make the writing harder. ("The writer should never write about the extraordinary," wrote James Joyce. "That is for the journalist.") The writer isn't the person who has the adventures or the horrible childhood or the drug addiction or the direct line to God. Some of that may help, but it's not compulsory. The writer is the scribe for those who live miraculous, ordinary lives—including, especially, himself. At the keyboard, you're the witness not the hero.

Some experience of life will help, of course. But some writers write perfectly well out of lives in which hardly anything happens. Wallace Stegner comments that Henry James led a life that stumbled from one inexperience to another. To be a writer, it doesn't matter what you've had to endure; what counts is how good you get at finding the poem in whatever goes on around you. The writer is the person, Stegner concludes, on whom nothing is lost.

But don't just write what you know. Write, specifically—as James Galvin has put it—what you *don't* know about what you do. Notice what disturbs and intrigues, haunts and beguiles you in whatever it is you have been given. Write whatever won't leave you alone. Enter its inner life. Don't deconstruct it, though. Just wander there. Write from inside that mystery.

 ## Try this

1 Write about something you don't know about something you do.
2 "That was when I woke up." Write three hundred words with this beginning.

3 "It is those we live with and love and should know who elude us," says Norman's father in *A River Runs Through It*. This seems true to me. Who, then, has eluded you? Write on that for ten minutes. Write a book about it! It would be a good subject.

Writing and wonder

In a class once, I found myself saying that to be a writer is not to know anything—except, of course, the odd thing about syntax and rhythm and voice. A writer is not an expert; to write is to practice wonder. Wonder, properly done, is an exacting discipline. It requires you to pay fierce attention for a long time and then to speak forth, forming up your questions into characters and your gleanings into stories and lines of verse. Re-enacting wonder, thus.

You'd better get reasonably knowledgeable, of course, about anything you want to turn your pen to; you'd better know your subject. But not to declaim upon it. It's not your expertise that counts; it's the quality of your wondering. You write as the guy or the girl who overhears the world where you are—I mean not just the physical world, but also what comes to you in thought and dream there—and you take it down and sometimes, when some of it means something, even if you're not quite sure what that is, you write about it.

 ### Try this

1 What do you wonder at? Write two hundred words about that.
2 What are you expert in? Write two hundred words about that.
3 Think of something you overheard this week that got you going —angered or saddened or gladdened or mystified you. Write something about that.

Finding your form

Writing is a marriage—not always happy—of grace and discipline. Some of the discipline is being in the world with your eyes and ears and notebook open. Some of it is turning your wondering into a piece of work and getting it done. Grace is what comes to you in your life to write about; and it is the language that comes along, the knowledge of how you must proceed, once you have given yourself to the drudge of grinding out sentences.

No one is smart enough to write a poem on their own. This, also, James Galvin said once. But the language is smart enough. One finds the poem one is not smart enough to write by finding the work—this small book of biography, this fragmentary memoir, this cycle of poems, this haiku, this novel of one's parents' love story, this detective fiction—that fits and serves the thing one feels moved to write. Once you have a job of work to spend your energy and hours on; once you have a book that needs some sentences to fill it out, then you have, as Jim put it, a plug to put into the wall where the language keeps its secrets.

You need a frame to get a painting started. You need to know where the edges are and how much space you've got to fill. To begin a book you need at least a subject. You need to work out what it isn't about as well as what it is. But you need to know more than that. You need an idea of its form.

To get this book done I needed to know what I thought I had to say; I had to know roughly how many words I had to say it in; and then how many rooms this house I was trying to build would have—how many chapters, that is, and what I thought each one was about. It didn't go according to the plan. It never does. But I had to know what I thought I was setting about; I had to have a task I could know well enough to think it might be just beyond me. Then I could sit and do it, and let the language visit me, already hard at work on just this book.

"I have not written a novel for seven years," wrote George Orwell in "Why I Write," "but I hope to write another fairly soon. It is bound to be a failure, every book is a failure, but I know with some clarity what kind of book I want to write."

At what kind of work, specifically, will the language find you? Are you writing a book (long or short?), an article, a short story or an essay? Are you writing a memoir, a fiction, an essay, a textbook, a guide, a prose poem, a collection of poems, a letter or a report? Are you writing a lyric or a narrative? And how will you structure your material—how will you arrange things; what is the frame upon which the whole work will stretch itself? How will you break up the narrative; when will you crowd, as Ursula Le Guin puts it, and when will you leap? How will you deal with the passage of time? How many chapters or parts will you have? Will you break up your material into small fragments or long, continuous chapters? Whose voice or voices will speak the work? And how will you begin?

▶ Try this

1 What kind of book or work do you want to write? Write some notes and then write three hundred words describing what it is, what genre, what kind of structure you think it may have, who's in it, who speaks it—all those questions I was just asking here.

2 Take a look through the books you admire. Look at their contents pages, if they have them. Look through them and notice how each one is composed. How does each one deal with the structural questions I mentioned just now? James Galvin's book *The Meadow*, for instance, falls into two parts. And each is made up of fragments of differing lengths, many of them as short as a paragraph. They chop from one time, one person, one place to another. How are your favorite books structured? Why have their authors gone for those structures? What are the advantages and disadvantages of each?

In the light of the variety of structures you observe among your favorite books, think about how you might organize your book or whatever it is.

A very good place to start

So how *will* you begin?

Often the words at the start get written at the end; sometimes it's only then that you know what it is you've written, and when you're ready to lead your reader into it. "The last thing one discovers in composing a work," wrote Blaise Pascal way back in 1670, "is what to put first."

So much turns on how your book or poem starts. Among other things, it's where you win or lose your reader. But because so much turns on it, you don't want to rush it, which is why you might put it off, at least in its final form, till last.

But there is some virtue in writing your beginning first. Gabriel García Márquez thinks so:

> One of the most difficult things is the first paragraph. I have spent many months on a first paragraph and once I get it, the rest comes out very easily. In the first paragraph you solve most of the problems with your book. The theme is defined, the style, the tone.
>
> (GABRIEL GARCÍA MÁRQUEZ, in George Plimpton (ed.),
> *The Writer's Chapbook*)

Most of a book's personality gets set up in its opening words. It's where the thing finds its voice—and makes up its mind (what it is). Or where, if it doesn't come off, it does not. Don't wait too long to give your work its voice or you may find it has none at all; if you wait until the end, you may find that what you graft onto the front doesn't agree with what follows. There are writers like me who cannot get going at all until they have an opening line. I have written books the other way around; this one got underway when I found my opening line.

David Malouf says he found a way to write his first novel *Johnno*, which he had carried around for a good while in his head, when an opening sentence occurred to him, spoken, as it were, in the same "open, undefended tone of poems I had written nearly a decade before," a plain statement of fact: "My father was one of the fittest men I have ever known." The tone gave him the first paragraph in the course of a morning, and the rest of the book in the weeks that followed. Find your beginning, specifically find your tone, and you will have found your book.

Listen to these great beginnings:

In a hole in the ground there lived a hobbit.

Call me Ishmael.

You won't know about me, without you have read a book by the name of "The Adventures of Tom Sawyer", but that ain't no matter.

"You too will marry a boy I choose."

I sing of arms and a man.

The real world goes like this.

In my younger and more vulnerable years my father gave me some advice that I've been turning over in my mind ever since.

He rode into our valley in the summer of '89.

The bride was a plain woman in a big hat.

But, you may say, we asked you to speak about women and fiction.

A story has no beginning or end.

He was an old man who fished alone in a skiff in the Gulf Stream and he had gone eighty-four days now without taking a fish.

She stands up in the garden where she has been working and looks up into the distance.

Mum says, "Don't come creeping into our room at night."

I had a farm in Africa at the foot of the Ngong Hills.

Mrs Dalloway said she would buy the flowers herself.

All happy families are alike but an unhappy family is unhappy after its own fashion.

It was the best of times, it was the worst of times.

Marley was dead: to begin with.

Some of these offer a striking image, some an image perfectly mundane (the woman in the garden, the woman heading out for flowers, the hole in the ground), perfectly turned; others are philosophical propositions; one is a landscape; each is personal (either in its voice or in its presentation of someone in particular—sometimes the writer, sometimes an old man, sometimes a hobbit, sometimes a bride, sometimes a dead man). Each is—and this is the point—a spoken thing, an utterance both natural and artful. Each, in its own way, ambushes you. It speaks; and what it says is *read me*.

Do what works for you; find your beginning, or let it find you when it's ready. But never stop listening for it. In it, you'll hear your book telling itself to you.

If no beginning comes, don't agonize. It will come later. It had better. Start on a section you feel ready to write. Keep working and keep listening out.

How will you begin?

 Try this

1 How many of those beginnings did you know? Which ones did you like? What are your favorite beginnings? Did the book live up to what that beginning promised?

2 Good beginnings are arresting or at least engaging in some way. They may be long, or they may be short. They may be concrete, or they may be abstract. They need to speak; and the best ones drop you straight into the midst of the story or the poem.

Think of an essay or poem or story you want to write. Think of some ways you might start it. Try them out. Write an opening paragraph three different ways and ask yourself, or someone else, which works best. You'll know best whether it really says (and in the right tone) what you mean to go on saying.

If you have a beginning, try two alternatives.

Listen like a thief

Writing, if I may paraphrase Kim Stafford, is faith in fragments. One can talk all one likes about the need to have a project, but sometimes one just doesn't. When that is so—and it mostly is—how do you sustain a writing life—and more to the point, a writing practice? Either you're writing or you're not; and it follows from what I've been saying about writing as work that one needs to keep at it, even when there seems so little to keep at and so little time to do it.

Kim's book, *The Muses Among Us*, proposes a kind of discipline for keeping on writing, part of which I have seen Kim perform. Keep a notebook handy, he says. And pull it out and write in it whatever catches most attention. Usually, with Kim, it's a snatch of conversation he overhears, or a thought he has when he's meant to be listening to something else. And then, each night, he says, or as often as you can, look back over your notes and find something that speaks to you. Sit and write whatever comes to mind about that. Begin, in this way, what may become, or may not, a poem or a lyric essay or a paragraph in a book. He elaborates a system that is practical and detailed beyond that, which goes something like this: write a postcard out of that idea; expand it into a letter; if you still like it, gather other ideas and bring them to the tale; find a title; write a draft; hear your key; redraft in that key; send the thing out to some people you can trust; rework it until you start to ruin it; send it out for publication and don't take no for an answer.

But get his book and hear it in his voice; read how he fleshes that out into a writing system. I have seen this man twice, now, compose a poem in short order out of the scrawl he entered into a handmade pocket book. I have heard him at more than one forum read poems that braided lines we had shared with each other and others had shared with us the past few days. Good poems, too, that he read to audiences who had not been there when these things were said, so that I know his poems worked as art.

The point is, *listen like a thief*; keep a journal and enter into it what you steal from the world; read it over now and then, maybe every night; see what it makes of you; see what you can make of it. Write the phrases that come to you from others or from wherever they come. Writing is an auditory art; a lot of one's inspirations will take the shape of phrases. Write them down and follow where they lead.

I have written, twelve months later in Darwin, poems from phrases that came to me from a river in Brisbane at Christmas; I have written, in my State library, poems whose skeletons walked into my notepad in Wyoming; I have written, in a cupboard in New York that was pretending to be a hotel room, stories from a scene I overheard on horseback in Idaho and scribbled on the back of a receipt driving home.

Be awake to the world. Take note of what it says. Take note so that a phrase or an idea will take note of you, and will stay. And work on you until it becomes your work.

Have, if you can, a big book to write. If you do, don't sit down each night or morning to write the whole book; sit down to write a fragment. Let it accumulate in splinters. But try not to stop making them daily.

If you don't have a big work, still don't stop. Make fragments your work. Keep writing them. Before long you'll have something that may resemble a book.

▶ **Try this**

1 In your notebook or journal, listen to people in meetings, in the train, on the television, at your breakfast table. Write down what they say. Take one of those phrases one night and spend twenty minutes writing a piece inspired by it.

2 Keep a journal. Don't worry too much what you have to write there, but write something every day. Keeping a journal gets you into the habit of writing. It makes it ordinary and everyday. You may find you become more fluent. You may find that keeping a journal also helps you observe things worth writing about.

3 Treat every email or letter as a writing exercise. Take every such chance to take a little more care over word choice and sentence structure than you might have in the past. Never miss an opportunity.

The art of interruption

Guard your solitude; you'll need it to keep piling up those fragments. Take yourself away somewhere quiet, if you can, when you have a book to finish. But let yourself be interrupted at your work. Sometimes. Mostly when you least want to be. In my experience, that's when the child walks in with the poem; that's when you were ruining your work and needed a break but didn't know you were or did; that's when the man comes to the door with your new boots with a story standing up in them already.

Hermes (messenger of the gods)—like all Greek gods, only more so —was perverse. Perhaps he still is. Expect him to deliver godly messages and shapely lines disguised as unwanted phonecalls and overdue bills. Don't carry on too much and rail against these things. Notice them and wonder. And write them down somewhere, and get back to work on the sentence in front of you.

Do you know that just as I wrote "was perverse" five minutes ago, my laptop delivered me a message that read "Word has encountered a problem and had to shut down. You may have lost some of your work." That Hermes, I tell you what! When I started my laptop again, all I'd lost was that one Hermetic sentence.

"You're writing about the process of composing, aren't you?" she asked. She was the photographer, the artist in residence, who had come up to introduce herself last night and who tonight was cooking me dinner in Kate House, by the river. "Are you writing anything about interruption?" she went on. "I know I just barged in on you up there, but you need to be interrupted sometimes so the work can catch its breath and decide if this is what it wants to be."

She's right. And the soup she made was the best food I'd eaten in two weeks.

 Try this

1 Have you ever found what you needed to say, or had some revelation about your work, because of an interruption? Write about it.

2 "There I was sitting there trying to work when . . ." Write for fifteen minutes from that beginning.

Strange is good

There's something strange about good writing. No one, you think at first, ever spoke like this. But soon, in what is odd, you recognize the sound of authenticity; soon you hear the sound of someone being who they are, of someone working hard to say exactly what it is they hear and what it is they think. What may strike you is the sound of someone doing more than merely muttering what first comes to mind. What sounds strange is what is true. In the work; in the mind and heart of its maker. Strangeness is a voice at its vernacular, wondering work.

Think Virginia Woolf, Ernest Hemingway, Annie Dillard, Cormac McCarthy, David Malouf, Peter Carey, Tim Winton, Karen Blixen, Antoine de Saint-Exupéry, Shirley Hazzard, Joan Didion, Barry Lopez, James Agee, Raymond Chandler, Toni Morrison, Brian Doyle, Mary Oliver, Joseph Conrad, Herman Melville, Saul Bellow, William

Faulkner . . . to make a random list. You'll find the strangeness in the syntax and the word choice, the verbs especially, and the rhythm that ensues. You'll find it in the tropes and metaphors. The turns of phrase. The prose is accomplished, but it is not quite orthodox. It refuses easy, conventional solutions:

Hell is like this. It's this cowering in the bottom of the cellar far from the smouldering trapdoor, between pumpkins and tubs of apples. It's the smell of a karri forest rising into the sky and the bodies of roos and possums returning to the earth as carbon and the cooking smell falling through the dimness like this. Trees go off like bombs out in the light . . .
    (TIM WINTON, *Cloudstreet*)

Nevertheless, life is pleasant, life is tolerable. Tuesday follows Monday, then comes Wednesday. The mind grows rings; the identity becomes robust; pain is absorbed in growth. Opening and shutting, shutting and opening, with an increasing hum and sturdiness, the haste and fever of youth are drawn into service until the whole being seems to expand in and out like the mainspring of a clock. How fast the stream flows from January to December! We are swept on by the torrent of things grown so familiar that they cast no shadow. We float, we float . . . (VIRGINIA WOOLF, *The Waves*)

This quality, the cadence of personality, flows from the deep instinct to say the thing freshly, to resist every cliché. It is the daemon of the artist that you hear; and you hear it not because she tries hard to let you, but because she knows no other way to write than to stand outside every norm and write every phrase as she has never heard it put before.

> But don't strain for strangeness. Don't copy it from someone else. Yours will be there in your own voice when you find your subject and get down to the hard work of uttering it fresh. Strangeness is personality laid unself consciously bare in words.

And if your writing sounds not quite like anything you've ever heard before, it could be a very good sign. (Or not, depending.) It will put you in some fine and strange company.

Try this

1 Who are your favorite "strange" writers? What's strange about them? What have they taught you?
2 Write two paragraphs about your father; write like you've never written before; write like you've never heard writing go before.
3 "Hell is like this." Begin like that. Write three hundred words or so.

Someone and somewhere

Writing must sound like it comes from some*one* and from some*where*.

A reader, like a listener in conversation, needs to hear a distinctive voice, or she will lose interest fast. The voice belongs to the work, really; it won't necessarily be how the author speaks in person or writes in other books. One listens to a book or poem, far more than one thinks. Reading doesn't merely happen with the eyes. If you can't hear a voice in a piece of writing, you'll put the thing down.

But a work also needs to sound like it's being uttered some*where* — like a conversation, again. Ethereal, ungrounded, dislocated writing does not engage us; it cannot. The location of a work may be the space we imagine the authorial voice speaking from (a desk or a hillside or a bath); or it may be the locale of the story, which may be quite a different place. It is as though a sentence, and indeed a whole work, needs to be native not just to its speaker but to the ground it speaks from (the ground, perhaps, of the author's being).

Every good work tells a place as much as it tells a person as much as it tells a story. *Out of Africa* is redolent of Africa as much as it is of Karen Blixen and Denys Finch-Hatton. *The Lord of the Rings* tells Middle-earth; E. B. White's essays and stories sound like New York and Maine; Tim Winton's *Cloudstreet* is something Fremantle has to say; Lawrence Durrell's *Alexandria Quartet* is the soul of Alexandria transcribed; *Anna Karenina* is Russia; *Johnno* is Brisbane; *A River Runs Through It* is Missoula, Montana; *Mrs Dalloway* is London.

To read is to go somewhere with someone (the narrator). Reading, among other things, is a field trip; a text is a geography.

So, how do you steep a work in a place? Steep yourself in that place, imagined or real; speak every phrase as though you were that place speaking. Recall the place in every phrase you make; hope that the place lives in every word, that the music of each sentence is the music of the place. Don't just write *about* a place; write *from within* it.

Try these devices:

- Speak your work (or some of its dialogue) in the vernacular of the people of the place. *Huck Finn* is the most profound and sustained instance of this.
- Conceive of the place as the real tale you're telling.
- Cast your place as a leading character in the drama.
- Learn the ecology and society, the culture and politics, the botany and meteorology of the place.
- Name some indigenous trees, some local hills, some rivers, some local winds, some festivals and foods.
- Observe the light, and put it in the book.
- Describe the scenery from time to time (more often than may seem, at first, natural or necessary).
- If it's night time, note what stage the moon's at in its cycle.
- Remember the weather and the lie of the land.
- Tell your readers, if this is an essay, where it is you're writing from, just as you might in a letter—what's the room like, which way does the window face and so on.

▶ **Try this**

1 Go for a walk (even if it's just around your room or house). Sit down and write a narrative of where you went and what occurred. See if you can imagine making your piece not only descriptive of that place, but like that place, in its structure and diction—in its music and feel.

2 "That's where I felt at home." Write three paragraphs on that theme.

3 "I came around the corner. The landscape opened up, and I thought, This is where I have always belonged." Write about such a place, if you have ever had that experience.

Figurative language

You don't need me to tell you—do you?—that if you're doing creative writing you're going to need some tropes.

You're going to need to write, in other words, more than merely literally. You're going to need to make your writing sing and your subject matter dance. You're going to need a lot of things, but above all you're going to need metaphors.

Don't hunt them; let them find you. What you're trying to do is to animate your prose or poetry with images from the real world—with color and sound, light and form, figure and emotion, act and deed and word. Don't try to trick things up, just because it's literature you're writing. Work hardest at getting down what your subject's really like; what really happened when. That's where you'll find the texture and mystery you need.

Paradoxically, though, if you want to write how something really is, you'll have to write it, sometimes, as it isn't. You'll have to use metaphor.

Henry, aged two and a half, sitting this morning on his ride-on train told us, "It's *like* a boat. But it *is* a train." Looks like he's got metaphor down.

A metaphor, of course, describes one thing in terms of another. If it's a simile, we liken the man to the eagle. If it's a metaphor, we say the man is the eagle. "God was throwing pebbles at the roof again"—that's a metaphor (for the sound of the rain I woke to this morning); "the lone pandanus stands like a crucifix just off the trail"—that's a simile. "I was of three minds, / Like a tree / In which there are three blackbirds," writes Wallace Stevens in "Thirteen Ways of Looking at a Blackbird," using a striking simile. When I say to you that language is an ecosytem and grammar is its logic, I offer you a metaphor. I do it to help you understand by asking you to look in a new way at what I'm talking about; I do it to animate and clarify my subject matter. Those are the reasons you want metaphors and figures of speech generally—to throw a light on the nature of the thing and to bring the thing, in your writing, alive.

"Summer sickens and grows long." There's a metaphor that helps you recognize a mood summer has and we have in summer.

Michael Palin is in the Sahara describing how water is drawn up from a well fifty feet deep and flumed into a date-palm orchard: "It's a method as old as the Bible—probably older," he writes. This is a rich and clever simile: it points out the antiquity and persistence of the scene; and it underscores something essential, ritualistic, even sacred about the work of these camels and men.

And here's John Updike contemplating the erect penis:

Men's bodies, at this juncture, feel only partly theirs; a demon of sorts has been attached to their lower torsos, whose performance is erratic and whose errands seem, at times, ridiculous. It is like having a (much) smaller brother toward whom you feel both fond and impatient; if he is you, it is you in a curiously simplified and ignoble form.

(JOHN UPDIKE, "The Disposable Rocket," *More Matter*)

Peter Roebuck, a poet among cricket writers, uses simile masterfully. This simile briskly evokes the difficulties of facing a spin bowler (read "pitcher" if baseball's your game):

The Sri Lankan batsmen found him harder to read than Finnegan's Wake.

(PETER ROEBUCK, *The Sydney Morning Herald*, January 27, 2006)

Here's a poet's paragraph about a place, flush with metaphor:

Elsewhere on the mountain, most of the green stays locked in pines, the prairie is scorched yellow. But Lyle's meadow is a hemorrhage of green, and a green clockwork of waterways and grasses, held up to the sky in its ring of ridges, held up for the sky to listen, too.

The granite boulder is only there to hold it down.

(JAMES GALVIN, *The Meadow*)

Don't work your metaphors too hard. The writing project is to tell how things are, not what they're like. (That's what Henry on his train was reminding me: it's *like* a clock, but it *is* this meadow.) Simile that distracts us from the thing itself fails its subject. So, too, metaphor that offers up an image that's hard to fathom—Charles Wright's simple simile "Clouds trail like prairie schooners" won't work for anyone not sure what a prairie schooner is (most readers outside North America); but so lovely and apt a phrase is always worth using, especially in a poem, regardless.

Stale metaphors are clichés. "Like a bull at a gate," "she could sell snow to Eskimos," "the wind whispered in the trees": we've heard all these before. They're not bad images in themselves, but they're tired now. Give them a rest.

Tropes aside, fill your writing with words that appeal to each of a reader's senses: sight, of course, but also sound and smell, taste and touch.

Michael Ondaatje is a master of this kind of sense-steeped prose:

> He could smell the oasis before he saw it. The liquid in the air. The rustle of things. Palms and bridles. The banging of tin cans whose deep pitch revealed they were full of water.
>
> They poured oil onto large pieces of soft cloth and placed them on him. He was anointed . . .
>
> Later, at the hospital in Pisa, he thought he saw beside him the face that had come each night and chewed and softened the dates and passed them down into his mouth. (MICHAEL ONDAATJE, *The English Patient*)

We have there sound and smell and touch and taste and sight (in its absence and then in what he thinks he saw, as well as in the palms and bridles and soft cloths that the patient feels or hears, and we see).

Some figurative devices have to do with the sounds the writing makes, not the images if offers. *Alliteration* is where you repeat a consonant (or like consonantal sounds) at the start (or in the middle) of a number of words in succession ("the sloop slid languidly around the loop of the lakeshore"). You do this to create a sound effect that evokes a mood or suggests a place or emulates the weather or the drama. Soft sounds suggest quiet; harsh sounds suggest violence or drama. When it's a vowel sound (or diphthong like *ou* or *au*) you repeat, the device is called *assonance*: *sloop* and *loop* and *shore* in my clause above, for instance. *Onomatopoeia* is the name for the device of using a word that sounds like the event or phenomenon it describes: *crunch, crash, bang, knock, yelp, wail,* and *scream* are onomatopoeic.

You can, if you like, allude to gods and myths and angels and saints, devils and monsters and dreams. You might pun. You might be ironical; you might understate or overstate. But above all, your writing must be rich in its words, especially its verbs, and alive with images and things. Try to get inside your subject or scene or idea, and write it from there—from the inside out. For that you'll need a lot of words so you can choose the most apt. Not something generic, but something that fits just that gesture or piece of furniture or woman's expression.

But make sure nothing you do just decorates your writing. It should serve your subject matter (by getting at its nature); it should help your readers (by pleasing them in itself and by making the reading more than a merely literal experience); it should animate your sentences (by giving them color and attitude and music).

▶ Try this

1 Write about a storm you've been in. Use some sound devices, some tropes and some images that appeal to every sense to capture it. Three hundred words.

2 Using understatement, write about a terrible sadness.

3 Using irony or humor, describe the worst date, or the worst boss, you ever had.

4 "I don't know what to say—you don't know how much this means to me," said the tennis champion after his victory. Put into words, without using the usual clichés (*it was like a dream come true*; *it hasn't sunk in yet* . . .) what he was trying to. Write about his feelings as you imagine them, or write about a moment of great joy you've known. Think about understatement. Think about fresh images. Try to say exactly what it felt like.

Rhythm section

And then there are the uses of rhythm.

English speaks in the rhythm of stressed and unstressed syllables. Énglísh spéaks iñ the rhýthm ôf stréssed añd uñstréssed sýllâblês (DA da DA da da DA-da da DA da DA-da DA da-da is the rhythmscape of that sentence. Speech is organized sound, a kind of irregular, semantic music. Literature heightens artistically the natural rhythms of the spoken word. When you write a sentence, you make a storyscape and an ideascape, but you also make a soundscape; you try to shape an apt and elegant topography.

> Music, Puccini wrote, is noise organized by wisdom. Writing, if you like, is noise slightly less organized by slightly more rational wisdom.

Poems are made of rhythm—of rhythm and (sometimes) rhyme and (always) image. More than prose, but a little less than music, poems are structures of carefully designed sound. But this book is not the place for a treatise on iambs and trochees, spondees and pyrrhics, dactyls and anapests, bacchics and anti-bacchics and choriambs; on beat and meter; on pentameter and hexameter; on feminine endings; on acrostic and villanelle and sestina. These are poetic forms and devices, large and small; and they all have to do with rhythm patterns. If you need to feel footsure among them, read about them in the books I recommend at the end.

No matter what you're writing, write it by ear. Edit each sentence, and every clause within it, until its rhythm is right. Until then, you won't have written the right sentence. Sound each one out until it moves just so: "All the fun's in how you say a thing," wrote Robert Frost. Can you hear it? Aĺl thĕ fún's ĭn hów yôu sáy â thíng; DA da DA da DA da DAA da DA? (A rhythm too metronomic for prose.)

Listen for rhythm; don't reach for it. Let it come. Rhythm's a thing you hear, not a thing you fabricate. In prose it must be loose; but it must be there. It should not rise and fall as regularly as this, for instance:

> There was movement at the station, for the word had passed around
> That the colt from Old Regret had got away.
> > (A. B. PATERSON, "The Man from Snowy River")

More like this:

In my hotel room the night before I leave Greece, I know the elation of ordinary sorrow. At last my unhappiness is my own.

(ANNE MICHAELS, *Fugitive Pieces*)

Hear the rhythms there: Iñ mŷ hôtel roôm thẽ night bêfoŕe Î leaṽe Greéce, Î knów thẽ êlátiôn oƒ órdiñaŕy sórrôw. Aî lást mŷ uñháp-pîneŝs iś ḿy oẃn; da da da DA da da DA da DA da da DA, da DA da da-DA-da da DA da da da DA-da. da DA da da-DA-da-da DA da DA. You could graph those two sentences, the ridges and foothills and hollows of their emotional and intellectual territory.

Then there's this:

I had a farm in Africa at the foot of the Ngong Hills.

Karen Blixen's sentence has a lilting and slightly more regular beat. One hears Africa; one hears the land's heartbeat; one hears drums. Reading her book *Out of Africa* is very largely an experience in topography and rhythm.

Her opening sentences goes: Î hád â fárm în Áfrîcâ ât thê fóot ôf thẽ Ngóng Hílls; da DA da DA da DAA da da da-da DA da-da DA DA.

Hear the prosey gait of Whitman's line "Alone and light hearted I take to the open road" Âlóne añd light héartêd Î táke tô thê ópên roád; da DA da da DA-da da DA da-da DA da DA.

Rhythm, Robert Hass has said, is more than a linguistic matter—it is deeply psychological. "Because rhythm has direct access to the unconscious, because it can hypnotize us, enter our bodies and make us move, it is a power. And power is political." Bad beat can kill your prose or get you killed; good beat can change the world.

"It is not for me," wrote T. S. Eliot, "but for the neurologists, to discover . . . why and how feeling and rhythm are related." But they are, he asserted. And he's right.

In the rhythm you'll find the soul in the voice of the work; you'll feel its politics and poetry. The writer amplifies—without distorting—the natural rhythms of speech and makes with them art that moves us. Maybe even changes us. So, listen to your sentences as they make themselves out; listen even harder as you revise.

Writing is utterance—chant and rant and litany. So much of it depends upon rhythm.

Try this

1 Listen to the way people speak. Turn on the radio or go for a ride in the train or the bus. Or wait till your children come home. Listen to the actual sentences people shape. Write some of them down, as exactly as you can, and chart their rises and falls. Do this now. Do it often, and keep note in your journal of what you hear.

2 Specifically, write a two-hundred-word piece sparked by some talking you overhear. It could be a conversation, but it doesn't have to be. It may just be a phrase.

Character

Capturing the character of a person is like capturing the character of a place. Be the place, be the person. Be what they are, as far as your imagination will let you. Inhabit them. Write, as it were, from inside their clothes, from inside their skin and mind and memory. Think in their words; move with their gait; sleep in their posture. Rise and fall the way they do.

Do as little exposition—talking about your character—as you can get away with. Don't, in other words, explain. And don't have your cast thinking too long and hard about who they are and how they got that way and how the world perceives them. Have them mostly act and speak in character.

How we speak is who we are; so is how we act. Catch your character at work, in solitude, in flagrante. And know how she speaks. Listen to her (or whoever in the real world resembles her); learn her lines. Ask yourself, when you write them down, if she is in them.

Become her inner life; be his childhood days and nights; be her broken adolescent heart; be the afternoon of his days on earth.

Our houses, by the way, are, sometimes, our souls made manifest. Our houses and the music we play in them, the food we cook (or not), the lighting we favor, the mess we make, the favorite chair, the rug. We can say as much about a person by describing his bedroom as we can by describing his face. Who we are is also where we are—and that, by the way, doesn't stop at the front veranda. Which takes us back to landscape.

Give me all that, some family history, some enacted relationships, and, of course, some strong hints about how your woman looks and what she wears—and I will tell you pretty soon who she is. No need to do that for me.

▶ **Try this**

1 Take a person you know. Write a couple of paragraphs in which you have the person doing something you've seen him or her do or you can imagine him or her doing—getting out of bed, driving a car, teaching a class, repairing the car, pulling on boots.
2 Have that person, or some other, speaking. Write down some actual sentences you've heard the person utter, exactly as he or she has uttered them. Write it up as a dialogue if you like, or a scene in which the person has to say those things.
3 How does your mother-in-law speak; your father; your best friend; your worst enemy; your second child? Write down some actual things they say.
4 Did you ever fall in love—or out of it—with someone because of the way he or she spoke, or one thing he or she said? Write about that.

Story, plot, and moment

Every piece of writing's got to be *about* something. But it doesn't have to be about much.

It doesn't take much to make a story—less still to make a poem. In terms of action, I mean. Hardly anything need happen. A baby cries in the night: that's a story. She never returned my call: there's another. He never left the valley he was born in: there's a third. A wife dies and her husband never gets over it: a fourth.

Story is the pattern of a thing—its rhyme and reason. Its rhythm and logic. It is what a moment or a memory or a girl's expression or a silence is *about*; it is the genius of the thing. And that thing may be just about anything. It may even be a place. Story is what makes these things what they are, and it is the way you try to tell that secret.

In *Steering the Craft*, Ursula Le Guin defines story as "a narrative of events (external or psychological) which moves through time or implies the passage of time, and which involves change."

Plot is simply one device a writer might use to carry a narrative forward. Le Guin defines plot as "a form of story which uses action as its mode, usually in the form of conflict, and which closely and intricately connects one act to another, usually through a causal chain, ending in a climax."

She goes on: "Climax is one kind of pleasure; plot is one kind of story . . . But most serious modern fictions can't be reduced to a plot, or retold without fatal loss except in their own words. The story is not in the plot but in the telling. It is the telling that moves."

A story needn't have much plot; it need not necessarily, though stories often do, explore a conflict, Le Guin continues. There are other kinds of story—of persistence, of memory, of loss, of discovery, of ongoing love, of healing. Of silence.

Some kind of conflict—some kind of dissonance or hint of danger, some kind of paradox or contradiction or unspoken disappointment or loss—gives a story traction in a reader's mind. It makes it true to life, for life often pulls us in at least two directions at once. There is what's happening, and there is at the same time what might have happened, and there are all the memory and anguish and hope we carry with us into what happens next. There's what we fear and what we hope and what we leave behind. That's how human life feels; that's how good stories often go, too. But the conflict they explore needn't be the muscular, life-and-death varieties that thrillers, for example, tell. The drama need not be high. It need only be human.

The reason one writes—the thing that makes a work endure, if it does—is all that cannot be reduced to plot. Story includes the plot, such as it is; but the plot is not the story. For the story's in the telling, not (or not merely) in the action it narrates. Long after you've forgotten most of what happened, a good book will still be happening to you. That's the real narrative: the way the telling moved you and moves you still.

One's writing needs to move (forward and back and up and down and in and out), but there are many ways, besides narrative, to set it and keep it in motion: there's the development of an idea; the playing of your writing's music, its beat and song, its shape; the shapely accumulation of vivid moments, images, thoughts and memories; the exploration of a landscape (physical or psychological); the shifting of points of view.

"Toward the end of her life," writes novelist Debra Magpie Earling, "the writer Katherine Mansfield focused her attention on small but powerful moments (both real and imagined) as the substance of her final work." She called those moments "glimpse memories." Mansfield "was convinced that life held extraordinary and life changing flashes of beauty that were the only stuff worth writing. Stories for her became small contained moments of being." Her idea was that you could make an entire literature out of moments in which "the whole life of the soul is contained"; literature could and should be accretions of such moments, in which nothing much might happen, but in which the world revealed itself as something altogether other than it had always seemed.

Partly because of the influence this idea exerted on Virginia Woolf, Mansfield's notion reshaped modern (literary) fiction, one way and another.

"The illusion is on me," says Bernard in Virginia Woolf's *The Waves*, "that something adheres for a moment, has roundness, weight, depth, is completed. This, for the moment, seems to be my life. If it were possible, I would hand it you entire . . . I would say, 'Take it. This is my life.'"

 Try this

1 "Take it. This is my life." Start like that and write a "glimpse memory." It could be a moment from your life or from someone else's.

2 Write a hundred words about perfect silence.

Not telling—a note on indirection

You can write a perfectly powerful narrative (or even a poem) in which you tell everything, just as it happened, one event after another. You might leave nothing material out. Or you can write a story that never describes the key events in so many words. Good stories often cover ground they never actually describe. They circle it and barely, or never, touch down. Writers learn to tell some, at least, of their story indirectly, implicitly, from above and below and all sorts of angles— any way but literally.

The art of telling by not telling, or telling from the side, at an oblique or acute angle, is called *indirection*.

Show; don't tell, they advise you in all the writing schools. But what you show may also be, most of it, an ensemble of sideshows. Lots of talking about the weather and the cut of the dress and the lie of the land, but a sustained kind of holding back from giving you the thing that is causing all this trouble.

Think of this, if you will, like sex. It's all the waiting and all the things that aren't in themselves actual sex (the central act) that make the thing so grand. One way to write good sex is to write the touch on the arm, the light in the room, the waking up after. That's indirection.

Delia Falconer's novel *The Lost Thoughts of Soldiers* is a good example. The author draws near to the central event of the story, and of her (anti-)hero's life—a misjudgment (was it?) on a battlefield—time and again, now from the man's deep past, moving forward to that day; now from the present morning, reaching back toward it; and now through the ghosted lives of friends he lost that day. She never describes exactly what happened. Yet it is that one moment the whole book tells. It fills the space the author leaves by not telling it directly. The book is an essay in indirection.

If you're telling a story, you must forbear; there are secrets you must withhold. You can't tell the whole truth. You can't get the whole plateau or war or journey or human life into one book. And you wouldn't want to. It wouldn't be a story then. Storytelling, in other words, *entails* indirection; storytelling is the aggregation of points of view upon—of approaches to and retreats from and hoverings above and tacks around—a central cluster of happenings (moments, lifetimes, crimes, battles, beginnings or endings) and people and locales. Storytelling asks you to leave most of your tale out; it wants you to let your readers imagine most of it themselves. You make a space; you articulate some of its features. You let the reader enter into it to find what she will find. You need to let her; you mustn't explain—at least, not everything.

For story is not exposition. What you embed in the story or the poem or the lyric essay, but never spell out, is the reason why; it is the meaning of it all. And you must let that mystery stand. Literature (including literary nonfiction) does that. It does not explicate the world; it frames the right questions and transmutes those questions into moments and plots and characters and songs.

That, in a sense, is what indirection is—the art of telling one thing by telling a bunch of other things instead. When you write literature you engage with reality metaphorically, figuratively, lyrically. A poem or a story is not a photograph. Writing, you give a reader a piece of the real world not by taking a picture of it, but by describing the photographer's childhood and love-life, how heavy her equipment was to carry in, and her mood as she opens and closes the shutter.

Fiction, in particular, is indirection. It does not represent reality—it tells (beautiful) lies. What it says is: this never happened. But nor is fiction simply fantasy. It describes, it comments on and reflects, the real world by inventing worlds that resemble it, loosely or closely. It alters reality to make reality come clear. It lies (if it's good) to tell the truth. Each story is a metaphor for an aspect of the real world. Fiction, in a sense, and among other things, is allegory. What it gives you is the real world, indirectly.

Let's say, then, that literature proceeds, more or less, indirectly. The more lyric the work, the more indirectly it works. And since poetry is quintessentially lyric, think how much more indirectly it will need to go—telling far more, and often something quite else, than it seems? It is what it suggests and doesn't ever quite say that makes a poem any good. Poetry is the art of saying it in other words.

What would you say this means, exactly?

The art of losing isn't hard to master;
so many things seem filled with the intent
to be lost that their loss is no disaster.

Lose something every day. Accept the fluster
of lost door keys, the hour badly spent.
The art of losing isn't hard to master.

Then practice losing farther, losing faster:
places, and names, and where it was you meant
to travel. None of these will bring disaster. . . .

                (ELIZABETH BISHOP, "One Art")

And what about this (and don't tell me it's about plums)?

"This Is Just to Say"

I have eaten
the plums
that were in
the icebox

and which
you were probably
saving
for breakfast

Forgive me
they were delicious
so sweet
and so cold

       (WILLIAM CARLOS WILLIAMS, "This Is Just to Say")

Indirection is a sort of letting be. You allow the world you're writing to come into being for your reader by leaving it well enough alone; by letting it create itself in each reader's mind by offering a few seemingly incidental figures and gestures on its behalf.

    Maybe indirection works so well on the page because it's how life goes. We proceed day by day in ignorance and uncertainty; we get glimpses of the truth of who we are and what we're doing and what our lives mean; we rarely (and usually too late) see the whole picture. Our lives—their climactic episodes, especially—make sense, if they ever make sense, only when we stand and look back at them. Indirection is, perhaps, the truest realism.

▶ Try this

1 Write about an event (actual or imaginary) without actually describing it. Write instead about the actions and moods of some of the participants some time after. Two hundred words.

2 Describe a man or woman (someone you know, maybe even yourself, or a character in your book) by describing a room in their house or a garden or a landscape they're attached to. Don't describe or characterize the person. Don't even have the person present. Two hundred words.

3 Imagine a man or woman with a secret. Imagine, if you like, your male character has fallen in love with another woman and embarked on an affair. Write a scene in which he arrives home and is greeted by his wife warmly. Somehow invest the scene with his guilty secret, without letting it come out. Tell the secret without telling it.

4 "I am what is around me," wrote Wallace Stevens. Write about a place you once lived, a place that shaped you; or write about the place you now live. Imagine that what you are really doing is drawing a picture of your soul. Three paragraphs.

Expository lumps

Indirection is, it turns out, a way to negotiate your path—and your reader's—through tracts of information your story can't do without —some facts about the place and time, the politics and culture and mores of your story.

Even in a story you have to do some exposition, though you need to do it without letting your reader fall from the story's spell. Such exposition happens best when it seems not to be happening at all. Ursula Le Guin talks about "expository lumps"—passages of straightout, unadulterated, unregenerate information—and how to avoid them. Good devices include weaving critical facts into the narrative or conversation; breaking it up into fragments (Ondaatje does this in his novels, where he supplies a lot of facts about bridge-building, archaeology, and the wind, for example) and spreading them through the book; putting the exposition in someone's voice or seeing it from someone's point of view; setting the exposition dancing by strong, lyrical writing. In short, find a way to *tell* the information in the same voice you tell the whole story.

Like this, for example:

In the morning they took him to the far reach of the siq. They were talking loudly around him now. The dialect suddenly clarifying. He was here because of the buried guns.

He was carried towards something, his blindfolded face looking straight ahead, and his hand made to reach out a yard or so. After days of travel, to move this one yard. To lean towards and touch something with a purpose, his arm still held, his palm facing down and open. He touched the Sten barrel and the hand let go of him. A pause among the voices. He was there to translate the guns.

"Twelve-millimetre Breda machine gun. From Italy."

He pulled back the bolt, inserted his finger to find no bullet, pushed it back and pulled the trigger. Puht. "Famous gun," he muttered. He was moved forward again. "French seven-point-five-millimetre Châtterault. Light machine gun. Nineteen twenty-four."

"German seven-point-nine-millimetre MG-Fifteen air service."

(MICHAEL ONDAATJE, *The English Patient*)

 ## ▶ Try this

1 Think about a technical task you are familiar with, but which may not be familiar to everyone (shoeing a horse, writing a sentence, cooking a particular meal, flying small planes, shearing a

sheep, climbing a mountain, caring for a loved one who has a disability, putting up a tent in a gale). Find a way to write about this without writing an expository lump. Two hundred words.

2 Tell a piece of history or science or theory that you need your readers to know about; but try to tell it slant. Indirectly in some way. Compose, perhaps, a scene in which a character wonders about it. Put some of it in dialogue. Two hundred words.

Pace

Some scenes go fast, and some go slowly. Some call for calm and others for excitement. Stories have dynamics. They need changes of pace.

How you pace your writing has everything to do with the style (and length) of sentence you choose (see "Sentences: a field guide" in Chapter 2) and the sound and personality of the words you flesh them out with. Think about which sentence styles work for suspense (segregating and freight-train mixed with the odd subordinating); which ones work for unsuspenseful action (probably all kinds, but especially freight-train and cumulative); which ones for exposition; which ones for description of a scene; which ones for reverie; and so on.

Know what kind of a passage you're writing and how you think it should move—a lope, a sprint, a meditation, a sleep, a making of love, a rocking of a baby, a getting out of bed and getting dressed, a grieving, a narrowly avoiding death, a sitting again where one has always sat and watched the days pass. Think then about the kinds of sentence that establish the velocity and rhythm each of those figures needs.

Feel how the drama and threat build from a bucolic start in this paragraph from Hemingway's *To Have and Have Not*: a languid compound–complex; then a run of five sentences, segregating style, building the pace; then a great, long compound–complex sentence with three main clauses and a load of short words like machine-gun fire, not to mention the "jump-jump-jump" and "bop-bop-bop-bop"; and then another action-compressed compound–complex to close. An astonishing performance.

Albert was on the stern cutting baits and Harry was at the wheel warming up the motors when he heard a noise like a motor back-firing. He looked down the street and saw a man come out of the bank. He had a gun in his hand and he came running. Then he was out of sight. Two men came out carrying leather brief-cases and guns in their hands and ran in the same direction. Harry looked at Albert busy cutting baits. The fourth man, the big one, came out of the bank door as he watched, holding a Thompson gun in front of him, and as he backed out of the door the siren in the bank rose in a long breath-holding shriek and Harry saw the gun muzzle jump-jump-jump and heard the bop-bop-bop-bop, small and hollow sounding in the wail of the siren. The man turned and ran, stopping to fire once more at the bank door, and as Albert stood up in the stern saying, "Christ, they're robbing the bank. Christ, what can we do?" Harry heard the Ford taxi coming out of the side street and saw it careening up on to the dock.

(ERNEST HEMINGWAY, *To Have and Have Not*)

Here's something more languid. It does its easy, nostalgic work through diction and rhythm and image and structure, a succession of temperate, regular clauses, full of short, familiar words.

The two women stood letting the breeze blow coolly on their faces, and they opened the fronts of their blouses a little to let it play on their breasts and under their arms.

And soon, very soon now, they would call them in to supper. But not just yet. They stood on the porch a while longer in the evening air seventeen miles out south of Holt at the very end of May. (KENT HARUF, *Plainsong*)

▶ Try this

Thinking about how to pace it, write a passage of three paragraphs or so telling

- a dream
- a chase
- a landscape and a journey through it
- a scene where a character takes a bath and thinks back on her or his day
- a scene describing a time, if you've had one, where you feared for your life

Points of view

If you're writing an essay, the point of view is yours. You're telling the tale—every piece of you, if Michel de Montaigne is to be believed; but not every piece of *it*. That's the way an essay goes; that's how we all understand it. There's someone sitting in a chair talking to you about how something seems to them, and the talker is the author. Essayists are not necessarily reliable, of course, and they are certainly not claiming any kind of objectivity. Their account is partial, in every sense. They claim merely the authority of first-person witness: I saw this, they say, and this is how it seemed to me.

So it is with most nonfiction—a history, a biography, a cookbook, a writing book. If you're writing it, the point of view is yours, and it's your voice we hear. If it's nonfiction, you're in the book, whether you like it or not. In journalism and other forms of more information-based nonfiction, the narrator is a quietly spoken, anonymous version of the essayist—she writes as a notionally detached expert or reporter. That is the characteristic point of view of journalism.

In literature other than mainstream nonfiction, the writer must choose whose viewpoint the story will be told from. The choices are a narrator outside the story (whom we shouldn't assume is the author, as we can in an essay) or one (or a number) of the characters in it. The author may wish to pass the telling, or at least the viewing, between the characters, in which case one says that the point of view switches. This can create interesting effects, and, in unsteady hands, cacophony. In his novel *Bleak House*, Dickens switches point of view between an omniscient narrator and one of his characters, Esther Summerson, who writes in the first person.

A writer will need to choose a point, or points, of view that fits the telling of her story or poem. She may shift her point of view, fraction it among her crew of characters, or hold it intimate—or lofty—and steady, close to her narrator's breast. Things turn, as you'd expect, upon her choice.

Here's the traditional range of choice.

First person

In this point of view, one of the story's characters tells it in the first person (I). *Moby-Dick*, *Johnno*, and *Huck Finn* are well-known examples. But there are so many on my shelves, particularly in twentieth-century fiction. The narrator may be a support actor—like Melville's Ishmael—or the main character, like Huck, or like Dante's poet in *The Divine Comedy*.

You'll only get part of the story, as it were—from the narrator's point of view. The narrator can only give you what he knows, sees, interprets, remembers, and intuits.

This narrative approach produces works that are one version or another of a memoir, fictive or real. F. Scott Fitzgerald's *The Great Gatsby*, Richard Ford's *Wildlife*, and William Maxwell's *So Long, See You Tomorrow* are three books that work this way.

This is the essayist's stance, too, of course. An essay is always personal in point of view and voice. But its narrator may not—indeed should not—be its hero. The essayist is really a kind of witness—engaged with but not starring in the events and ideas the essay discusses.

In this point of view, in fact or in fiction, someone addresses you directly. They don't just report; usually they confess. This is the most intimate point of view. And it can cloy fast on a reader who likes a little more personal space.

"Most of what I'm going to tell you, I know," says Kent Haruf's narrator in *The Ties That Bind*. "The rest of it, I believe." And he ends:

I'm done talking now. I've told you all I know.

Only, before you leave, before it gets full dark, you have time to drive over there a half mile east and see what remains of that yellow house.

Barry Lopez's narrator in *Desert Notes* is even more solicitous:

I know you are tired. I am tired too. Will you walk along the edge of the desert with me? I would like to show you what lies before us.

A narrator can be much less welcoming and reliable than this. Salinger's Holden Caulfield, for instance:

If you really want to hear about it, the first thing you'll probably want to know is where I was born, and what my lousy childhood was like, and how my parents were occupied and all before they had me, and all that David Copperfield kind of crap, but I don't feel like going into it.

(J. D. SALINGER, *Catcher in the Rye*)

David Copperfield, referred to so irreverently by Caulfield, is a classic of limited first-person narrative. Marilynne Robinson's *Gilead* is written in the first person in the form of a long letter from the narrator to his son. Her narrator talks only indirectly to the reader, therefore, and one feels as though one is prying a little into the beautiful, formal intimacy between father and son.

 Try this

Write about the birth of your child or the first time you knew you were in love with someone or the moment you got news of a death; and write it from the viewpoint of someone involved (yourself or someone else) in the first person.

Limited third person

Here, too, the story is told by someone in it; but this time it's told in the third person, which waters down the intimacy of a first-person telling. Because one doesn't relate to *he* or *she* as one relates to *I*, a telling in the limited third person will sound more detached than in the first. Again, you get only the story that character is in a position to tell you.

The limited third person, Ursula Le Guin notes, is the dominant point of view in contemporary writing. It allows room for the detachment that characterizes modern writing. Graham Greene wrote most of his novels from this point of view: Scobie's in *The Heart of the Matter*, for instance. Cormac McCarthy wrote *All the Pretty Horses* from John Grady Cole's point of view in the limited third person. *Tom Sawyer* is told from Tom's point of view, pretty much, and in the third person; Kipling's *Kim* is told from Kim's point of view; and *The Shipping News* from Quoyle's.

Try this

1 Rewrite, in the limited third person, what you wrote in the last exercise.

2 Write about something you are ashamed of, or something you find it hard to write about, in the third person. Sometimes it is a way to achieve the detachment you need to write about such things.

Omniscient or engaged narrator

This is the way all stories once got told—by an anonymous small-time god with a good view and an intimate acquaintance with the cast.

Think most children's literature and all the myths and legends. Think most contemporary popular fiction. Think *The Iliad* and *The Odyssey*, *The Epic of Gilgamesh*, *The Canterbury Tales*, *Don Quixote*, *A Tale of Two Cities*, *The Mayor of Casterbridge*, *War and Peace*, *The Jungle Book*, *The Tale of Peter Rabbit*, *Pride and Prejudice* (most Victorian fiction, where these "involved authors," as Le Guin calls them, predominated, intervening often in the narrative with asides of the "Dear reader" variety and expressing sympathy or its opposite for their characters), *Washington Square*, *Mrs Dalloway*, *Doctor Zhivago*, *The Grapes of Wrath*, *The Lord of the Rings*, *Harry Potter*.

The teller stands outside the story, taking no part in its action, but he knows and sees everything. In this approach, the narrator knows how everyone thinks, why they act, how they feel, what the whole thing means; one experiences the story from inside the heads and hearts, and from the standpoint, of many of its characters. Though he is mostly offstage, the narrator is not detached.

Sometimes the narrator alludes to himself in the first person (this happens in *Peter Rabbit*, *The Canterbury Tales*, and *Don Quixote*, for instance) but only in his role as storyteller, and not very often. "I am sorry to say," writes *Peter Rabbit's* narrator, "that Peter was not very well during the evening." Generally, though, the engaged narrator doesn't walk out on stage. His telling *is* the stage, the means by which we get to hear and see the drama from many angles, in many voices.

In such books, the viewpoint—the sympathy or attention of the narrator—shifts between the characters, without the book ever belonging to any one of them. Think how the focus moves among the players in *War and Peace* or *The Aeneid*, *The Lord of the Rings*, *Doctor Zhivago*, and *Cloudstreet*. (*Cloudstreet*'s narrator sometimes addresses his characters directly and, in the end, I think, reveals himself as one of them.) And think how the story passes, in *Cold Mountain*, from Inman to Ada and back, chapter by chapter.

This is certainly the most taxing point of view for a writer to handle, since it includes everything and everybody. It may be hard to find a voice for the book since there's no character into whose life you can step, or in whose idiom you can speak. And yet the book must still speak. What manner of man or woman is telling this tale?

Detached narrator

This is a very noir point of view. By contrast to the engaged narrator, the detached narrator stays right out of the story, and he tells it with cool detachment, not presuming to interpret or even understand a character's motives or inner life. The reader gets only the kind of description, delivered in a disinterested kind of way no matter how gruesome or heartrending the events, that a bystander might supply. "Camera-eye" and "fly-on-the-wall" are other names for this approach. McCarthy's *Blood Meridian* is a good example of this point of view.

There's emotion there, pain and terror and grief and joy, but you're not going to emphasize it. You're going to let it rise up all on its own out of your quiet, deadpan delivery. This style is the embodiment of restraint, the antithesis of sentimentality.

No one was alive on the hilltop except the boy Joaquín who was unconscious under the dead body of Ignacio. Joaquín was bleeding from the nose and from the ears. He had known nothing and had no feeling since he had suddenly been in the very heart of the thunder and the breath had been wrenched from his body when the one bomb struck so close and Lieutenant Berrendo made the sign of the cross and then shot him in the back of the head, as quickly and gently, if such an abrupt movement can be gentle, as Sordo had shot the wounded horse.

(ERNEST HEMINGWAY, *For Whom the Bell Tolls*)

The challenge is to make your readers care about the fate of your characters without your expressing sympathy for them. Writing from this point of view proceeds by indirection—it describes mostly action and expression and gesture; and it employs dialogue; but it withholds commentary and lets surfaces speak for much else (feeling and psychology and motive) that goes unsaid. Sometimes, of course, it is by withholding commentary that you allow the sadness or the horror or the grief or wonder to be for a reader. One shouldn't assume that authors who write this way are coldhearted; they write this way, most often, to get out of the way—to let the real story (the grief or the horror or the lust or the wonder) arise, if it will, in the reader, as though the reader were telling it himself.

 Try this

1 Write a scene from breakfast this morning, or from work this afternoon, involving at least three people. Write it first as the engaged narrator; rewrite it, next, in the viewpoint of the detached narrator.

2 Use the viewpoint of the detached narrator to write about something sad or bad or ugly: a time when you or someone else suffered; a car accident you observed; a war scene; an image of horror from the television. Try it out on a loved one, when you're through. See if they're moved, or if they think you're just callous.

Observer–narrator, first person

In this approach, the narrator is a bit-part player in the story she tells. What she tells you is something she witnessed; the story is not really about the narrator, or not chiefly. One might almost understand Melville's Ishmael in this role in *Moby-Dick*. Maybe even Nick in *The Great Gatsby*—for this is Gatsby's book, really, as *Moby-Dick* is Ahab's and the whale's.

The difficulty writing fiction from this viewpoint is working your narrator, plausibly, into enough of the action to tell you enough of the story.

Try this

> Write a scene in which a husband leaves his wife, from the point of view of a six-year-old girl who wanders into the end of the yelling and watches her father carry a suitcase out the door and drive away.

Observer–narrator, third person

Here, too, the narrator is a bit-player, but they speak as a *he* or a *she*. Tolkien uses this device now and then through *The Lord of the Rings*, observing great councils and marches to war from the point of view of one of the small people, usually a hobbit. He does this, for example, in "The Ride of the Rohirrim", in which the hobbit Merry wonders and overhears great discussions, then joins the ride to battle, observing it from the saddle behind one of the warriors.

Notes

1 A writer might not want to stick to one of these points of view for the length of a book. You might write most of it as a detached narrator, bits of it in the voice of a character or two, then move for a while into an essayistic first person. Many modern novels (and poems) have played with point of view in this way and produced striking works. It's risky, though, as you can imagine. I mentioned Dickens's *Bleak House* as an example earlier. Cormac McCarthy's novel *No Country for Old Men* is told by his characteristic detached narrator, but strung with a narrative in the first-person voice of Bell, the sheriff, who's part of the action.

2 You can use a multiple first person. William Faulkner's *As I Lay Dying* is written in the first person but from many points of view. Each chapter is spoken by one the relatives of Addie Bundren, whose death and lying in state gives the novel its name. Peter Matthiessen uses this device, too, in *Killing Mister Watson*.

3 In real life, all categories blur. It's hard to pin some books down to one of these points of view. Ondaatje's narrator cares about Kip and Hana almost too much to sustain the detachment of the telling to

the end of *The English Patient*. It's a good idea, though, as a writer, to choose one mode and stick to it. You won't find the work's voice (or voices) until you know where it's being spoken from and by whom.

4 The second person, *you*, is not one of the traditional points of view. It doesn't have much history, but it's had some popularity since the seventies, waning now. Just who *you* is can be elusive, which may explain the attraction. It could be the writer (we all address ourselves as *you* sometimes). It could be the reader or all of us. Really, *you* is a version of the detached first person: *one*.

▶ Try this

1 Write a scene from childhood that involves at least three characters. Write that scene three times, each time from the point of view of a different character. Then write that scene again from the viewpoint of the omniscient narrator.

2 Write a scene from the viewpoint of a person you find it hard to like or hard to understand—a radical cleric of some description, say; a prime minister or president; a drug trafficker; a teenager; somebody of the opposite political persuasion; someone simply of the opposite gender; a supporter of the football team you care for least. That person ought to be involved in the scene. You might be, too. Three hundred words.

3 Write about a dream you can recall. Write it from the viewpoint of a character (human or otherwise) who was not identifiably you in the dream.

Write with nouns and verbs

At primary school they encourage you to use describing words. They're trying to help you notice more about the world—its colors, its highs and lows, its speeds, its textures and designs—and get it into your words. But when you grow up, your writing teacher will probably tell you to stop using so many adjectives and adverbs.

"Write with nouns and verbs" is one of the elements of style. Those are the load-bearing walls, so make them bear the load.

Good writers ration their modifiers to get the primary parts of speech (nouns, pronouns and verbs) doing the work they're made for. (Remember the "who does what" I talked about in Chapter 2?) "Fewer curves—more straight lines," a teacher once chided me in a life drawing class. "It has to feel like there are some bones beneath those lovely hips and boobs you've drawn." I turned the page and straightened the lines, and the drawing suddenly came true. Nouns and verbs are the straight lines; they are the skeleton of your story. Adjectives and adverbs are the curves. Less, in the case of modifiers, definitely amounts to more.

So Ursula Le Guin proposes an exercise, and I have used it for a long time now myself; this is how my version of it goes. I've often witnessed writing students produce astonishing pieces of work in response to it; and often what they wrote felt, to them, like the strangest, most unnatural thing they had ever done. That's not necessarily a bad thing. Sometimes we need someone else to tell us that what we've done is fine. So here it is; see what you produce; see how it makes you feel.

 Try this

> Write a descriptive passage—say, a journey, such as the one you took to or from work or something more momentous, or take a walk outside and come back and write the way you went—using NO adjectives or adverbs. None at all. Write two hundred words.

Unwriting

Writing, says Thomas Kane, consists of thinking about it, doing it, and doing it again. And again and again.

Writing is a process; it's iterative. It happens off the paper, and on the paper, and off the paper again. First you make some kind of plan (I spoke about this as "Finding your form," and I speak about it a bit more in Chapter 6). Then you embark on the writing. This is the draft, the emergent work. In time, if you persist, you reach the end of that: you've got the story told, you've got the poem close to its home port and sunk it; you've written every room of the house you intended to build.

That's when you start doing it all again.

You need to work as hard as you can, in your draft, to avoid having to write any of it again; but you will always have to. No one pulls it off the first time. Some sentences may stand unchanged from start to finish. But most of them will change or go.

The writing, in fact, isn't over until you've written most of what you first wrote a second time and a third time and a fourth. Until you start to wreck it, Peter Matthiessen said once.

You edit for sense and syntax and coherence and punctuation and rhythm. You tidy up. You burn back. You make sure the work keeps on talking in its own true voice, but no longer than it should. You unwrite and unwrite until only what you meant to write remains; you erode the work until it is itself.

This is editing. The main thing to know about it is that it must be done. And you'd better be the one who does most of it.

And then, just when you think you've uncovered, by all this unwriting, the best work you're capable of writing, along will come your editor and show you all the many ways in which you haven't.

 ## Try this

Take a piece of work you wrote recently—perhaps one of the exercises here. Rewrite it; make it shorter. But aim mostly to make it more like the thing it's meant to be.

CHAPTER 5

ATTITUDE

On manners and your reader

I don't know if that grocer on my shoulder digs all the references, but other than him, I write pretty much for myself.
S. J. PERELMAN

The room where I work has a window looking into a wood, and I like to think that these earnest, lovable, and mysterious readers are in there. JOHN CHEEVER

Manners

This is a short treatise on good manners.

I've noticed that the people with the best manners remember them whomever they're speaking with. I've noticed they treat everyone much the same. They're never obsequious, nor are they gruff, or not for long. They have a sense of humor, and they seem perfectly natural and at ease in every kind of company—as though this is how you'd catch them just being themself.

Good writers are like that on the page. They are well-mannered, not mannerly. Nothing they say feels like affectation. They are naturally civil and frank, kind and careful and precise. Every reader matters to them equally, but only as much as is relevant. They privilege no one in particular; they address each of us as a kind of everyman or everywoman.

You have a reader; don't forget her. Treat her with respect, but not too much, no matter who she is.

Treat her as an adult (unless she is in fact a child), and write as if you were having with her the best conversation you've never had with anyone. Affect nothing but respect, ease of manner and comfortable self-assurance. If you must adopt an attitude, adopt that one. Be relaxed, thoughtful, compassionate, generous, dignified, informal, respectful. That should work for just about anyone.

And it sounds like good manners to me. It also sounds like democracy in action. It sounds like respectful egalitarianism. Like true civility. Let's write the way we'd like society to run.

Good writing is not mannered and stilted—it's not inflected with overanxious politeness, nor with false *bonhomie*, nor with false confidence, nor anything faux or excessive. No false elegance; just elegance. Good writing is calm and cool, and it remembers its manners. Everyone likes to be treated with a relaxed mix of dignity, grace, and respect by someone who knows what he's talking about but isn't trying to show it off. That's the kind of attitude writers want toward their readers.

Don't feel obliged, beyond reason, to use the industry jargon. Write in a way that pleases you and says what you have to say clearly; in any given field the best writer is the one who uses the least of that field's arcane idiom. Think, as Aristotle said, like a wise person, but talk like an everyman, conversing with a friend.

On the other hand, if you're responding to a tender or filling out a job application, be sure to address your response to the phrases used. But spell out neatly what you take each of them to mean and relate your expertise to that; reframe the question in your own words and address it. ("Our Understanding of Your Needs" is a heading a client of mine uses for this kind of reframing, followed by "Our Expertise" and "What We Propose to Do.") There are few things worse than the application that keeps on repeating the phrases used in the specification document. Interpret; don't just parrot. No one (at least no one I'd want to work for, let alone read) likes a parrot—except of the wild kind.

Write the way it goes when some expert has the courtesy to think his content through for his audience before he stands to speak; write what you're called to write, as that considerate expert might speak it, in language an intelligent non-expert grown-up like you could follow. No such expert would compromise the complexity of his subject matter or the sophistication of his thinking about it; but in his diction and structure, he makes the complex simple. In the hard work he performs transposing difficult ideas into lucid and vivid speech lies his truest professionalism and courtesy.

Take that kind of care. Never never "dumb down"; never feel obliged; never pander; never fawn; never patronize; never bully; never ever. Hold up your end of a clear-headed conversation.

Treat every reader pretty much alike. Speak in the intelligent vernacular, and explain anything—deftly, not patronizingly—you think she may not know. Treat every reader as an intelligent grown-up. Someone just like you, in other words. And if it's a functional kind of thing you're writing, bear in mind that she'll be in a hurry. So don't muck about. Check in (with yourself, since your reader is not there to check with) to see if you think she's keeping up or growing bored or nodding off or hunting for a dictionary. Apologize; adjust; keep going.

Write for everyone. Remember your manners; work out what you want to say; and write. Forget about your readers, beyond that.

When it comes to your readers, I advise a benign, polite neglect.

 Try this

Make a list of the different classes of readers you have (for example, your boss, your teacher, the examiners, the customers, the board, the public, the regulatory authorities). Then make a list of the qualities they would all look for in your writing.

Eighty/twenty

You see, we're all pretty much alike. As readers, I mean.

If you want to know whom your readers resemble, look in the mirror. Though your reader is—and this is vital—*not* yourself, every reader is very *like* you. In this way: regardless of how much or how little they know, regardless of their rank and interest, readers are more than likely intelligent adults with too little time on their hands. Like you. No one wants to be left in the dark—do you? No one wants to be baffled. No one wants to be left waiting till the end of a long document to find what it's about and whether, and how, it concerns them. No one wants to be spoken down to, and few of us enjoy being treated obsequiously. Most of us want to hear a thing said plainly and elegantly, with circumspection and intelligence and with our interests in mind. We want the act of reading to take as little time as possible and to yield as much meaning as possible in that time. And none of us wants a struggle.

You may have heard of the "eighty/twenty" rule. Twenty percent of my work, for instance, returns me 80 percent of my income; and vice versa. It's a general rule of business life. Eighty percent of every car the company makes is the same; we tailor the 20 percent almost infinitely to cater for a variety of genuine or engendered tastes. And so it is with writing. Eighty percent of what every reader needs from a piece of writing is the same, no matter who they are and no matter how expert. Eighty percent of the writer's effort ought to go into catering for those *common* needs. Which are what I've been talking about from the start: clarity, economy, grace, order; and if it's a work of literature, readers want in addition, mystery, suspense, levity, wisdom and beauty—heartbreak, perhaps, and a little romance.

But then, and I'm talking mostly about functional writing here, there's the other 20 percent—the almost infinite ways, of relatively minor importance, in which each reader, or each class of reader, differs. We need to think about that; but only 20 percent of our writing energy and time ought to go into it. *Everything* doesn't depend upon the reader we have in our sights; 20 percent of everything does. If you ignored, in other words, the individual needs of every reader almost completely, but worked hard at writing with grace and clarity for the average intelligent grown-up, you'd please most of your readers—including the fussiest, whose needs fall into the 20 percent. Your supervisor, your examiner, your boss, the lawyers, the technical experts, for example. They, too, need you most of all to make sense and to get it right and not to take too long about it; compared to that, anything else they want matters much less and shouldn't cost you too much effort.

I say all this because we live in times when market segmentation has become a dogma and when we think of readers as consumers to whom each message (our product) must be, as though it were soda, discretely

> So expend your energy tailoring a message for its audience like this: spend 80 percent of your effort (by far the bulk of it) doing what you always do, regardless of whom you're writing for; spend 20 percent of your effort tailoring. That should do it.

positioned. I say all this because I notice people tying themselves and their writing in knots in an effort to write every document "in a different style," as they put it. Hardly anybody's good enough to do that— to repackage the same message effectively for each market segment, for each imagined class of reader. And, oddly enough, the people most addicted to the notion are often, in my experience, the least nimble at performing it; they have so narrowed the range of words in which they feel free to speak (these business units and government agencies and scientists, for instance) that they can't find another way to say a thing that needn't have been said so differently anyway.

Instead of merchandizing your message, enlarge your vocabulary. Get yourself, thus, a richer resource with which to perform the subtle, but often marginal, adaptations you'll need to position your prose for its sometimes multiple, sometimes pernickety readers. Don't knock yourself out differentiating each message; work hard to make each piece of writing manifestly and universally clear; then finesse it—tool it and trim it delicately—to cater for your best guess at what your reader likes or needs.

Writing clearly is hard enough work; you don't want to waste your energy tap-dancing and tailoring and spinning. Spend your writing effort writing so that *everyone* might understand. Eighty percent clarity; 20 percent fiddling. Get that equation backwards, and you stop making much sense to anyone.

Remember: benign neglect. Write clearly for everyone. Dedicate yourself to clarity, economy, and grace.

Try this

- Write a short autobiographical note suitable for three different audiences (your best friend, say, your old high school magazine, and a court of law). Think about what it will take to write this overfamiliar subject matter so it satisfies each. Think about what words you can assume knowledge of. Think about using examples. Think about not summarizing, but rather, supplying the detail and color and life of who you are. And just how different would these audiences actually be?

- A TV station wants to interview you on Monday for five minutes as part of a series about the work life of ordinary citizens. This is morning television, for a wide audience. Work on a script describing the work you do, in words fitting for that audience.
- Your child's class has invited a parent each week to come in and tell them about the work that parent does. These are ten-year-olds. Write a script suitable for that audience.

Hard to please

All of this applies—only more so—when you're writing literature. Good art isn't made to measure. You need to write the book that only you can write. The book you think everyone wants is a book other people have written or are writing already. Such books don't last, and you'd like yours to, wouldn't you? Original books endure, though derivative books, easy ones, often succeed more fully in the short term. Paradoxically, the book that no one is looking for—because no one has written it yet—is what everyone wants to read. You won't find out how to write that one by asking readers what they want.

Write to please yourself; make yourself hard to please.

William Faulkner—a writer's writer, admittedly, but a Nobel laureate and one of the masters—said: "Mine is the standard which has to be met, which is when the work makes me feel the way I do when I read the Old Testament . . . That makes me feel good. So does watching a bird make me feel good."

John Cheever says he writes for the kind of men and women who live and read "quite independently of the prejudices of advertising, journalism, and the cranky academic world." He's writing, one fears, for a shrinking market.

But those are the people I write for, too, those strangers in the woods. Apart from them, these civilized and independent-minded people, one's fellow men and women, one writes for no one, not even oneself; I think I write to make the work what it seems to want to be. I hope that if it's good, if I keep it human and musical, there'll be some people who get it. And maybe I'll be one of them.

Frame of mind

Voice expresses self; tone expresses mood.

That's true of speaking, and it's true of writing. My voice is my voice no matter what state of mind or health I'm in. I am who I am regardless of my indifference, anger, jubilation, cheek, anxiety, disinterest or devil-may-care; and my voice betrays me. But you know which mood I'm in because its tone changes.

A good conversation is marked by the particularity and personality of the voices involved in it. It's the same with writing. How you communicate should not only make sense for your reader; it should be true to you. Every piece of writing should sound as though someone were speaking it. So yours should sound like you. Not because you're someone special; just because you're the writer, and these are meant to be your words.

The moment you find yourself trying to sound like someone else is the moment your writing loses its voice and loses its readers. It will be stilted; it will ring false; it will sound like as though it were composed by a machine or a committee. Or, worse still, by a politician. Writing like someone else is both difficult and dull. If your writing is not in some way pleasing to yourself—and it won't be unless it sounds at least a little like you—you'll tire of it. And if you're bored, you can be certain your reader will be, too.

Even at work, or in college, writers should be allowed to write in their own voice. No matter what kind of document it is, it will work better if it speaks; and it will not speak if its author tries to write as though she were the organization. Corporate entities, last time I checked, did not have the gift of speech; they have to leave that to their people. In reality, as the law knows, you write, in an organization, as one of its officers, and that's how each policy writer, consultant or customer service executive ought to sound. But how each of us plays that role, conforming to the same code of conduct and style guide, will differ from person to person. And so it should.

Outside a professional context, as I said last chapter, try to sound like no one but your deepest, truest, fullest self. Not like your idea of how a writer should sound.

Writing well, particularly at work, or for one's cause, or when there's any kind of money involved, or politics or relationship, asks of you some serious emotional intelligence work. You need to know the mood you're in, so that your don't let your mood do the writing. Don't let anger or anxiety choose your nouns and verbs and especially your adjectives. Get those feelings in check. Set them aside and write as though you were the cool (and respectful) customer I was talking about before. Even if you're not. How do you pull that off? Choose the kinds of word and structure good talkers, including you, employ in well-mannered conversation. Fool yourself into being the kind of person who can conduct such a thing right here on the page.

▶ **Try this**

1 Do you let your people write in their voices? Does your boss let you? How? If not, why not? How might you help them write well in their own way?

2 A client—call them ABC Inc.—contracted with you six months ago to write their annual report. You worked hard on the job. Much of the information you were promised never materialized, and you had to make a nuisance of yourself among the employees, lining up interviews and requesting spreadsheets, job descriptions, strategic plans, and so on, just to be able to get the document done. You have succeeded, against all probability. Although the client was late with the first two (of four) instalments of the agreed fee, they paid each in the end.

Now the job is done—on time. The client has signed off on your draft and complimented you on its high standard. You know that it complies with industry standards. You have ten years' experience in this work, and reports you have written have won several awards.

You have pressed the client twice for payment of the outstanding two instalments (50 percent all up) of the fee, and so far you have received no response. Two months have passed since the submission of the report. Now you receive a letter from the organization asserting that the report is below the standard they had expected and demanding that you rewrite significant parts of it as soon as possible.

The task is to write them a letter in response. Think hard about what you want to achieve and what tone you need to strike. How do you feel? Think about writing down what you would like to say, to get it off your chest, before writing the kind of letter that might serve your interests better.

Empathy's not everyone's strong suit

Writing is, among other things, a practice of empathy. While being most utterly yourself—the master of your subject, the engineer of sturdy sentences, the project manager of complexity and nuance, the manager of the risk of misunderstanding—you must also be someone else: someone who doesn't know what you know, who only knows what you say, and who only knows what you mean if your words make sense to them. You must sound out every phrase you make as though you had not made it. You must hear what you say as though it were not you who said it. You must write as though you were not only writing this, but reading it.

> A good writer is a careful and a critical listener. You are your own work's first and most important reader. If you don't listen to it carefully, it's probable no one else will.

So it's going to help to be good at not being merely yourself. Alas, not everyone is equally gifted at that.

If you're not, it may help to cast someone in the role of your reader and speak your piece for them. Since a good piece of writing will go like a good conversation, cast someone with whom you converse well; think of someone you're used to treating in the way I've described earlier. A good friend. A work colleague. Someone who listens well. Someone with whom you feel you talk fluently and intelligently. Sit them (imaginatively, if not actually) in the listening seat and talk, regardless of who your actual reader is.

Gertrude Stein said, "I write for myself and for strangers." If you're good with strangers—people with whom there is often much less to feel inhibited by—write for a stranger. (And, as ever, for yourself.) Write, as S. J. Perelman does, for the grocer on your shoulder.

Or write, as I once heard a writing teacher suggest, for your mother. Now there's a man who must have had a good relationship with his mother. But I like his model. I think he meant that one treats—ideally, and sometimes actually—one's mother with respect and informality. And if one can strike that unusual balance—respect and informality, even love—one will get the writing right.

Try it. Write for Nelson Mandela or Madonna, if it helps. Write, like John Steinbeck, for your dogs, or for your favorite horse. Write for someone who isn't yourself but whom you don't have any trouble conversing with in your mind. Write with confidence and ease, with informality and simplicity. Don't dumb it down; keep it smart and short.

▶ Try this

1 The next thing you have to write—board paper, letter to the council, letter of resignation, tricky email—sit down and begin it as though it were an email to a friend. Or to your mother, if you have that kind of mother.

  Once you find the tone and voice for that, the strategy for organizing your thoughts, keep it going through the actual document. See if it helps.

2 Take a piece of writing you have to do. Think of its reader or readers. List every concept and word you can think of that

someone other than yourself might be unfamiliar with. Write down the expressions and concepts you are absolutely sure this particular reader will understand. Write down as briefly as you can what it is that you want them to understand from reading your piece. Now have a go at writing it, keeping your reader in mind, being careful to spell out anything that may need to be explained.

You're not here to judge

Many of my clients—particularly those who write, regulate or administer policy or whose work it is to assess the work of others—have trouble getting their tone right. The writing I read from them oscillates between harsh judgment at one end and vague circumspection at the other. Reading, you feel the weight of the writer's judgment (either overtly overstated or, worse still, aggressively implied) or else you have no idea what they have concluded, so persistently do they withhold anything like an opinion. (Frequently, to make matters worse, the vaguest reports are often the longest; they spend page after page trying to avoid uttering anything resembling the harsh conclusion they imagine they're obliged to have reached. One client of mine spent fifty pages of executive summary and well over 150 pages of report proper *not* saying anything so straightforward as that the relevant agency under review had overspent its budget by some millions of dollars.) No one wants to read writing heavy with judgment or vague and snide with judgment withheld. We don't want it blunt or circuitous or sneering. We want it straight and calm and clear.

I think these writers mismanage their tone because they misconceive their role as writers. The writer is not there, no matter what function his or her organization performs, to stand in judgment—or to withhold it. She is there to tell the story of what she finds. Like the scientist or historian or journalist (in the old days). She is not a shock jock or politician; she is not a dictator, a pharisee or a judge—at least, mostly she's not a judge. Praise and blame are not the game the writer, especially in an organization, plays. Don't think of your bottom line as whether the agency (or the person or the process or the philosophy or the product) has passed or failed, and how terrible it is, if the latter. Your opinion about that is immaterial; what one needs to know is exactly what the agency, for instance, is doing and how that corresponds with what they're meant to be doing. Your task is gap analysis.

One of my clients tells their people to make their reports fair and true and balanced. As long as "balanced" has nothing to do with political spin, that sounds like a good formula to me. That would entail writing that gives the material facts dispassionate analysis, that considers all sides, and covers all relevant options.

If you know you're not there to judge, you're likely to resist a judgmental tone, or, conversely, a tone that's meek and apologetic—or embarrassed or arch or evasive about everything you can't bring yourself to say. Write like a literate scientist. The right tone for all your writing is what would work for mum: dignified, calm, clear-headed, confident, humane.

It's hard to find examples of such writing in public life. It's easier to find blunt and evasive instances, but I'll offer you, instead, an instance where I think the tone is pretty good.

Aviation plays a prominent role in Australian business, trade and tourism, as well as meeting important community needs. Australia generally has an impressive aviation safety record. However, any loss of confidence in aviation safety could have serious detrimental repercussions for the industry. The Civil Aviation Safety Authority (CASA) is responsible for the regulation of aviation safety in Australia, except for aviation security. A well-documented and transparent safety surveillance and enforcement regime that ensures targeted and adequate industry coverage, as well as consistency and fairness for all, is necessary for CASA to demonstrate that it is effectively performing its functions under the Act.

Overall, CASA has improved its management of aviation safety compliance since the 1999 audit, particularly in areas such as the identification of risks at the operator level; the frequency and coverage of surveillance; and enforcement of the Act. CASA has adequately addressed the majority of the recommendations from the 1999 audit and has partially implemented the remaining relevant recommendations.

(Australian National Audit Office, Aviation Safety Compliance
Follow-up Audit: Civil Aviation Safety Authority, 2002)

This conclusion is simply written and reasonably plainspoken; it is
concrete and straightforward. It is about as readable as such writing
ever gets, mercifully free of the usual dull and abstract litanies of corporate governance, accountability, transparency, service delivery and
performance management (though, perhaps only because of the
scope of the inquiry). It nearly flies.

CHAPTER 6

SHAPELY THOUGHTS
On thought, planning, structure, and paragraphs

If this book of mine fails to take a straight course, it is because I am lost in a strange region; I have no map. GRAHAM GREENE

Have a plan—don't stick to it

The garden wall is made of sandstone, off-cuts from a quarry at the foot of the dividing range. "We've hauled tons of rock from there," says Rhyl. She's a sculptor, and this wall, which encloses a terrace of flagstones at the front of the house, is just one of the things she's made from all that scree. Three hundred gargoyles in the university quadrangle are some others.

This is the kind of wall you shape as square as a hedge—a yard high, a yard thick—out of chunks of rocks as irregular and fractal, as left-overs from a mullock heap. It's a chaotic mosaic, finished plumb, through three dimensions. Four, if I include the morning and all the time it took to make the rocks, which compose the wall. And I'm sitting on it in the shade of jacarandas on a hot morning, and I'm talking to Rob over the sound of water falling from an iron pipe into a fishpond.

Rob's a potter and a builder, and he's Rhyl's partner. He used to dream impossible forms and wake to make them. He's imagined just about everything—the extensions to the house, the shaded verandas, the gates—that I can see from where I sit. But it's Rhyl who's done most of the heavy lifting lately. She's a woman used to hauling and forming up, and Rob's legs are giving him trouble. His circulation is bad. He has ulcers that hurt so much he can't stand long in the heat.

So he's sitting in the shade, and he's saying, "I don't like to draw things up too tidily. I have an idea of what I want a room or a garden to look like, of course, but I've learned to let the site tell me what goes where. It's not till you start working that you discover what you have to do—where to put the window or the path or the step. It's not till you're hefting rock and timber in the sun that you learn how the land falls and where the best shade is and where you want to flop down in the late afternoon."

I look around at what that technique has conjured here.

"Have a plan—don't stick to it," I say. "That's what I tell my students sometimes. Discover the real work you need to write by writing it. Have a plan to make sure you start. But be prepared to wander off the chart."

"That's what I'm talking about here," says Rob.

All creativity shuffles, thus, between order and chaos—making a wall or a bronze statue, a gargoyle or a paragraph. Let the work catch you in the act of executing a well-laid plan. If it doesn't find you doing that, it probably won't find you at all. Then let it tell you what it really needs to be.

 Try this

Did you ever try to make a cake or build a cabin or make something from scratch that turned out better than you planned because you abandoned the blueprint? Write about that.

Random walk

You know the kind of thing I mean: a random assemblage of sentences amounting to something much less than Rob and Rhyl's water-garden. Reading prose that's carelessly composed feels like being led on a random walk by someone who's trying to find out where they're meant to be taking you. It's the rubble, not the garden wall. It's unpleasant. How to avoid that kind of composition—how to impose just enough order on your writing—is what this chapter's about. It's about structure.

You want your writing to cohere. You want it to hang together, as though it could hang no other way. And you want this because your reader wants it. When we read, we need to sense a design holding the narrative, if it's a narrative, together and moving it along. Lack of order, too much repetition, no forward movement or logic—these qualities kill a work.

So how do you make your writing cohere? How do you move from the pile of rubble you start with—your gathered and disorderly thoughts and the need to make something of them—to the wall around the garden and the small and shapely universe it contains? How do you do your thinking so that when it's done, you're just about ready to write? How do you move from the chaos of research and conception to the necessary order of the written thing? For thinking needs to stay wild; if you micromanage it, it dwindles to a sad trickle. It can't be forced; it needs to be allowed. Writing, on the other hand, must be tidy—at least, it must end up seeming so. How do you get from the wilds to the garden? That's what this chapter's about.

I hold these six things to be true and essential. I never leave home without them.

1 *The rough guide.* A rough plan will serve you better than an elaborate one. Writing has a way of making itself up as it goes along. No one can know where it will go at the outset.

2 *The tight thesis.* On the other hand, a tight thesis will serve you better than a loose one. Know what you're trying to say and keep on knowing it, and keep on refining it, and keep on saying it, in all its subtlety and complexity, sentence after sentence. (If it dawns on you in the writing that you're not saying that at all, then remake your thesis and start writing again.) Know where you stand and where you mean to go, and be clear about it. Writing is not a fishing expedition or a sleepwalk. It's a hike with a map and a compass and plenty of time.

3 *Have a point and make it upfront.* There are many ways to organize thought on paper, but if in doubt, write every document

SHAPELY THOUGHTS | 199

and every part of it deductively. Start, in other words, with your main point, justify it and explore it. This is probably not the best way to write a novel or a poem, but it's good for just about everything else.

4 *Coherence happens sentence by sentence.* The hardest and most vital work of coherence happens at the level of the sentence. Concentrate on making your sentences good, one after another. Nothing—no amount of mindmapping and planning—matters more than this. Sentence making is the ultimate structural discipline. Ask yourself how each sentence you write advances the story you're telling, the thesis you're demonstrating, the argument you're making, the love you're proclaiming, the recommendations you're submitting, the policy you're proposing. Get to the end of it rhythmically, economically and competently. Then join it to the one that follows (having already thought hard about how it follows from the one before).

5 *Paragraphs make perfect.* The second hardest and most vital work of coherence happens at the next level up: the composition of tidy paragraphs, each transparently part of the whole; each entire; and all elegantly interlinked.

6 *Link everything to everything else.* This is not a new point; it's a way of summarizing the others. Every sentence and every paragraph should link to the one before it and point to the one that comes next. Your readers must know, as they read each clause and sentence and paragraph, why they are reading it and why they are reading it here and why they are reading it now; and they must hear in it your main point reprised, advanced and clarified.

Arrive before you begin

Arrive at your document before you start writing it.

Get done, I mean, with the messy business of gathering facts and interpreting them and working out what they all amount to and what you want to say about that, before you take up the pen. Know just what it is you mean to say before you start to say it.

"There's one thing I say to my people here," the senior man at my client said to me, "more often than anything else, and much more often than I'd like. It's this: do your thinking properly off the paper, so you can express it clearly, simply and briefly on the paper. Can you talk to them about that?"

"I will," I said. And I did.

Writing is usually both clearer and shorter when it's been thought through first. "What am I saying here; exactly what have I concluded; and what response am I looking for?" Unless you've got answers to those questions at hand, put your hands back in your pockets.

Order your writing by getting clear about these things before you set out:

- What are you saying (exactly)?
- Why are you saying it (what is your purpose; what decision or change or action are you looking for)?
- What context makes your point relevant?
- What evidence justifies your conclusion?
- Why does your conclusion matter?
- For whom does your conclusion matter?
- Whom will your conclusions affect and how?

No reader wants to stumble along with you, looking in every place you looked, at everything you found; readers don't want to accompany you staggering toward some sort of conclusion about all that— or no conclusion at all. What they want is what you've made of things. What they want is the story. It's up to you to make it convincing. Interpret, analyze, critically assess, and conclude. That's what you're there for. Give them the benefit of your considered thought. Don't let them loose in your data and ask them to do your thinking for you.

An axiom of communication theory tells us that when we compose any kind of message we move through four phases: data to information to knowledge to information, again. That is, I gather data; I analyze and interpret it and discover what it means; I become so familiar with the material facts and arguments and findings that I enter into a state of knowledge; then, when I speak, I inform my listeners so that soon enough they, too, may know the subject almost as well as I do.

One travels that arc from chaos to order whenever one writes. And most of the journey takes place off the page. Most of it is thinking and design.

> When you write you organize ideas. Don't offer up data. Tell a story; make it good and true; know what it's about and what it's for; tell it well; let it make sense; and hope that wisdom may arise.

 Try this

1 Use that list of critical thinking questions (see p. 39) to think through the next tricky thing you have to write.
2 Think of something that gets your goat, and use that list of questions to plan a short opinion piece—a rant—on that topic. Write the piece, if you like. But most of all, plan it.

Chaos theory

Talk all you like about planning; the truth is we discover our writing by writing. We do our hardest thinking making sentences.

A sentence makes the meaning it makes out of the process of its own unravelling. Out of a process itself chaotic—the thinking of thoughts and the embarkation upon one's sentences—a writer discovers what it is she's really trying to say and how she needs to hang it together. She makes sentences and stitches them together so that it will seem they all come out that way the first time and as though the thing could not be said any other way.

Try this

If you didn't write the opinion piece in the last exercise, write it now. Notice how you get lost sometimes trying to flesh out your notes into sentences; notice how you sometimes find a fresh idea or refine a loose one in the process of composition.

Thesis/antithesis

I mentioned before (see p. 181) Thomas Kane's notion that writing is work performed in three movements:

- thinking about it
- doing it
- doing it again

But the thinking, though it comes first, never stops. And as soon as the thinking starts, you begin to write (if Kane is right about writing's three stages), because you begin to pose questions, shape theses, and frame issues—*in words, in phrases, in sentences*. When you organize ideas, to invert what I said before, you write.

Thinking need not be orderly. High-calibre thought is mildly chaotic, unconstrained by fixed ideas. But like a wild habitat, a mind will have its own organizing principle. Thought proceeds, I think, in a kind of dialectic shuffle.

Thinking always begins, I think, with preconception—not a pre-judgment, but a notional conclusion (an hypothesis), which the thinking tests. If the thinking is good, the testing will be sound and relentless, and the hypothesis may fail; indeed, a good thinker sets out to try—to see if she can disprove—a thesis. A good thinker keeps making new theses until she gets one that stands, that's justified and sustained by the material facts.

This is how a writer should think—and she should probably finish most of that thinking before she sits down to write. A writer's thinking is an exacting kind of hike, a purposeful kind of wander—not an aimless walk among facts. The writing picks up where—and it articulates *what*—the thinking arrived at.

So, don't begin to write without having put yourself and your findings through this kind of process. Go into the data with a question in your pocket, an embryonic thesis to test. Keep your mind open; be tough on yourself; keep asking yourself what you make of things at this point, and where your hypothesis is weak; keep testing and refining.

> When you've got to the end of such a process, you should have something to say—something clear and defensible. Unless it's a literary work, say it, and say it at the start. The wandering is over. You have arrived. Announce where you've arrived at and demonstrate how and why—that's what the paper's for.

Even if you're writing a poem or an essay or a story, it still seems like a good idea to have a notion of what it's hoping to say (even if it says it indirectly or by implication), and to have it from the start. Know your throughline, and keep following it, even if you never once articulate it; this is how it goes best in literature. Indirectly.

If, when you start writing, you feel you're hunting for a conclusion—if you don't yet have your pitch, your thesis, your message down—then that's a draft you've got there. Don't mistake it for prose. What you're doing with your fingers on the keyboard is getting your thinking finished.

> What readers want is *writing*—information and guidance. They want the benefit of your thinking, not the thinking itself, raw and unstructured. They want orderly thought.

 Try this

Take something you're researching or thinking about now or something you know a fair bit about. Ask yourself what you really want to say about it. Make it a short statement—a sentence or two.

A wild kind of order

If you've finished your research, it's time to grow wise about what you think you've found and to turn it into a story that makes (beautiful) sense to your reader. It's time to find the bones and make from them a skeleton and drape it with your tale. It's time, in other words, to get organized.

And you should do that however you like; just don't get too orderly too fast. Forget your hierarchies of headings; don't compose a list. Not yet. No one ever thought creatively or clearly in a dead straight line, from first point to last. Let the writing itself throw up the kind of outline some of us try to make at the outset. A detailed outline is a product of a well-written document—not the other way around.

What you want now is a loose kind of map. The first task is not to structure your *document*; it's to find the order in your thoughts and sketch it. You move from thinking into writing by articulating first the pattern of what you know, what you've made of the data—the topics you need to cover and what they all amount to.

A loose-jointed kind of skeleton, a more gestural kind of anatomy, serves you best in the transition from research to writing. Anything tighter tends to stop your thinking—and indeed your writing—short. It maps, if I may revert to my other metaphor, too narrow a territory; it confines the search; it limits the journey. Sketchier plans keep the right-side of one's brain on the job—the hemisphere that recognizes patterns and generates ideas. The right brain is good at the big picture; it discovers and unearths and connects. The left brain analyzes and orders what the right brain perceives and conceives. Once we have the shape of things, the left brain sets about naming them and setting them in the right kind of sequence; it connects the hipbone to the thighbone and so on, until the bones resemble a skeleton for the writing to flesh out.

A mindmap is a device for integrating these two brains of ours; for seeing the wood from the trees; for discerning the pattern in what we know; for naming the parts; for deducing topics we have to cover; for working out what they amount to; and for loosely articulating all this, so that one is ready to write.

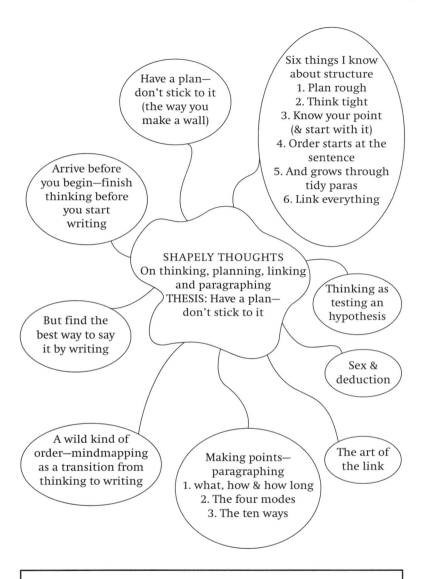

The mindmap is a wild kind of ordering—neat enough to launch us on the finer kind of thinking, the deeper kind of discovery, we do when we write, but not so neat it hobbles us.

Take your subject. Write it down at the center of a sheet of paper. Free yourself from syntax and logic. Just ask yourself what you know and what you want your audience to know about that. Write the answers in short phrases roughly encircling your subject; make a network of nodes. Do this until you have on paper all the topics you feel you need to write about.

Then ask yourself what all of those points add up to. What are you saying in this document by making each of these points? What are they all about? This will be your thesis sentence.

You can use a mindmap to plan an entire book and each chapter in it; each paragraph, if you like. (I'm working from one right now—the one on the previous page—which I drafted the day before yesterday to get my head around this chapter.) And you can use one again and again, whenever you start wondering what the hell you thought you were saying at this point.

The web of ideas becomes a rough map that guides the writing. And the thesis sentence becomes your starting point—your throughline. But the mindmap has less value as a map than as a process; the better you make it, the less you're likely to need it. It gets your mind into gear. It organizes you, so that you're ready to start making a wall— and following where it wants to go.

▶ Try this

Imagine you have to make a short speech at Toastmasters on one of these topics:

- The secret of good writing
- The secret of good parenting
- Your three rules for leading a good life
- Why men are redundant
- The basis of a happy relationship
- The consolations of solitude
- The consolations of landscape
- The uses of reading
- The politics of Intelligent Design
- Anything else that comes to mind for you

> Mindmap your thoughts. When you have a mindmap, summarize
> your thesis briefly. Go ahead and begin to write your speech, if you
> want. Begin it with a short paragraph that states your thesis, jus-
> tifies and explains it.

SEX and the working writer

You've made your mindmap, and you're ready to write. How are you going to start? And how are you going to organize what you have to say under each topic your map has helped you plot?

If in doubt, think of sex. Well, think of it this way:

1 State (S)
2 Explain (E)
3 Explore (X)

Everything I know about SEX I learned from one of my clients, the same one who told me to tell his people to get their thinking done before they started their writing. He told me SEX had changed his life when someone told him about it. It made a writer of him. It's a simple rhetorical model that will take you a long way—in writing at work anyway. It's a model for a whole document and for all of its parts— each chapter and paragraph, I mean.

1 *State* your conclusion, the bottom line, what the thing's about (take two or three sentences if you need to, but keep it brief).
2 *Explain* yourself (briefly again): why is this so; why is it important; what problem does this conclusion solve; what background made it necessary to come to a conclusion about this thing?
3 *Explore*. As you expand into this explanation you begin the work of X (exploration). And that work may take you several paragraphs. Indeed, one's whole document is really an extended exploration of your statement and justification. Begin each paragraph with its main point.

SEX is just one way to compose a paragraph. It's an instance of deduction: you begin with your conclusion and justify it. Within a document—in the course of the long or short exploration of your opening statement—you may want to employ many different kinds of paragraph, some of them starting with their main point, others circling around it, finishing with it or explaining it with examples.

But most functional documents go best when they proceed deductively—when they say upfront not only what they are about but what they conclude. Don't make 'em wait till the end to find out who done it. Unless it's a detective novel you're writing.

Two people win when you start with your conclusion: you and your reader. *You* win because you focus your mind and make yourself write an orderly document that is a piece of directed exposition; a thesis orders you. *Your reader* wins because he gets an orderly document that begins by telling him what he most wants to know—which is why he should read on.

Writing clear thesis statements upfront is hard work. That's why so few people write them. You don't want to be blunt or judgmental; nor do you want to be generic and qualified. A good thesis is not a statement of whether something is wonderful or terrible, or whether you like it or not; it's your conclusion about exactly how you see something—for example, not that the war in Iraq was a disgrace or a necessary evil, but just what it achieved and why; not that there are many things one might do to sustain a loving relationship, but that Rilke had it right—love will prosper if each of us is the guardian of each other's solitude. A thesis is what you make of the evidence; it's your summary of what you've found. It should be clear and short and engaging—perhaps even intriguing. And it should open out into the exploration the rest of the document undertakes.

These thesis sentences don't help much:

A number of factors contribute to good writing. (Vague and useless. What is the one thing you could say about good writing, which would include all those factors?)

This report proposes a number of options available to the State of Oregon by way of improving the operation of its ports infrastructure to take advantage of the growth in international trade. (What are they?)

Opinions have always differed about the qualities of Mark Twain's *The Adventures of Huckleberry Finn* and about its impact on American literature. (What is the nature of those opinions, and on balance, why do you think the book matters?)

The department has manifestly failed to implement an adequate response to the recommendations of the last audit report. We find the department's conduct unacceptable. (Too blunt and judgmental; what has the department done?)

The jury is still out on climate change. (So when do you think we can expect them back; and what uncertainties are they discussing?)

Let me translate the first few. These are more like thesis statements. The makings of good SEX:

Writing is like the best kind of conversation. It goes well when it sounds like speech; but it must be more carefully orchestrated.

The consultancy brief asked us to address this threshold question: would a combined ports structure in the State of Oregon yield significant improvements? Our answer is yes. This study shows that a single ports corporation will position Oregon to seize the opportunities presented by the expansion of global trade and the improvement of port logistics.

All modern American literature comes from one book by Mark Twain called Huckleberry Finn. (ERNEST HEMINGWAY)

Most of the writing I review suffers from want of a thesis. Politics is one reason writers in business and government won't say what they mean at the start (or anywhere, sometimes). Inductive habits of thought are another. Loose and hasty, anxious thinking is a third—*I won't tell you what I've concluded because I haven't concluded anything yet, and I can't bring myself to admit it.* Don't be anxious; don't outsmart yourself; don't make long recitals of background and methodology first; don't ignore your reader. Just work out what it is you're saying, and say it—remembering the manners we spoke of in the last chapter —upfront. Say it; say why; then explore the topics you need to explore to justify your thesis.

Try this

Rewrite the remaining two thesis statements above. Recast my attempts at the others, too, if you like.

Pieces of string

A paragraph is a meaningful assemblage of sentences. It is what SEX leads to.

A paragraph is all the sentences you need in order to make—and then to justify and explore—your point. But just *this* point—the one you articulate in so many words in your statement or thesis sentence, the one best said (outside literature) first.

Knowing when each paragraph is over—knowing when enough is enough—can take a long time to master. Each paragraph is a rock—just this rock—in the wall. And in a good wall, the size and nature of the rocks vary.

So, a paragraph is a collection of sentences that tells one piece of a larger story. Like a sentence, each paragraph will name something and say something about it. A sentence contains a subject and a predicate, a paragraph an issue and its discussion—but not necessarily in that order.

A good paragraph may be one sentence long or ten. It's unlikely, these days, to go on for twenty. Because we find ourselves in an age of short attention spans and information fatigue, your paragraphs probably want to be shorter today than they did a hundred years back. But there's no perfect length, and each paragraph oughtn't to be the same size. I mention this because there are people out there telling students that five sentences, and no more, make a paragraph. That sounds like a recipe to me—a recipe for pretty ordinary writing. It's not a question of how many sentences you've got; it's whether you've got the right ones, and only the right ones, laid out in the right order to say the thing you think you're saying.

Practice: you'll get the hang of it. Read good writers. Notice how they do it. Notice that in good writing paragraphs vary in length and form and manner depending on what their author has in mind for them; notice that variety is part of the large-scale music of a good piece of writing.

Because it's graceful to vary the structure and style of your paragraphs (just as it is to diversify your sentences), let me list the species. My purpose is not to have you cast every paragraph you write in one or other of these molds; each is a way of mustering one's thoughts and sentences, and each has a long and virtuous history. Each is a shapely way of saying something, and since we have many points to make or stories to tell whenever we open a laptop, it would be good to know a few different routes. The shape one chooses should depend on what one is trying to say and why—and knowing even *that* would be a breakthrough for most of us.

The four modes

If you exclude the vital but mystical business of making rhythm and other semantic musics with your words, a thing you cannot plan for with quite the precision I'm going to describe; if you also pretend that writing ever could or ever should observe such orderly distinctions—there are four ways to proceed when you open you mouth on paper to utter a paragraph. You may tell, you may describe, you may argue, or you may explain. And so, there are four modes of making a paragraph.

- *Narration*, in which you recite a sequence of events—this, of course, is the storytelling mode, good for novels (where your purpose is not to explain but to recite) and those parts of more functional documents where you need to say what happened.
- *Description*, in which you pan, like a camera, across a room, a crime scene, a new product, a woman's face, a meeting, a moment, a flood plain.
- *Argumentation*, in which you put a case and defend it by use, especially, of logic—a mainstay in the law, politics, marketing, and education, although one is always, in a sense, arguing for a position.
- *Exposition*, in which your purpose is to explain, analyze, and inform.

I'll have most to say here about the expository paragraph because exposition is what one does most of the time in functional writing—in school, college or university essays; in academic or technical papers; in business, scientific or professional reports; in business letters; in policy statements and so on. But even in that kind of prose, you're also going to need to narrate, describe, and argue.

If you're writing journalism, you'll learn to swing easily from one to the other (least of all argumentation, since that is not what a journalist is supposed, except on the op-ed page, to be embarked on).

If it's literature you're writing, you won't want to be doing much pure exposition. Expository lumps, clumps of analysis or large tracts of fact spoil a good story, song or poem. But in practice, all writing organizes ideas; all writing makes points, offers up ideas and elaborates them, directly or indirectly. So everyone—even the poet, very often the novelist, always the essayist—does exposition.

A pragmatic note: in real life, few paragraphs are pure. While one can identify examples that just narrate or just describe, that just argue or just explain, most paragraphs do a bit of everything. Where a writer pursues no design, where she forgets what story her paragraph sets out to tell, this kind of rhetorical hybridizing can ruin a paragraph; but, as long as you write with your eyes open, impure paragraphs are more than passable. They are, in fact, what good prose is made of, for they speak with the characteristic cadences of natural thought and utterance.

These categories, then (the four modes here, as well as the ten kinds of exposition, which follow), are simply analytical tools. They help you design more orderly paragraphs. But real paragraphs can walk *and* chew gum. Lively writing everywhere—in novels and essays, newspapers and college papers, speeches, brochures, and textbooks—will often explain, insist, describe, and narrate, all in the same paragraph. Try describing a room or a landscape—narration creeps in as soon as someone or something moves. Try narrating an event without describing the players and the scene, without explaining what is going on.

As well as being one of the finer passages of prose you'll ever read, this paragraph by Norman Maclean argues and explains, it narrates, and it describes; and perhaps the way it manages all of them so deftly is the reason it is so fine. It shows and it tells with exquisite care. It has one idea, and it tells just one story. But it uses landscape, drama (recalled and enacted), dialogue, reflection, and proposition to get the telling done; it seems to contain the whole world.

A river, though, has so many things to say that it is hard to know what it says to each of us. As we were packing our tackle and fish in the car, Paul repeated, "Just give me three more years." At the time, I was surprised at the repetition, but later I realized that the river somewhere, sometime, must have told me, too, that he would receive no such gift. For, when the police sergeant early next May wakened me before daybreak, I rose and asked no questions. Together we drove across the Continental Divide and down the length of the Big Blackfoot River over forest floors yellow and sometimes white with glacier lilies to tell my father and mother that my brother had been beaten to death by the butt of a revolver and his body dumped in an alley. (NORMAN MACLEAN, *A River Runs Through It*)

Here's a paragraph where nothing much happens except weather and a road. But the description is also a narrative of vital events, of which a small human drama—finding a place to bury a lover—is part.

We stood in silence in the long grass, and I smoked a cigarette. Just as I was throwing it away, the mist spread a little, and a pale cold clarity began to fill the world. In ten minutes we could see where we were. The plains lay below us, and I could follow the road by which we had come, as it wound in and out along the slopes, climbed towards us, and, winding, went on. To the south far away below the changing clouds, lay the broken, dark blue foothills of Kilimanjaro. As we turned to the north the light increased; pale rays for a moment slanted in the sky and a streak of shining silver drew up the shoulder of Mount Kenya. Suddenly, much closer, to the east below us, was a little red spot in the grey and green, the only red there was, the tiled roof of my house on its cleared place in the forest. We did not have to go any farther, we were in the right place. A little while after, the rain started again. (KAREN BLIXEN, *Out of Africa*)

But here is some (more or less) straightforward narration:

She hurries from the house, wearing a coat too heavy for the weather. It is 1941. Another war has begun. She has left a note for Leonard, and another for Vanessa. She walks purposefully toward the river, certain of what she'll do, but even now she is almost distracted by the sight of the downs, the church, and a scattering of sheep, incandescent, tinged with a faint hint of sulfur, grazing under a darkening sky. She pauses, watching the sheep and the sky, then walks on. The voices murmur behind her; bombers drone in the sky, though she looks for the planes and can't see them.

(MICHAEL CUNNINGHAM, *The Hours*)

And another opening paragraph of description from the start of a very different book:

Will you look at us by the river! The whole restless mob of us on spread blankets in the dreamy briny sunshine skylarking and chiacking about for one day, one clear, clean, sweet day in a good world in the midst of our living. Yachts run before an unfelt gust with bagnecked pelicans riding above them, the city their twitching backdrop, all blocks and points of mirror light down to the water's edge. (TIM WINTON, *Cloudstreet*)

Here's a decent piece of argument:

But, in a larger sense, we cannot dedicate—we cannot consecrate—we cannot hallow—this ground. The brave men, living and dead, who struggled here, have consecrated it, far above our poor power to add or detract . . . It is rather for us the living, rather, to be dedicated here to the unfinished work which they who fought here have thus so nobly advanced. It is for us to be here dedicated to the great task remaining before us—that from these honored dead we take increased devotion to that cause for which they gave the last full measure of devotion—that we here highly resolve that these dead shall not have died in vain—that this nation, under God, shall have a new birth of freedom—and that government of the people, by the people, for the people, shall not perish from the earth.

(ABRAHAM LINCOLN, *The Gettysburg Address*, 1863)

Hear the rhythms, notice the care, with thought and word, upon which that great short speech depended.

And here's a nice piece of exposition:

Writing is often discussed as two separate acts—though in practice they overlap, intermingle, and impersonate each other. They differ in emphasis, but are by no means merely sequential. If we do them well, both result in discovery. One is the act of exploration: some combination of premeditated searching and undisciplined, perhaps only partly conscious rambling. This includes scribbling notes, considering potential scenes, lines, or images, inventing characters, even writing drafts . . . If we persist, we discover our story (or poem, or novel) within the world of that story. The other act of writing we might call presentation. Applying knowledge, skill, and talent, we create a document meant to communicate with, and have an effect on, others. The purpose of a story or poem . . . is not to record our experience but to create a context for, and to lead the reader on, a journey. That is to say, at some point we turn from the role of the Explorer to take on that of Guide. (PETER TURCHI, *Maps of the Imagination*)

 Try this

1 What's the organizing idea or story in each paragraph I've quoted above? (Some may seem to have more than one.)

2 Write a description of:

- your bedroom or the place where you work
- your mother's face

3 If you could change just one thing in the world, what would it be and why? Make an argument for that.

Ten ways to make a point

There are ten ways to make a point—more if you hybridize. There are ten ways to develop a point into a paragraph. You can develop your point by

- rephrasing it in various ways
- illustrating it with examples
- likening it to something else by
  - analogy or
  - comparison
- distinguishing it from something else by contrast
- explaining
  - what caused it or
  - what it causes
- defining it (and explaining your definition)
- analyzing it
- qualifying it

A note: although most of the sample paragraphs below (as well as the ones I've just quoted) begin with their main point (topic sentence) and develop it in one of the ways I've listed, you may lodge your paragraph's main point anywhere—beginning, middle or end. When you put your topic sentence somewhere else than first, you relax your rhetoric into something more like talking. And you vary the formula, which can be pleasing. So, have a point, and let it organize your paragraph, but don't feel compelled to begin with it.

1 Rephrasing

You make the point over and again, phrasing it a little differently each time. This can be a powerful and, if you let it get away from you, a dull way to write a paragraph. This passage from Jim Crace's novel *Being Dead* really makes an argument, by saying the same thing in different ways, again and again: everyone and everything dies; the landscape deals with it; the landscape is made of death and dying, and—dead or alive—we are part of the landscape. Exposition and argument have their place in literature, if you can do them this well:

It is, of course, a pity that the police dogs ever caught the scent of human carrion and led their poking masters to the dunes to clear away the corpses for "proper burial," so that the dead could be less splendid in a grave. The dunes could have disposed of Joseph and Celice themselves. They didn't need help. The earth is practised in the craft of burial. It gathers round. It embraces and adopts the dead. Joseph and Celice would have turned to landscape, given time. Their bodies would have been just something extra dead in a landscape already sculpted out of death. They would become nothing special. Gulls die. And so do flies and crabs. So do the seals. Even stars must decompose, disrupt and blister on the sky. Everything was born to go. The universe has learned to cope with death. (JIM CRACE, *Being Dead*)

2 Illustration

Illustration is a sibling of restatement, and sometimes it's hard to tell them apart. When you illustrate, you make a point and then offer up an example or two or however many it takes to explain or exhaust yourself. The second paragraph of Karen Blixen's *Out of Africa* is a long recital of lovely examples of what she claims in her opening sentence.

The geographical position and the height of the land combined to create a landscape that had not its like in all the world . . .

In the opening of her essay "The Little Virtues," Natalia Ginzburg uses the same technique (perhaps more analytically, because she is making an argument). This is also a good example of the contrasting style.

As far as the education of children is concerned I think they should be taught not the little virtues but the great ones. Not thrift but generosity and an indifference to money; not caution but courage and a contempt for danger; nor shrewdness but frankness and a love of truth; not tact but love for one's neighbour and self-denial; not a desire for success but a desire to be and to know.

(NATALIA GINZBURG, "The Little Virtues," *The Little Virtues*)

3 Analogy

One way to help readers understand what you mean is to offer an analogy. In place of or in addition to the image or idea you want your readers to grasp, you describe a second thing—a thing perhaps more striking to them. Your purpose is to invest your subject with some of the power and strangeness of the analogous subject; your purpose is, as it always is with metaphor, to enliven your subject and waken your readers to something remarkable about it, by reference to a second subject that is manifestly lively and memorable in precisely the respect you're saying your real subject is. To your readers you say: think of this familiar thing I'm talking about as though it were this other (more lovely or remarkable) thing. John Updike, for example, writes an opening paragraph—he writes an entire essay—asking us to think of the male body as a rocket designed to deliver a payload and in the process release a man from time and self for the duration of the mission ("The Disposable Rocket," 1993).

Brian Doyle runs a good line in analogy, too. Here's a typical paragraph, also on an anatomical theme:

Or think of the heart as a music machine—not a far-fetched idea, for the heart runs on electric impulse and does so in a steady 4/4 rhythm. A musician friend of mine maintains that the 4/4 rhythm, standard in popular music, feels right, normal, because it is the pace of our hearts, the interior music we hear all day and all night. We are soaked in the song of the heart every hour of every year every life long.

(BRIAN DOYLE, *The Wet Engine*)

4 Comparison

A less striking kind of likening happens when you compare what you're saying to something equally familiar to a reader. The idea, here, is to point up the essence of the thing you mean by reference to another essence *like* it. You're hoping that the quality you're referring to becomes clearer when it is seen to belong not just to this one case but to a class of two or more. The car drives like a boat, you might say; or she sings with the passion of Maria Callas and the precision of Joan Sutherland; or the market is behaving the way it did before the 1987 crash.

The bush was like the sea, a rooted, tideless sea. It presented to the first settlers the same anonymity, wild and strange. Its dangers, more passive, were just as real. It closed like water over those who penetrated it. It went on and on across a continent as unlimited as an ocean. A specialized knowledge was needed to navigate it, but it could not be learnt at a marine college. A generation had to grow up in it. It took exactly a generation before a way over the mountains was found and the interior unsealed. This may not sound reasonable, but it has its own logic.

(MARJORIE BARNARD, *A History of Australia*)

5 Contrast

Another way to make something clearer is to contrast it to its opposite. The most remarkable and sustained instance of this technique I know is Natalia Ginzburg's essay "He & I," in which every paragraph contrasts herself and her husband. "He always feels hot, I always feel cold," she begins, and so she carries on. (Her subject, I think, is really the difference—and the relationship—between the two of them, not merely herself and her true nature, as understood by contrast to her husband.)

James Thurber is, as ever, talking rather more about himself than his subject, in this case Salvador Dali, to whom he contrasts himself,:

> Let me be the first to admit that the naked truth about me is to the naked truth about Salvador Dali as an old ukulele in the attic is to a piano in a tree, and I mean a piano with breasts. Señor Dali has the jump on me from the beginning. He remembers and describes in detail what it was like in the womb. My own earliest memory is of accompanying my father to a polling booth in Columbus, Ohio, where he voted for William McKinley.

> (JAMES THURBER, "The Secret Life of James Thurber,"
> *The Thurber Carnival*)

6 *The cause of things*

The strategy here is simple, even if the research and thinking behind it are not: something happened; here's why. This kind of paragraph discusses the cause of something.

Here, Louise Erdrich poses a question of causality (why am I depressed?) discreetly and obliquely (like a good literary stylist) and answers it:

> I have no profound reason to be depressed and have always hated and despised depression, fought it with every argument I can invent, tried my best to walk it off, run it off, drink it out, crush it with leaves and solitude on the Plains or in the accepting Northeastern woods. But the deaths of three of my grandparents, within months of one another, seem to trigger a downward trend I cannot stave off even with a baby in my arms. Somehow, over all these miles, I must have been sustained by my grandparents even more than I knew, because the silence in their wake roars over me, their absences shake me, and it seems as though something within me is pulled deeply under, into the earth, as though I still follow after them, stumbling, unable to say good-bye. (LOUISE ERDRICH, *The Blue Jay's Dance*)

Historians are interested in what happened and how and why, and you can find among them some nice examples of paragraphs shaped in search of the causes of things. Here, for instance, is Eric Hobsbawm in *The Age of Revolution*:

The French Revolution was not made or led by a formed party or movement in the modern sense, nor by men attempting to carry out a systematic programme. It hardly even threw up "leaders" of the kind to which twentieth-century revolutions have accustomed us, until the post-revolutionary figure of Napoleon. Nevertheless a striking consensus of general ideas among a fairly coherent social group gave the revolutionary movement effective unity. The group was the "bourgeoisie"; its ideas were those of classical liberalism, as formulated by the "philosophers" and "economists" and propagated by freemasonry and in informal associations. To this extent "the philosophers" can be justly made responsible for the Revolution. It would have occurred without them, but they probably made the difference between a mere breakdown of an old regime and the effective and rapid substitution of a new one.

7 *The effect of things*

Instead of—or after—talking about the cause of a thing, one talks about its consequences: because this happened, because she took this step, because he thought this thought, all the world changed thus. Here's an instance from the close of Natalia Ginzburg's "The Little Virtues." It explores what happens when a parent has retained a sense of her own calling (beyond parenting); and what happens when she has not.

And if we ourselves have a vocation, if we have not betrayed it, if over the years we have continued to love it, to serve it passionately, we are able to keep all sense of ownership out of our love for our children. But if on the other hand we do not have a vocation, or if we have abandoned it or betrayed it out of cynicism or a fear of life, or because of mistaken parental love, or because of some little virtue that exists within us, then we cling to our children as a shipwrecked mariner clings to a tree trunk; we eagerly demand that they give us back everything we have given them, that they be absolutely and inescapably what we wish them to be, that they get out of life everything we have missed; we end up asking them for all the things which can only be given to us by our own vocation; we want them to be entirely our creation, as if having once created them we could continue to create them throughout their whole lives . . .

(NATALIA GINZBURG, "The Little Virtues," *The Little Virtues*)

And here's half of the second paragraph—a recital of consequences —from Leo Tolstoy's *Anna Karenina*:

Everything had gone wrong in the Oblonsky household. The wife had found out about her husband's relationship with their former French governess and had announced that she could not go on living in the same household with him. This state of affairs had already continued for three days and was having a distressing effect on the couple themselves, on all members of the family, and on the domestics . . . The wife did not leave her own rooms and the husband stayed away from home all day. The children strayed all over the house, not knowing what to do with themselves. The English governess had quarrelled with the housekeeper and had written a note asking a friend to find her a new place. The head-cook had gone out right at dinner-time the day before. The under-cook and the coachman had given notice.

8 Definition

When we define something—a word, a term, an issue, a problem—we place bounds around it. We restrict meaning in order to promote clarity. Dictionaries, of course, define words—what they mean by general agreement and in the light of their history; what they mean in specific contexts.

A defining paragraph proposes a definition of something; then it goes on to justify and exemplify and elaborate that definition. "A paragraph is a meaningful gathering of sentences," I offered above, and went on to explain what I meant. "History is the discourse of context," I might begin; or "ecology is the science of relationship." Each takes a large idea and tries to characterize it; each begs for explanation. "A weed is a plant out of place," goes a famous gardening truism. Whose place? Why is it out of place? Who says? That's what the paragraph should say.

Here's Michel de Montaigne proposing a brave, frank, and contentious definition of marriage:

A good marriage, if such there be, rejects the company and conditions of love. It tries to reproduce those of friendship. It is a sweet association in life, full of constancy, trust, and an infinite number of useful and solid services and mutual obligations. No woman who savours the taste of it . . . would want to have the place of a mistress or paramour to the husband. If she is lodged in his affection as a wife, she is lodged there much more honorably and securely. When he dances ardent and eager attention elsewhere, still let anyone ask him then on whom he would rather have some shame fall, on his wife or his mistress; whose misfortune would afflict him more; for whom he wishes more honor. These questions admit of no doubt in a sound marriage.

(MICHEL DE MONTAIGNE, "On Some Verses of Virgil,"
The Complete Essays)

Here's a famous defining paragraph, admittedly only a sentence long. It's from a novel, and the rest of the novel explores it. Talk about SEX!

It is a truth universally acknowledged, that a single man in possession of a good fortune must be in want of a wife.

(JANE AUSTEN, *Pride and Prejudice*)

9 Analysis

We use *analysis* broadly to mean hardheaded critical consideration of something. Every expository paragraph ought to be analytical in that sense. But there is a narrower meaning of analysis, and it lends itself to a particular kind of paragraph: one breaks one's subject down to its components and explains each of them in turn. You take the engine apart to see how it runs. With luck, it still does when you put it together again.

(I am in the midst of a sustained piece of analysis, as it happens, writing this book—what is writing; what are its parts and how do you master them; what, specifically, is a paragraph and what are the many ways of writing one?)

Okay, I'm going to cheat now. I want to include some of George Orwell's "Why I Write" because it's so good. The whole essay explores the question its title asks; specifically, it is an extended and astute analysis of tendencies that lead one—himself, in particular—to write.

I abstract the paragraph that follows from five paragraphs in the original. It is a fine example of how one might write an analytical paragraph:

I think there are four great motives for writing . . . (1) Sheer egoism. Desire to seem clever, to be talked about, to be remembered after death, to get your own back on grown-ups who snubbed you in childhood etc. . . . There is . . . the minority of gifted, willful people who are determined to live their own lives to the end, and writers belong in this class . . . (2) Aesthetic enthusiasm. Perception of beauty in the external world, or, on the other hand, in words and their right arrangement . . . Desire to share an experience which one feels is valuable and ought not to be missed . . . (3) Historical impulse. Desire to see things as they are, to find out true facts and store them up for the use of posterity. (4) Political purpose—using the word "political" in the widest possible sense. Desire to push the world in a certain direction, to alter other people's ideas of the kind of society that they should strive after.
  (GEORGE ORWELL, "Why I Write," *The Penguin Essays of George Orwell*)

If you look back a few pages, you'll find that the passage I quoted from Peter Turchi's *Maps of the Imagination* as an example of expository prose is, specifically, a classic piece of analysis.

Here's a more down-to-earth example of analysis. It breaks down a process—the way rivers behave—into the factors that make them behave thus; it then breaks those two factors into their parts and considers what they, in turn, are made of:

The way a river looks and behaves depends on the terrain through which it flows—whether the slopes are steep or gentle, whether its channel is in solid rock or in loose, unconsolidated material—and on the sediment load it carries. The load is the mineral material carried along by the flowing water; it consists of everything from boulders to rock dust to tiny clay particles caused by the chemical decay of rocks, plus small amounts of organic material such as dead leaves and twigs; it is the material that becomes sediment or alluvium once it has come to rest. (The word sediment is sometimes used to mean all deposited material, regardless of whether it was transported by water, wind, or glacial ice. Alluvium means sediments deposited by rivers.) (E. C. PIELOU, *Fresh Water*)

You'll find plenty of analysis in legal writing and textbooks and manuals. What are the parts that make the whole what it is; how does the system work; what are we talking about exactly? That's how you proceed when you write analysis.

10 Qualification

Here you make some kind of a bold statement and retreat from it.

Here's a novel that begins with qualification:

In a hole in the ground there lived a hobbit. Not a nasty, dirty, wet hole, filled with the ends of worms and an oozy smell, nor yet a dry, bare, sandy hole with nothing in it to sit down on or to eat: it was a hobbit-hole, and that means comfort. (J. R. R. TOLKIEN, *The Hobbit*)

Phillip Lopate's essay "Against Joie de Vivre" begins with a classic example:

Over the years I have developed a distaste for the spectacle of joie de vivre, the knack of knowing how to live. Not that I disapprove of all hearty enjoyment of life. A flushed sense of happiness can overtake a person anywhere, and one is no more to blame for it than the Asiatic flu or a sudden benevolent change in the weather (which is often joy's immediate cause). No, what rankles me is the stylization of this private condition into a bullying social ritual. (PHILLIP LOPATE, "Against Joie de Vivre," *The Art of the Personal Essay*)

So does Robert Benchley's "My Face," which makes me realize what a classic essayistic device this is, particularly for kicking off with:

Merely as an observer of natural phenomena, I am fascinated by my own personal appearance. This does not mean that I am pleased with it, mind you, or that I can even tolerate it. I simply have a morbid interest in it.
(ROBERT BENCHLEY, "My Face," *The Art of the Personal Essay*)

There's the qualification right at the start, and again in the second sentence. The final sentence summarizes what this qualified fascination amounts to.

At the risk of sounding uncertain of yourself, this kind of paragraph, which goes better with a touch of humor and self-deprecation, sounds like a fairly humane kind of conversation. It may grow dull if you repeat it, though. Move on, as ever; explore in all these ways.

▶ **Try this**

1 Write an expository paragraph on the education of children or your relationship with your spouse, using each of these paragraph types:

- definition
- analogy
- illustration

2 Think of a problem that concerns you at home, at your child's school, at the place where you're studying, where you play sport or where you work. Write three paragraphs about it, the first descriptive, the second expository, the third argumentative.

3 The newspaper I read most mornings includes on its back page a column of six hundred words called "Heckler." In it, each day, a reader complains engagingly about some social habit or other —the way parents scream from the sidelines, the rituals of Christmas, motorists who drive slowly in the fast lane, the misuse of words, the way everyone kisses you socially these days, even on first meeting you, for example.

Write a short Heckler about something that exercises you. Write three or four paragraphs, and employ different approaches in each.

The art of transition

You have to lead your reader on.

Every paragraph you write, every sentence in a way, is part of your exploration—by indirection, by meditation, by argument, by wondering walk, by analysis—of whatever it is you've said (or implied) that you have to say. Every paragraph is part of the telling of a story you've reduced to one or two lines and uttered (or implied) somewhere. Every sentence is a piece in the one puzzle. But which piece of what puzzle and why you've put it just here must be plain on the face of every word and phrase you write.

Good writing holds its reader's hand and leads her through the unfurling of itself, pointing back to the last step and forward to the next, showing her the map, reminding her of the destination. Good writing is a coherent journey back to the place where it began. It's a circle. It's a wall whose logic is implicit in every stone.

In good writing, a reader finds it hard to get lost. (I should add that in a novel or other work of literature, getting your readers lost, keeping them wondering, throwing them off balance, and all that are part of the writer's purpose; but a good creative writer convinces his readers that he, at least, knows exactly where he and the piece of work are headed.) In loose and hasty prose, not only does the reader lose her way; the writer loses his as well, or never knew quite where it lay.

Unity (making every stone suggestive of, and of a piece with, the whole wall) and *flow* (making each stone distinct and sequential) characterize good writing; and they stand in tension. The one is about sameness; the other is about change. Linkage is how you resolve them: you keep saying new things, you keep carrying the story forward, but you never stop helping your reader understand how each new development (argument, qualification, example, plot twist) is related, and how all are related, to the whole. *Transition* is how you make your writing both hang and flow.

Good writers know about transition. They know how to lead you deftly on. Michael Pollan knows more about it than most. Here are three impeccably coherent paragraphs from his book *The Botany of Desire*:

The garden is still a site for experiment, a good place to try out new plants and techniques without having to bet the farm. Many of the methods employed by organic farmers today were first discovered in the garden. Attempted on the scale of a whole farm, the next New Thing is an expensive and risky proposition, which is why farmers have always been a conservative breed, notoriously slow to change. But for a gardener like me, with relatively little at stake, it's no big deal to try out a new variety of potato or method of pest control, and every season I do.

Admittedly, my experiments in the garden are unscientific and far from foolproof or conclusive. Is it the new neem tree oil I sprayed on the potatoes that's controlling the beetles so well this year, or the fact that I planted a pair of tomatillos nearby, the leaves of which the beetles seem to prefer to potatoes? (My scapegoats, I call them.) Ideally, I'd control for every variable but one, but that's hard to do in a garden, a place that, like the rest of nature, seems to consist of nothing but variables. "Everything affecting everything else" is not a bad description of what happens in a garden or, for that matter, in any ecosystem.

In spite of these complexities, it is only by trial and error that my garden ever improves, so I continue to experiment. Recently I planted something new—something very new, as a matter of fact—and embarked on my most ambitious experiment to date. I planted a potato called "NewLeaf" that has been genetically engineered (by the Monsanto corporation) to produce its own insecticide. That it does in every cell of every leaf, stem, flower, root, and—this is the unsettling part—every spud.

Experiment in the garden is the topic here—the general idea; his particular experiment; mankind's experiment with GM crops. Notice how Pollan strings that topic through the sentences of each paragraph through words that allude to it: *experiment, try out, methods, discovered, risky proposition, my experiments, unscientific, control for every variable, nothing but variables, complexities, trial and error, planted something new, my most ambitious experiment.*

Notice the way Pollan makes neat transitions from one paragraph to the next. He does this through the word or phrase with which he starts each paragraph: *Admittedly* points us back to the first paragraph; *In spite of these complexities* points us to the ideas he has pondered in the second paragraph; *Recently*, which begins the second sentence of the third paragraph, links all he has said on the topic so far to what he is about to say. After a trim transitional word— *Admittedly*—which opens the second paragraph, the subject of the first sentence is *my experiments.* This subject contains the book's topic, now familiar to us. That sentence ends with the new ideas he wants to take us to in this paragraph: *variability and control.*

Look at the structure of the third paragraph. It starts, again, with a transitional phrase linking it to the last paragraph. The first sentence ends with words that take us to the new idea in this paragraph: his ongoing experimenting, and this experiment with "NewLeaf" in particular. The second sentence moves from experiment to newness to *my most ambitious experiment to date.* The opening of the third sentence, *I planted*, explains that personal experiment, and the rest of the sentence tells us more about it, making sense of the claim in the previous sentence that this was his most ambitious experiment so far. *That*, which opens the last sentence, points straight back to the last words of the previous sentence. If you want to make your writing cohere, master transitions.

In pursuit of coherence, try these three things that Michael Pollan does so well in these three paragraphs:

- Use transitional words and phrases (between sentences and paragraphs).
- Allude to the main idea often in the words you use.
- Pick up in sentence two the idea with which you ended sentence one, and so on.

Make your prose as you might make a drystone wall. You're not concreting the pieces; they just have to fit and stay fit. How will you chisel each stone, how will you turn it and set it down so that it sits conformably with its neighbors and carries the wall forward? And have you left space—just enough—between the stones?

▶ Try this

1 Look back on the "Heckler" column you wrote. Rework it to improve its flow and transitions.
2 Imagine you have to write a report for your boss or partner on what you've learned from this book about writing well.

- Make a mindmap.
- Work out an embryonic thesis statement.
- Write the opening three or four paragraphs on this topic, focusing hard on linkage, on both unity and flow.

3 You want to write a book. Or you have written one. Now your agent has asked you to draft three hundred words for her, the basis of the pitch she will make to publishers. Use a map of some kind. Think hard about what your thesis or throughline is. Draft four or five paragraphs pitching your great work, starting with "This book tells a story of . . ."

AMEN

An epilogue on beauty, honesty, and civility

Harry Potter's all right, I guess. He's a place to start. But let's not stop with him.

I'm glad he's done so well. But the scale of the success J. K. Rowling has achieved—let alone what Dan Brown has managed with a much less accomplished work—can fool an inexperienced reader or an aspiring writer. Writing can be so much more than this—not more difficult, but more beautiful, more musical, more accomplished, more exacting, more capable of changing and improving us all.

I'm not talking about writing that is beautiful or experimental or shocking for its own sake. That would be self-indulgence; and we have enough of that already. The writing we need may be plain or extravagant, but it will be carefully made and mindful of its readers (of their humanity, of their hope for wisdom and music and meaning). I don't want it to be purple, but I'd like it to sing. My book has been a short cry—a yelp—for grace. It hopes to encourage a more accomplished, artful, and honest kind of prose—writing that aims to do more than merely get a tale told.

"The good writer," John Steinbeck said, "works at the impossible. There is another kind who pulls in his horizons, drops his mind as one lowers rifle sights." We have enough workmanlike, merely functional, writing. We have too much careless prose, too much that is haphazard, too much that is tone-deaf. We have, at the same time, too much self-conscious writing, turned out in a kind of literary or academic, professional or tribal patois.

I wrote this book because I long, and I don't think I'm alone, to read more sentences so well formed, so perfectly uttered, they make one weep—in their form and rhythm, in their topography and amplitude and in the truthful spaces onto which they open. Let plots take care of themselves; it's time more writers spent more care shaping astonishing sentences. Elegant, shapely, heartbreaking—in the way a mountain range can be, or a horse, a woman's form, a child's voice, the posture of a tree, or the taste of a glass of wine. And it's time more publishers understood the deeper hunger among readers for works that sing. We have been drugged long enough by narrative; we have grown used to merely competent prose.

Most of us don't work quite hard enough at making elegant, clean, strange, and lovely prose because it's plain hard work. Elegant and— in its place—striking prose wants more courage and technique than most of us can muster and sustain. And it's no good writing a bad sentence for every good one. "A work that aspires, however humbly, to the condition of art," wrote Conrad, "should carry its justification in every line."

That is the kind of exacting discipline, the kind of aspiration, this book's been about.

But I think we need better writing for political as well as artistic reasons. For the struggle to improve our sentences is the struggle to improve ourselves.

In these times, more than ever, we need a little depth and care, generosity and poise. We need a little perspective and honesty and restraint. And politically, a little low-voltage rage. We need, in other words, to rediscover the syntax of civility and the diction of democracy.

FURTHER READING

Colman, Ruth. 2005. *The Briefest English Grammar Ever!* Sydney: UNSW Press.

Dillard, Annie. 1989. *The Writing Life.* New York: HarperCollins.

Eisenberg, Anne. 1992. *Guide to Technical Editing.* New York: Oxford University Press.

Evans, Harold. 2000. *Essential English for Journalists, Editors and Writers*, rev. edn. London: Pimlico.

Fowler, H. R. & Aaron, J. E. 1995. *The Little, Brown Handbook.* New York: HarperCollins College Publishers.

Goldberg, Natalie. 1986. *Writing Down the Bones.* Boston, MA: Shambhala.

Hale, Constance. 1999. *Sin & Syntax.* New York: Broadway Books.

Hirsch, Edward. 1999. *How to Read a Poem.* New York: Harcourt.

Huddleston, Rodney & Pullum, Geoffrey. 2005. *A Student's Introduction to English Grammar.* Cambridge: Cambridge University Press.

Ivers, Michael. 1991. *The Random House Guide to Good Writing.* New York: Random House.

Kane, Thomas. 2000. *The Oxford Essential Guide to Writing.* New York: Berkley Books.

Le Guin, Ursula. 1998. *Steering the Craft.* Portland, OR: Eighth Mountain Press.

Lindberg, Christine (ed.). 2004. *The Oxford American Writer's Thesaurus.* New York: Oxford University Press.

McQuade, Donald & Atwan, Robert (eds.). 2005. *The Writer's Presence*, 5th edn. Boston, MA: Bedford/St Martin's.

O'Conner, Patricia. 1996. *Woe is I.* New York: Putnam.

  1999. *Words Fail Me.* New York: Harcourt Brace.

Oliver, Mary. 1994. *A Poetry Handbook.* New York, Harcourt.

  1998. *Rules for the Dance.* New York: Houghton Mifflin.

Plimpton, George (ed.). 1989. *The Writer's Chapbook.* New York: Viking.

Siegal, Allan & Connolly, William. 1999. *The New York Times Manual of Style and Usage*, rev. edn. New York: Times Books.

Stafford, Kim. 2003. *The Muses Among Us.* Athens, GA: Georgia University Press.

Stegner, Wallace. 1988. *On the Teaching of Creative Writing*. Hanover, NH: University Press of New England.

Strunk, W. & White, E. B. 2000. *The Elements of Style*, 4th edn. Boston, MA: Allyn & Bacon.

Thompson, Anne. 1994. *Purpose & Pattern*. Toronto: Oxford University Press.

Turco, Lewis. 2000. *The Book of Forms*. Hanover, NH: University Press of New England.

Watson, Don. 2003. *Death Sentence*. Sydney: Random House.

Williams, Joseph M. 1990. *Style*. Chicago: University of Chicago Press.

Zinsser, William. 1998. *On Writing Well*, 6th edn. New York: HarperCollins.

INDEX